Hindsights

the autobiography of an unknown artist

Stan Erisman

Hindsights

Published by Stan Erisman
Publishing partner: Paragon Publishing, Rothersthorpe
First published 2021

© Stan Erisman 2021

The rights of Stan Erisman to be identified as the author of this work have been asserted by him in accordance with the Copyright, Designs and Patents Act of 1988.

All rights reserved; no part of this publication may be reproduced, stored in a retrieval system, or transmitted in any form or by any means, electronic, mechanical, photocopying, recording or otherwise without the prior written consent of the publisher or a licence permitting copying in the UK issued by the Copyright Licensing Agency Ltd.
www.cla.co.uk

ISBN 978-1-78222-835-6

Book design, layout and production management by Into Print
www.intoprint.net
+44 (0)1604 832149

Cover illustration: *A Cry*, oil painting #21, by Stan Erisman, 1972

The Foreword to the *Hindsights* series can be found in Book 1, *Natural Shocks*.

Slings and Arrows

To be, or not to be, that is the question:
Whether 'tis nobler in the mind to suffer
The **slings and arrows** of outrageous fortune,
Or to take Arms against **a Sea of troubles**,
And by opposing end them: to die, to sleep
No more; and by a sleep, to say we end
The heart-ache, and the thousand **natural shocks**
That Flesh is heir to? 'Tis a consummation
Devoutly to be wished. To die, to sleep,
To sleep, **perchance to Dream**; aye, there's the rub,
For in that sleep of death, what dreams may come,
When we have shuffled off this mortal coil,
Must give us pause. There's the respect
That makes Calamity of so long life:
For who would bear the Whips and Scorns of time,
The Oppressor's wrong, the proud man's Contumely,
The pangs of despised Love, the Law's delay,
The insolence of Office, and the spurns
That patient merit of the unworthy takes,
When he himself might his Quietus make
With a bare Bodkin? Who would Fardels bear,
To grunt and sweat under a weary life,
But that the dread of something after death,
The undiscovered country, from whose bourn
No traveller returns, puzzles the will,
And makes us rather bear those ills we have,
Than fly to others that we know not of.
Thus conscience does make cowards of us all,
And thus the native hue of Resolution
Is sicklied o'er, with the pale cast of Thought,
And enterprises of great pitch and moment,
With this regard their Currents turn awry,
And lose the name of Action.

– William Shakespeare, Hamlet's soliloquy
from *Hamlet*, act III, scene I

Slings and Arrows
Book four in the Hindsights series

Stan Erisman

CONTENTS

Chapter 1: Roads not taken 1

How I was recruited for a job at a prestigious private school and why I turned it down; how an influential gallery owner offered to make my career as an artist and why I turned him down; how these milestones looked then and look in hindsight; and how family visits highlighted our growing separation from our past.

Chapter 2: Down to the bone 15

How a trip to London and conscious exposure to the arts took us to a new level of examining and questioning the first premises of our beliefs and the nature of belief, and how difficult it is to abandon beliefs strongly held – or subtly instilled.

Chapter 3: In this together 31

How our focused efforts to connect with Bob, to create a home out of his hovel, and to grow in his friendship began to show results in his emergence from depression; how my painting continued to inspire and be inspired by Jeanette, and encouraged by Bob; and how Bob's encyclopedic knowledge and deep interest in learning enriched and enthralled us.

Chapter 4: Glacial flow 50

How I began making more visceral analyses of Biblical stories by using them as motifs for my paintings; how the unfolding of the Watergate scandal contributed to our questioning the noble motives of our homeland; and how my research for writing *Hindsights* led me to see – in retrospect only – a few early signs of powerful and pathological anxiety in Jeanette.

Chapter 5: Lurches and surges 67

How the sudden death of my dad affected Jeanette deeply; how it was closely followed by the totally unexpected cancellation of my draft order of 1970; how we suspected that the two events might be related; how a visit from Poland adversely affected Jeanette; and how my painting continued to challenge and nourish us.

Chapter 6: Grasping and grappling 80

How my conversations with Bob, my musings with Jeanette, my correspondence with my brothers, and my retrospective analysis of the Bible culminated in a painting that embodied my inability to believe in the existence of a good god; and how my continued painting aimed to resolve this question further, to help deal with my grief – and Jeanette's.

CHAPTER 7: The missing tapes 101

How we began exchanging audio tapes with Bob, and how my discovery of these tapes during my research for *Hindsights* gave me painfully belated insights into the dangerous trends in Jeanette's troubled mind; and how we began planning a trip to the States now that the draft was abolished, my induction order cancelled, and I was thus no longer a fugitive.

CHAPTER 8: Testing the water 114

How our five-week trip to the US in the summer of 1974 shocked us into realizing first how massively the US had changed since 1969, then how much *we* had changed; how we were made to feel unsafe, unacceptable, unwelcome and unsuitable in our native land; and how much this experience added to our feeling that Sweden was now our home.

CHAPTER 9: Shifting void 138

How we took a cheap and wonderful trip to Rome (to "purge" ourselves after the US); how we began looking for a bigger place to live; how utterly disappointed we were to be cheated by a realtor; how my emergency appendectomy terrified Jeanette; how Jeanette's dad died suddenly in November; and how his horrifying funeral traumatized Jeanette.

CHAPTER 10: Moving 159

How we found a dirt-cheap ruin (from 1864) in which we saw the potential for a home; how a friend helped us cut red tape and navigate many difficulties; how life in a run-down neighborhood gave us an entirely different experience and would require all kinds of skills I lacked; and how previously unexplored aspects of our naiveté served us well.

CHAPTER 11: Tearing 178

How we began by tearing out that which was cracked, broken, rotten or disintegrated; how each new round led to the discovery of previously hidden layers; and how it took most of 1975 just to reduce our ruin to a skeleton before we could turn to the equally daunting but joyous task of building our dream inside that shell.

CHAPTER 12: Intensity 205

How we prepared an insulated concrete slab after drains were installed, began putting up studs, preparing for new windows, new joists to replace the rotten ones, wallboard, etc; how we took a week off for a culturally intensive trip to London; and how Jeanette's mood swings were intensifying as well, without my understanding the seriousness at the time.

Chapter 13: «You can picture Jeanette» 228

How we installed our kitchen cabinets, got the staircase and began tiling the floor in the fall of 1976; how Jeanette's moodiness was becoming palpable and led her to quit her part-time secretarial job; how she withdrew more and more into herself in early 1977, how desperately I didn't want to see that; and how I was finally forced to see the utter horror of it when she took her own life.

Chapter 14: No place to go 242

How total despair engulfed me, destroyed my will to live, gave me no rest, no place to go despite the best intentions of Bob and others; how I traveled in agony to Basel, then to the US and back; how I was a raw and open wound; and how my only reason for not taking my own life was my inability to believe that anything could ever reunite me with Jeanette.

Appendix 1: Our home at Korngatan 262
Appendix 2: Paintings 19-78......................................266
Appendix 3: Jeanette's poetry....................................284

CHAPTER 1

Roads not taken

I couldn't have known, on June 28th, 1972, that four years and nine months later my darling Jeanette would be dead. I couldn't have lived under that obscene death sentence, knowing. It would have been terrifying, paralyzing, debilitating, grotesque, outrageous; I would have spent every hour of every day raging, raging against the countdown on the light of my life, vainly trying not to allow *any*thing to happen – good *or* bad – out of fear it would ultimately lead in that inexorable direction. Nothing would have been the same. Perhaps nothing ever *is* the same as what it could have been, might have been. *Of all sad words.* Maybe nothing is even the same as what it is. Maybe nothing remains the same as it was when it happened or while it is happening. The experience is not the memory or the memoir. The territory is not the map. You can't step into the same river once.

* * *

I knew nothing of any of that in 1972. I perceived no foreboding. We'd heard about a break-in at the Democratic National Headquarters at the Watergate complex in Washington DC in May, and certain questions about possible links to Nixon's henchmen were beginning to make the headlines, but there were no real direct links to the Oval Office yet (not that we'd have been surprised about anything like that from "Tricky Dick").

Our focus on the US as the most and perhaps only important source of news in the world had been decreasing rapidly since we arrived in Sweden. That trend accelerated rapidly in June 1970 after I was drafted, declined the invitation to go to war, and thereby became a fugitive from "justice". We were now exposed to a different kind of criticism of US government behavior (other than the student protests movements we'd witnessed in the late 1960s). Swedish, British and Swiss media representing mainstream thinking (or close to it) in those countries gave different, broader, deeper perspectives than we'd encountered before.

Still, the biggest cloud on our horizon in the summer was the arrival of Jeanette's kid sister Rosanne and their cousin Maureen, both now around 20. Maureen seemed to us to follow her leader Rosanne in every way. They would be staying with us from June 28th until July 17th, nearly three weeks, departing five days before Jeanette's 28th birthday. Jeanette had occluded feelings; although there was never any question that she would make them feel welcome, she told me she felt that she and Rosanne had never bonded terribly well. Jeanette thus felt some degree of apprehension. Rosanne always treated me, intentionally or not, with mild disdain. Jeanette never commented on it directly, but made it clear to me that it was something she didn't appreciate one bit.

Prior to their arrival, we hadn't heard from Bob for an unusually long period. I wrote him and offered to come down to Basel on the train myself and spend some time with him during Rosanne's visit, but Bob wrote back saying that he'd been awfully busy at work, and still was. I didn't get off the hook. I was, however, capable of playing the gracious host if I had to.

Both Jeanette and I had become accustomed to Bob's company in an unexpected way and to an unexpected degree. Our visits with him raised the bar for social conversation to a level unlike any other social conversation either of us had ever experienced; we now felt ourselves hoping and expecting that *any* conversation with anyone else would comprise a significantly lower proportion of idle chit-chat and a correspondingly higher proportion of in-depth talk: philosophical issues, world events and political controversies, historical milestones and perspectives, the evolution of values, art, music and science. In other words, we sought substance, things that *mattered*, things we felt were essential ingredients of life (unlike gossip), and therefore also necessary for making social interaction meaningful and mutually rewarding: worth the bother.

Those were the very topics that most of the members of our families, especially Jeanette's, almost always strove to avoid. Rosanne was no exception. Jeanette and I had been discussing such topics with each other, deeply and earnestly, to the best of our growing abilities, more or less from the first day we met, when she was 20 and I was less than a month past my 19th birthday. Rosanne was now 20; her age alone was thus no excuse.

For the first few days, Rosanne and Maureen made a lot of comments about TV sitcoms, soaps and various series they followed in the US. When we told them we'd never seen those shows, they looked at us as if we'd moved to some ravine in Appalachia. If their comments happened to concern a show we'd also seen on Swedish TV, and they wanted to see it too, they moaned that our offering was two seasons behind the US. (The fact that they could hear the undubbed soundtrack was simply their presupposition and thus equally unappreciated.) And if we *could* watch one of their vacuous shows yet didn't like it, they moaned about our dullness.

We tried mentioning a couple of British (and Swedish) series we followed and asked if they'd seen them. They couldn't see the parallel, nor why they or anyone else would ever want to concern themselves with anything as foreign as foreign, and that included British. And if we mentioned the Vietnam War or anything critical of the US and its policies or questionable historical behavior, we met a wall of silence or a dismissive sneer.

I couldn't paint while they were at our place, not because our apartment was too crowded, but because of the invisibility – of me, of my paintings, of anything important to either Jeanette or me. But we temporarily reset our social intercourse bar, put our lives on hold, went on outings and sightseeing, locally and in Copenhagen, without learning anything, kept our conversation in the comfort zone of our guests without straying from the surface because the surface *was* their comfort zone. In other respects, we simply endured until their departure in the morning on July 17th.

Mom continued her devious trickery to push Evangelical Christian messages on us. One ruse we'd noticed (from the first time she tried it) was that she kept sending us Swedish hymns to translate – many of them! I knew exactly what she was up to; she obtained the Swedish versions from bilingual friends of Swedish descent (who could have made the English translations themselves if they hadn't already). But Mom clearly wanted to "sneak" her messages into our consciousness. Jeanette was more naïve at first, but not for long. Sometimes we had fun using literal translations where possible, or more specifically, where they gave funny or absurd results. (Readers who know Swedish will understand why "Åldersklippa" would be a hilarious way to express "Rock of Ages"; perhaps "Geriatric Boulder" would convey the spirit of such intentional mistranslations....) Our purpose was, of course, to get Mom to see that her ruse wasn't working.

The farther away I got (in distance, time and outlook) from the religious beliefs of my family (and to some extent my own through my childhood brainwashing), the less sense they made to me, like discovering that the "wisdom" of a purchase – such as buying a wildly colored shirt or sombrero or fez when visiting a place where such things are sold and worn – may magically disintegrate in your closet and leave you wondering two years later what the hell you were thinking, if indeed you'd been thinking at all.

I suppose the religion of my upbringing would have simply become irrelevant for me and faded politely into the background had my mom and brothers not constantly nagged about it, dragged it back to my attention, relentlessly shoved it in my face, like picking at a scab before the wound has healed. But that's what they were continuing to do. And had religion been a purely benign force in the world, it might have teetered off my daily radar anyway, but religion was certainly by no means benign. It remained and remains a primary source of armed conflict in the world.

As a child, I always felt that *"Because I said so!"* didn't qualify as an answer to a serious question or challenge, and I resented it. I was therefore not going to do likewise and meet my family's challenges with a dismissive wave of the hand. In the interests of truth I felt I was first obliged to seek and be able to provide real answers to why I questioned or did not believe what they did, why I would no longer take that road. Unlike my family, however, I had no equivalent ready-made bank of non-religious clichés to draw upon. If they felt that *"Because the Bible says so!"* was an adequate answer to anything, I was determined to be prepared to point out a few of the other things that that same Bible says – things that would turn out to make the purveyors of religion squirm in discomfort. That turned out to be amazingly easy.

On July 20th, just three days after the departure of Rosanne and Maureen, I got a phone call, out of the blue, from the headmaster (or rector or principal) of Grennaskolan, offering me a full-time job starting the following month. My spontaneous reaction was one of excited amazement, as though a suppressed inner longing for some type of job security might at last be fulfilled. After all, my situation at the two language schools I'd been working for – Hamadi's and Demaret's – was devoid of assurances of any income at all beyond the nearest couple of weeks.

I didn't have the faintest idea how this rector came to contact me, through what channels, or what he knew about me, because I certainly didn't know a thing about him and not much more about his school. But he seemed to know some people who knew me, possibly some who were once pupils of mine. I'd at least heard of the venerable school up in Gränna, a small town about three hours' drive north of Malmö, just north of Jönköping. We drove through Gränna with Dad and Mom in 1971 on our trip to find the birthplaces of two of my mom's grandparents. The seat of learning in question was a prestigious and exclusive boarding school primarily for high-school students whose parents were foreign diplomats, industrialists, or just rich. I also knew that nearly the entire curriculum was conducted in English.

When this rector, whose name I've forgotten, phoned me and introduced himself, he painted a glowing picture of the school and its setting, and what my job would be and what a jaw-dropping (relatively speaking, of course) salary I'd be making, and could I please get on a train on Sunday and come out to meet him at his summer residence in the picturesque countryside in the southeastern corner of Skåne, known as Österlen. He would pick me up at the train station in a tiny town called Tomelilla. I agreed, and went.

He invited me to coffee and cookies in his home, in the best Swedish tradition (well, perhaps not the best; there would then have to have been *seven* different kinds of cakes or cookies). He wasted no time getting into the details of the job, hastily looked through my résumé, which I'd compiled for the occasion. He said he felt perfectly satisfied with my credentials and qualifications. I asked about the possibility of work for Jeanette as well, and he said there would certainly be at least part-time secretarial work for her at the school, perhaps more if she wanted it. And we wouldn't have to worry about housing – we'd have our own lovely quarters: a lovely apartment on the lovely grounds, and everything sounded lovely and rosy. I told him it sounded great, but that of course I'd have to discuss it with my wife first, and would get back to him within a couple of days. He reminded me of the urgency to fill the vacancy, so I promised to phone back the next day and let him know.

I was (and to some extent still am) the kind of person who, when visiting a supermarket, sometimes tends to start scurrying around, gleefully filling my shopping cart with all manner of exciting new items, and then, when approaching the check-out counter, begin wondering *Do I really need this?* and *What do I want with that?* and *Surely I don't need any of those?* – and then start putting stuff back on the shelves.

Jeanette and I felt we'd earned our serious-discussion and logical-decision-making merit badges, so as soon as I returned home late that Sunday afternoon, I told her all about the offer. We went straight to it, starting with the affirmatives. *Yes, the job sounds great. Yes, our financial situation would be vastly improved.* Then there were a couple of maybes or unknowns: *Would we enjoy the work itself and the school environs?* and *Would working for a school with admissions perhaps based as much on wealth as on merit be something we could feel comfortable with?* And finally we came to three outright negatives: *Did we move to Malmö to end up in a location several hours more remote from the heart of Europe than we already were?* and *Would this location still be convenient enough for Bob to come and spend time with us?* And finally, the deal-breaker: *Would I have enough time to paint?*

Following this fairly rational analysis, there was no doubt in our minds that the only thing for me to do was to phone back the next day and say sorry, but no thanks. The headmaster was appalled, baffled and perplexed. The inscrutable road we were on suddenly offered us a silver fork, which would have changed our future in countless and unforeseeable ways; we took the other fork instead, the stainless steel fork, and felt good about it.

Three days later, on July 27th, Al and his family arrived for a five-day visit, in connection with a fairly extensive family stay in England, where Al was involved in a book project at the mathematics department at Oxford University or something like that. It was our first meeting since Jeanette and I left Vancouver three years earlier, and it was obvious to Jeanette and me (and probably to Al and Nancy as well) that the gap between us was now more like a chasm.

Al was in many ways still the same guy he'd been ever since a certain Thursday night in the fall of 1960: the born-again fundamentalist Meeting member, protector of the faith, torn between wearing his proselytizing zeal on one sleeve and his underlying good-naturedness, human decency and word-game enthusiasm on the other. But he was also different. He was now an Important Person at Boeing, with a growing number of other irons in the fire as well – particularly within the field of mathematics – and was showing more signs than ever of discomfort regarding the Meeting's insistence on the literal interpretation of every word in the Bible.

The mere fact that Al was reading the works of the Christian apologist Francis Schaeffer, rather than relying solely on John Nelson Darby and the approved stars of the Plymouth Brethren, seemed to allow him to convince himself that he was open-minded on the subject of religion. And the fact that Al sent me a Schaeffer book and requested me to comment on it might have further contributed to Al's conviction of his open-mindedness. But the fact that I did read the book carefully and commented on it extensively, and pointed out to Al many of the uncomfortable fallacies I'd discovered in it, in combination with the fact that Al refused to respond to my comments at all – convinced me otherwise.

Most of the increased differences between Al and me were because Al was largely in the same place (our childhood indoctrination) in terms of religion and

I was most decidedly no longer anywhere near that place. I knew that Al was still reading his Bible every day. But was he ever reading it critically, or only for the possibility to gain a little more wiggle-room, to find a loophole or two in the stranglehold of literalism? Although I'd also read the entire Bible many times over as a child, since I left Oak Park I'd only read it in connection with finding specific refutations of the arguments of people like Schaeffer – people who bend over backwards so as not to have to open their minds or question the foundations of their beliefs. I hadn't yet fully confronted all the divine atrocities found in that book, nor challenged the first premises of acceptance – the unchallenging, blind acceptance that is required to make Jehovah's moral depravity defensible and "holy".

Bob and I had been hovering around the edges of freedom (for about a dozen years in my case, and closer to twenty in Bob's), as if afraid to let go of the last of the emotional ties to the fundamentalist Christianity of our upbringing. *Discredophobia* – the fear of ceasing to believe – was continuing to manifest itself. Our discussions (by letter and whenever we met) intensified the process, and Al's visit made me realize that simply finding arguments against the wobbly logic of Schaeffer was no longer enough. I would soon have to read the Bible again, if for no other purpose than to examine what it *really* said.

Discredophobia is a very real thing. If you've been imbued, saturated, carpet-bombed, immersed and held under, or if you've been subjected to any other form of physical or psychological coercion – *especially as a child!* – it's likely to take a monumental effort to extract yourself from it as an adult. It makes no difference whether it's Christianity, Islam, Hinduism or any other life-encompassing set of beliefs, you'll do everything possible to hang onto it, go to any lengths to defend it (to others or only to yourself), anything to avoid examining the crumbling foundation of fables, lies, deceit, threats of doom, promises of reward (usually not nearly so powerful as the threats). You may even experience overwhelming panic at the very thought of ceasing to believe. And like other phobias, the fear turns out not to be warranted once you get on the other side of it. It's not rational. It doesn't make much sense after all.

The day Al and family left, August 1st, with my job situation still unstable despite being quite a bit less than full-time, and with my painting situation going full blast, I brought up with Jeanette the question of whether now might be a good time to revisit the notion of selling some of my growing number of paintings at a gallery. Jeanette's spontaneous reaction was a look of horror. She *loved* my paintings, all of them, and she didn't want me to sell *any*, except maybe to Bob, who fully appreciated and loved them too. We could certainly do with a supplementary source of income, but would the price to achieve it be too high?

People who'd visited our apartment and seen my paintings displayed a broad range of reactions: from no reaction at all, to furtive glances when they thought I wasn't watching, to polite expressions of acknowledgment, to hesitant praise, and occasionally (rarely) to an eruption of praise and perceptive questions. Some of those in the latter groups were also asking when I was going to have an exhibition. I had to tell them I didn't know, nor was I actively thinking about it. Some accused me of "hiding" my paintings away at home. I found it hard to see any significant difference between *my* "hiding" them by having them on *our* walls, and *their* hiding them by having them on *their* walls, except that Jeanette and I seemed to appreciate them much more than anyone else. But didn't I want to be famous? some would ask. The mere thought of fame made me shudder; my adolescent days of Hollywood aspirations of stardom were far in the past by now.

[*To anticipate possible questions about why I'm publishing* Hindsights, *and whether that doesn't imply a quest for fame of some or any kind, the answer is a resounding* NO! *Publication is to get my story out there, to make it available to those who might benefit from knowing that someone is on their side, and to tell my story as truthfully as I can possibly tell it.*]

Still, I thought it could at least be interesting to test the water. I had quite a bit more to show now, compared to when Jeanette and I were going around to a few galleries in Malmö in 1969 with my rolled-up paintings in a tube, soon after our arrival in Sweden. With Jeanette working at least part of most days, we decided that I would make a few gallery visits on my own, provided I didn't make any decisions without consulting her first.

One of the first places I visited, on Thursday, August 3rd, was Galerie Börjeson, which had opened just a few years earlier and was already on its way to becoming one of Malmö's most prestigious galleries. I'd been there a few times to view and admire the Picassos, Mirós and Chagalls, as well as the Max Ernsts and Vasarelys, but had never spoken with the owner. The entrance was on Hamngatan, in a fairly old and vaguely auspicious building at the corner where Hamngatan empties onto the main square, Stortorget. The ground-floor exhibition room, with its large display window facing Hamngatan, was not terribly large. But there was a black spiral staircase that led to a huge, open, L-shaped gallery upstairs, bright, with large windows facing both Hamngatan and Stortorget. The owner, Per-Olof Börjeson, was a man in his forties wearing a suit, with dark, somewhat curly hair (the owner, not the suit). He was sitting in his glass-walled cubicle office at the top of the stairs. There was nobody else in the gallery when I nervously entered that weekday mid-afternoon. I cleared my throat and he looked up at me from behind his cluttered desk, peering over the glasses perched far down on his nose. He asked if he could help me with anything. I told him I was an artist and wanted to see what he might think of my work. Then I held out my catalogue within his reach, and with a somewhat puzzled expression he leaned forward, took it and opened it without saying anything. I stood there waiting for a few seconds. I saw and heard him catch his breath. Then, without taking his eyes off my catalogue, he motioned for me to sit down on the vacant chair opposite him, which I did. He continued looking with what seemed to me like mounting interest, as if his mind were spinning rapidly. At that point, there were only about 20 paintings in my catalogue, seven of which I'd already sold.

Then came all kinds of rapid-fire questions: where was I from, how long had I been in Sweden, how long had I been painting, what did painting mean to me, what were my plans, where was I living, had I ever exhibited, on and on. Then he stopped, leaned back in his executive office chair, clasped his hands over the catalogue in front of him and said he'd like to *see* these paintings – he'd like to come to my home and see them in person. I wasn't expecting that kind of reaction *at all*, particularly in view of all the brush-offs Jeanette and I experienced in '69, but I told him yes, certainly. He asked if he could come to our home the next day, in the afternoon. That would be fine. He asked if he could keep my catalogue with him until then, to study it some more. I hesitated a second, but quickly agreed after remembering that Bob had a copy.

When he arrived the next afternoon, Jeanette was also at home (she only worked in the mornings). Börjeson swept into our small entrance hall, which normally didn't allow a lot of sweeping, and handed me back my catalogue without losing stride. He was slightly out of breath from the four flights of stairs, or perhaps he wasn't expecting to see Jeanette there. He instantly stopped to introduce himself to her and rattled off all the polite pleasantries we'd come to expect when meeting a Swede for the first time. His manner was thus fairly formal, yet effusive: far less formal than the Swiss, but far more so than Americans – a bit more like Canadians.

Then he turned his attention, all of it, to the paintings, staring intently at each one for at least a full minute before moving on to the next. His tour took him into all three of our rooms. He appeared lost in thought, stunned. Some 20-30 wordless minutes later, when he'd finished his tour, he seemed to be having a hard time finding words. He was shaking his head in short,rapid twitches, and muttering "*This is ... these are ... I'm ... This is <u>great</u> stuff! I don't ... I've got to ...,*" and then he drew a deep breath, shook his head once more and firmly blurted, "*I'm going to get back to you, I'll call you, in just a few days! I'll have an offer.... Don't ...!*" And then he turned and left, just like that, scurrying down the stairs without looking back.

Jeanette and I stood there speechless for half a minute, wondering what had just happened. He clearly *liked* them, we agreed. He *seemed* to like them *very* much, but not knowing him, not being able to calibrate any correlation between his true feelings on one hand and his facial expressions, choice of words, body language and tone of voice on the other, our assessments could be nothing more than conjectures, shots in the dark. We had no idea whether he would get back to us as he said, much less what he was going to get back to us *about*, or what kind of offer he might have been referring to.

Suppose he wanted to put on an exhibition and sell my paintings, I wondered aloud. Jeanette wrinkled her nose in distaste, or perhaps it had more of a defensive twist. Did I *want* to do that? Did Jeanette? Was I *ready* for that yet? Would I soon be? Would I *ever* be? But our questions just swirled; there were no answers, nor could there be until his offer – whatever it might be – was on the table for us to decide on.

The following Monday, August 7th, Börjeson phoned in the late morning, while Jeanette was still at work and I was painting. He asked me, with considerable excitement in his voice, if I could come to his gallery at once to discuss his offer. I quickly put aside everything I was doing and cycled at higher than normal speed, which was normally high. When I arrived, he was almost more breathless than I was. He announced, effusively, that he was going to make me an offer he'd *never* made to *any* artist before. He *loved* all my paintings – they were totally *unique* in his experience – and he wanted to put them *all* on display in his gallery, a separate exhibition, a one-man show. Then he wanted to arrange exhibitions for my paintings in Copenhagen, Stockholm and Hamburg, for starters. I would get 50% of the sales price for any paintings sold. He paused, perhaps waiting for this to sink in, or for me to respond, or just so he could catch his breath.

While he'd been talking, I felt the blood draining from my head a little, and thought it prudent to sit down. I'm sure my jaw must have been hanging open. I was completely unprepared for and overwhelmed by the magnitude of such an offer. I managed to control my voice enough to ask if I'd have to sell them *all*. Oh, no, he assured me, just the ones I *wanted* to sell. I indicated that I understood, although I didn't. Then he went on. I could also turn over *everything* – or anything I wanted – to him of the paintings I would be painting in the future. Oh, yes, and he would draw up a three-year *contract*. That word scared me a little. But he assured me that the only stipulations of the contract would be about benefits for me; I would have no other obligations under the contract than to agree not to exhibit in other galleries than those arranged by him for three years, the period of the contract. There would be no minimum or maximum number of paintings. I wouldn't be working under pressure. It was sounding more and more tempting – like a dream come true.

Then came his final point, the icing on the cake. As an added incentive, he would pay me 100,000 Swedish kronor, up front, as a bonus – just for signing. That amounted to about *three times my entire income* for that year! I think he almost expected me to scream *YES!!!* right there on the spot, but I knew that this was a life-changing decision. I had to have Jeanette in on it. Besides, I suddenly found myself pushing a shopping cart full of ramifications at high speed towards the check-out counter. I told him that I needed a little time to digest it all, and now it would be my turn to get back to him.

It took quite a few minutes for my heart to stop hyperpounding after I left the gallery. I had to slow down on my way home so as not to crash into a bus from behind or a wall head-on. Back at our apartment, I began pacing furiously from room to room, sometimes squealing with delight, sometimes anxious and pensive. I was desperately trying to give my rational mind a chance to get a word in edgewise, above the roar of my emotions.

I must have had a weird expression on my face when Jeanette came through the door that afternoon. Her first thought was that I might be seriously ill, but an instant later she knew it was something quite different. When I told her about Börjeson's offer, it was her turn to have to sit down. Her reactions were similar to mine: first overwhelmed by the sheer magnitude of the offer, then jubilant about the recognition of my talent implicit in that offer, then pensive about the potentially life-changing complexities of signing, then skeptical about whether she or I or we wanted all that we perceived such a stupendous contract might entail at this point in our lives, then repeating all of the above in chaotic non-sequence. And she was also *extremely* proud of me.

Yet another sea-change was facing us. A potential life-changing decision had to be made. There were several emphatic *yes's*: the money and the *security* it entailed (it was hardly a question of wealth, not that we'd ever sought *that*); the unlimited time to paint it could give me; and the opportunity to leave the language-school racket behind, at least for several years. We looked long and hard at these significant advantages, until they turned and bent in the undergrowth. The *maybe's* were more complicated, and some of them bordered on *no's*: the threat of fame (once my adolescent Hollywood dream abated, I've always seen fame as a threat); the potential risk to my artistic integrity in view of the fact that I was playing around with a few different styles, and might be influenced to paint in the style that sold best rather than the one that was most important to me at any given time; whether I might have a problem with rejection if my paintings didn't sell well; the disappearance from my life of paintings dear to me and Jeanette, to buyers more interested in wall decorations or investments than in content. And finally, there was one decisive no: the *feeling of freedom*. I was well aware that the contract proposal was uncommonly generous in allowing me to turn over only those paintings I wanted to, and only as many as I wanted to, but I couldn't escape the feeling that I'd be painting for Per-Olof Börjeson and not (or at least no longer solely) for Jeanette – or for myself.

It was at that moment that I realized to what a great extent the flight of my art was borne on the wings of Jeanette, influenced by her moods, thoughts, feelings and broodings, supported by her love for me and mine for her. She was truly my muse. (Farther down the line, some people would say they thought that my paintings influenced her; in truth it was vice-versa.) Perhaps that was why she was adamant about keeping my work out of what she loathingly called "the market".

I had to admit that my teaching work, no matter how much it could feel like drudgery at times, was in fact *a way for me to buy my freedom to paint without the need to sell*, with no other influences than my muse and my own musings, to let it take whatever directions it did, to go with my own flow – and hers. And that was what I needed.

I never considered myself an expert on what "art" should be – my undergraduate course in aesthetics made it clear that millennia of philosophers have failed to produce a consensus on the very definition of art, let alone on what criteria can be considered valid for assessing whether a particular work of art is "good" or "bad". My personal favorites were just that – personal favorites – whether or not they were universal favorites, majority favorites, also-ran favorites or nobody's favorites. People's opinions about a work of art are, of course, valid – as statements about those people, statements that don't necessarily say anything at all about the work of art. I had my own paths to explore, to try to say things I felt were important, or at least meaningful to an audience that was unknown, possibly indifferent, even hostile.

I phoned Börjeson two days later, after Jeanette and I had first given ourselves time to discuss his offer over and over. I told him I was sorry, but I wasn't yet ready to take that step. To say he was disappointed would be a monumental understatement. His tone was furious – or livid, if that can be a tone of voice – and hurt: "*such a generous offer and you just throw it back at me!*" He sounded as if he'd taken my answer as a great personal insult, when in fact I felt incredibly honored. But after all was said and done, Jeanette was relieved. And so was I (mostly).

I'd thought of Robert Frost's poem *The Road Not Taken* in connection with our decision about Gränna, and about what a difference *not* going made to our peace of mind. And now here was yet another decision of even greater magnitude. In fact, none of the roads we'd chosen, in our lives as individuals and in our life together, felt particularly travelled by. Think how many *what-if's* there are in a lifetime, how many misinformed, uninformed and uninformable decisions form everything that follows forever!

Already, many of my truly life-changing decisions were the result of feeling I had no choice. I obviously hadn't *chosen* to move to Glendale when I was seven months old, nor to move to Oak Park when I was five, yet both places formed me profoundly. I hadn't *chosen* to be born in the USA, or to be born White, or to be born at all, for that matter. I hadn't chosen what aptitudes and congenital conditions I might have, I hadn't *chosen* to be born into an exceptionally religious family, yet I knew I had to get out of there to survive, and "far away" was the only thing I knew about the choice of San Francisco. I didn't *choose* for the US to stick its nose, its bombs, and its troops (and try to stick my neck) into a civil war in a place called Vietnam. But because the US did, I had to get the hell out of my native country too.

In hindsight it has become clear that even the smallest, most innocuous decision can have a life-changing impact – the proverbial beating of a butterfly's wings in the Amazon. You come to a city intersection and want to get to the corner diagonally opposite. Should you cross left first and then right, or vice-versa? Add an out-of-control vehicle and the decision might be a matter of life or death. Free will? What's that? What kind of wine goes best with it? If you cannot possibly know the consequences of your decision before it has become irreversible, *fait accompli*, are you still accountable? To what, or to whom? And why?

In the space of just three weeks, we'd made two major new decisions (and confirmed one older one) not to take certain roads: the road to Grennaskolan and the road to commercial success as an artist. We'd also been confirming more and more that we wanted no part of the road to religion. All three decisions were ultimately about choosing freedom instead of anything that gave even the slightest feeling of bondage – insomuch as we actually had the freedom to choose at all. I've never felt I had any occasion to regret those choices, and I feel quite certain that Jeanette felt the same.

CHAPTER 2

Down to the bone

After those emotionally wrenching decisions, both Jeanette and I felt we needed a break, and what better place to take it than London? We loved that city the last time we were there (Jeanette's second time, my first), in December '69, even when much of it was closed for Christmas and we were chilled to the bone. Now, in August 1972, we were sickened not only by the almost daily revelations of underhandedness and treachery relating to Nixon and Watergate, but perhaps even more by the US polls showing that the American electorate seemed likely to re-elect the bastard. London was the antidote for that as well. We were ravenous for its offerings of history, its museums, its theaters, its pubs, and for another round of being in an environment with our almost-native language all around us.

Two competing Danish charter travel companies – Spies and Tjæreborg – were currently vying for Swedish vacationers' business, offering incredibly good and cheap package deals to England's capital city (among numerous other destinations, such as Mallorca and similar places of interest to sun-worshippers, which we never were). When we discovered that a last-minute booking for a whole week in London, including the flight and a fairly good hotel with breakfast, would cost us as little as 99 Swedish kronor, we were sold. Our flight left the Copenhagen airport on Sunday evening, August 13th.

During our week there, we went to a couple of concerts – also cheap back then – and spent a lot of time in the National Gallery at Trafalgar Square, as well as the Tate along the Thames, and the Natural History Museum. The latter turned out to be costly, as I mislaid the Asahi Pentax single-reflex camera that Bob bought us to enable us to keep him supplied with good-quality photos of my latest paintings. It was gone forever.

A number of the paintings we saw in London were disturbing to me, in a painfully good sort of way: they helped to open my eyes to things I hadn't wanted to consider. The skills of the artists were breathtaking, but I always tended to spend most of my time with the Impressionists and thus never bothered much about earlier works. But this time I did. A number of the Old Masters' paintings depicted gruesome scenes of murder, mayhem, suffering, treachery and other biblical motifs. Since I was well-versed (and well-chaptered) in the Bible, I not only recognized the actions depicted, but also knew that the artists in no way exaggerated the horrors of the biblical accounts in question – on the contrary.

The paintings disturbed Jeanette too – particularly the massive painting called *The Deluge*, painted by Francis Danby in the late 1830s, with its angel weeping over the death of a small child – a child that *God chose to drown* along with the rest of humanity (and animals). Seeing it close up, vividly and unflinchingly portrayed, made it agonizingly real. Even if you don't take the Noah's ark story literally, how is there a good figurative interpretation? And if the Bible is *the* source of information about a god that people are supposed to, compelled to, worship...?

I found myself wondering how much else I'd been overlooking. Reading those biblical stories over and over was one thing; seeing a few of them graphically rendered was beginning to bring home to me what they were really about. The subject was easy enough to identify: *Genesis*, chapters 6-8. But I'd never seriously pondered the ramifications of a God *choosing* to drown the whole of mankind, every last man, woman and child, except for eight people!! How could I have read this so many times as a child and not seen it as the act of a raving psychopath? Why hadn't I seen the atrocity of such things before, despite having read those texts, over and over? It occurred to me that it was *because* I'd read them over and over as a child, they'd become mere sounds before I even understood the words. I'd been mesmerized, then immunized against the impact of what they actually said; repetition turned frightening content into mere cadence; learning was lambasted by liturgy. What the hell kind of god did my parents worship – and urge me, command me, indoctrinate me to worship?

Scene after scene of the slaughter of innocent people – no small children were spared – began springing to my memory from paintings I'd viewed in Chicago, Madrid, Amsterdam and London, as well as in my collection of art books. My memory began linking them to the biblical accounts I read mechanically as a child, rote memories I could now evaluate with my conscious adult mind for the first time ever. Case after case of God-sanctioned, God-commanded and God-inflicted treachery and atrocity began popping up, things I would have to look up and confirm when we got home to my Bible in Malmö.

Then I remembered a statement attributed to Jesus: *"Verily I say unto you, Except ye be converted, and become as little children, ye shall not enter into the kingdom of heaven."* (Matthew 18:3). That was it! The biblical god didn't want anybody using their mind and discovering his barbarism. Just accept, don't ask questions. So why have a brain?

Down to the bone

For centuries, the Catholics blamed *all* Jews for the role a few Jews many generations ago *allegedly* had in the crucifixion of Jesus. (Funny that they didn't blame all Romans, but perhaps that would have been tricky, as they were Roman Catholics....) And the Protestants blamed *all* Catholics for the role the Church officially had in the Inquisition. But nobody seems to want to give *Him* responsibility and blame for the mass slaughters of the Old Testament that he had committed, ordered, or condoned, or *His* promise of eternal torture of nearly all of mankind in the New one.

Jeanette seemed even more upset than I was about these things. She and I had long discussions as we walked through Hyde Park together, trying to figure out why many people continued to cling to such barbaric beliefs. Did clinging to barbaric beliefs prevent or impede societies from becoming less barbaric? Was it because Tradition dictated that it should be so? We'd seen plenty of examples of how tradition could be really (and sometimes viciously) despotic, commanding and commandeering a complete shutdown of free and rational thinking in order to gain the acceptance and subservience of otherwise rational human beings. It made no sense at all, as if the whole world *were* a stage, full of sound and fury. But it signified a lot to the victims. We were shaken.

As far as I knew, my entire family – including aunts, uncles and cousins (with the notable exception of Bob) – still fervently believed (or claimed to believe) in the literal truth of nearly every word of the Bible. I had a brother with a doctorate in mathematics, another with two degrees in engineering, yet based on their most recent accounts of their beliefs to me at that time, they both still believed in a *literal* Noah's ark, heaven and hell, the works. Could anything but indoctrination and brainwashing explain how that was possible?

A week is nowhere near enough time to see London, of course, especially if you're also trying to think and to process everything ganging up on your brain. It took us several days to get beyond the museum-induced mental exhaustion and discover that there was also an amazing buffet of theaters with seats that even we could easily afford. Now I understood much more clearly why Jeanette was eager for us to come to Europe instead of settling into middle-class life in some North American suburb.

I also confirmed Jeanette's assessment that English food – cuisine – was one thing England was famous for not being famous for. [*A lot has happened since 1972!*] Instead, we gravitated to Italian, Greek, French and Chinese restaurants, and were well rewarded for our efforts. In our exploration of Soho we saw quite a few Indian restaurants as well. Neither of us had ever tried food from India before, but our adventurous spirits carried us across the threshold of one such establishment, where the strange and wonderful scents wafting from its cobalt-blue exterior made our mouths water and drew us inside.

Many of the words on the menu were unknown to us, and few of the names of the dishes sounded even remotely familiar. We'd heard that Indian food could be pretty spicy (read "hotter than hell"), but I was unafraid, since I'd always tended to prefer a lot of heat in my Mexican food back in California. We perused the menu and noticed that each dish was marked with a varying number of chilies – the more chili symbols displayed, the hotter the dish. I hesitated a little: maybe not the very hottest on the first try? Instead of the Madras lamb curry (five chilies) I went for the Vindaloo lamb curry (four chilies).

Our waiter looked startled when I told him my choice. "*Hab you eaden Indian pood bevore?*" he asked in nearly monotonal surprise, despite the look of great concern on his face. "No," I replied, "but I like hot Mexican food." He frowned and wrinkled his brow. "*Mebbee you sould dry somding nod so hod?!*" I looked up at him and smiled cheerily, "No, thanks, I'd really like to try *this* dish!" "*OK*," he replied, shrugging and turning away, "*bud I warned you!*"

Jeanette's order was much more conservative (one chili), but we were both enjoying the totally new sights and fragrances of the dishes being served all around us, getting hungrier by the minute as we sipped our beer and nibbled on some delicious na'an bread, dipping small pieces of it into a selection of tasty sauces (all of them new for us), one of which brought tears of heat to our eyes. After an unhurried time to absorb the tastes and smells and exchange our impressions of them, we saw our waiter heading for our table with our respective main courses, which by now we were awaiting eagerly. He placed them in front of us, wished us enjoyment, and retreated to a discreet vantage point about five meters away.

My eyes were already feasting on the chunks of tender lamb in a rich dark sauce, resting on top of a bed of beautiful pilaf rice. My nose soon joined the sensory symphony as I reached for my fork, gently filled it and raised it to my mouth, my nose urging me on. The first sensations of taste were absolutely divine – for about three seconds. Suddenly, every pore in my body opened, *spat*! I was instantaneously soaking wet inside my clothing. My mouth was on fire. There was panic in my eyes, accompanied by tears of sheer terror. I lunged towards my beer. The waiter came rushing over from his lookout post, "*No, suh! Nod your *beer, suh – dad make id worse! You dayg yogurd!"* He placed before me the small dish of yoghurt and cucumber he already had in his hand, as if he might possibly have anticipated the outcome of my first-ever encounter with a hot Vindaloo curry.

He was right; the yoghurt quenched the worst of the flames almost instantly, but I was still in quite a state. Sweat was flowing down the back of my neck like a rushing tributary to the greater river of sweat already inside my collar, swirling all down my back, making my underwear feel like it was squishing with sweat. My socks were splashing in it, as though some psychopath had locked me fully clothed in a Finnish sauna (temperatures of 110°C [230°F] are said to be not unusual in Finland; I've only experienced 100°C, in Sweden).

Gradually the heat began to subside and, being the daredevil I still was at that stage in my life, I commanded myself to shake off the momentary discomfort – if one may describe being dunked in a vat of molten lead as discomfort – and I proceeded, by which I mean I reasserted my command over the dish of Vindaloo curry before me.

At one point in this purgatorial meal, when our waiter stopped to ask how things were going, I asked him if *he* also found this dish extremely hot. "*Oh, no, suh!*" he replied, surprised. "*Por me is beddy biled – by chidren eed dis,*" gesturing with his hand at the level of his thigh to indicate how small the children in question were. I found it incomprehensible.

At the same time, strangely, there was no denying how delicious the dish was. It was just that I'd never before associated "delicious" with excruciating pain. But as I proceeded, to the last syllable of pilaf rice, I found that I could taste what I was eating and that the taste was every bit as good as the smell promised it would be before the Vindaloo ever wrought rude mayhem inside my mouth and body.

Jeanette and I went to a concert that evening. I continued to sweat throughout each movement of whatever piece we heard. My ears kept filling up as if the concert hall itself were undergoing enormous fluctuations in altitude. When we went to bed, my mouth was still tingling, but I was experiencing no pain, presumably due to the release of endorphins. The next morning, with my ass firmly planted on the toilet seat, I yearned for some of those endorphins, or at least some yoghurt with cucumber, to assuage the effects of the flame-thrower that had now reached the other end of my alimentary canal. [*During a trip to London some four decades later, I encountered that same Indian restaurant, went in, ordered the same Vindaloo lamb curry, and found it too mild; I had to ask for extra chili. Heat is relative to what one is used to!*]

When we returned to Malmö, I got out my Bible and began reading: "*In the beginning God created the heaven and the earth.*" For the first 18 years of my life, I'd been trained to read every last word of this book literally, and swallow it all without question. Now I knew I was reading a myth. At first, the story was merely bizarre, starting with a water-covered earth apparently all mixed together with a firmament, meaning the heavens. *But, what the...?* This was the *starting* point, *before* the first day of creation, the heaven and earth that apparently were already there before creation had begun. Even though I'd been reading it literally, I'd never noticed that.

Light was created on that first official day, and despite the sun not being created until the fourth day, the first three days all had an evening and a morning; again, something I hadn't noticed before. Men and women were created on the sixth day and instructed to get out there, to multiply "and replenish the earth" (Genesis 1:27-28; how does one *re*plenish something that's never been plenished?), but Adam and Eve weren't created until *after* the six days of creation were all over, plus the day of rest, which means until the next chapter; so, contrary to the nearly universal belief (as far as I'd ever heard Christians and others talk about), the Bible does *not* say that Adam and Eve were the first people! (That sequence of things, at least, resolved the conundrum raised in the movie *Inherit the Wind*, when the defense attorney asks where the wife of Cain came from. People had already been multiplying outside that garden for generations!) Did nobody read what was *there*, in black and white? Or was it just me?

As I continued reading, I found that nearly every verse seemed to contain absurdities and fallacies, but they were all pretty benign and silly in the first two chapters. It wasn't until chapter three that the truly foul nature of this God, this Jehovah, Yahweh, would start to reveal and assert itself and completely contradict anyone's notion of an all-wise, all-powerful and all-good God.

After being given all-too-easy access to it, Adam and Eve are commanded *not* to eat the fruit of the tree of knowledge of good and evil. God apparently never had kids before. Anyone who's interacted with kids knows that if you let them do (or have) five things and tell them not under any circumstances to go near the sixth, guess which one they'll be interested in? It's human nature! And don't say anything about Original Sin – Adam and Eve didn't have it yet! The only reasonable conclusion is that God *doesn't* want them to remain totally amoral (how are they supposed to know that eating this fruit is evil, without knowing what "evil" means?)! A serpent (created by God, by the way) persuades Eve to eat the forbidden fruit and to give some to Adam. For this, God condemns them and all their progeny to suffer forever. What a guy! Praise the Lord! God is love!

It gets worse. After a few hundred years of begetting, and a few dozen more *non sequiturs*, Noah comes along. By this time, the all-wise and all-powerful Jehovah is pretty fed up with the *entire* two-legged species He's created, since He's obviously failed to create them in accordance with His own quality specifications, and decides to undertake His first-ever genocide: kill *everybody* (except eight people: Noah himself, his three sons, and their four respective spouses). God is going to drown *everybody* else – including all the animals – except for one male and one female of each species.

After God has made enough rain to drown them all, He keeps everything submerged for five months. The first thing Noah does once the flood has subsided enough to allow disembarkation is to take "of every clean beast and every clean fowl" (implying that God also created dirty ones) and kill them – as burnt offerings to the god who'd just nearly wiped out the entire planet. (So much for the survival of *those* sacrificial species!) Then, just to demonstrate once again what a nice guy He is, God creates a rainbow as a *covenant* not to kill everyone again, at least not *by water*! (There's no mention of fire here, not even in the fine print. He's got a whole bag of tricks; just wait till you get to Revelation!)

Noah is so thrilled he takes off all his clothes, gets plastered and passes out. One of his sons (Ham) sees his father naked and tells his brothers. When Noah wakes up, he doesn't blame *himself* for his drunkenness or for his nakedness. He doesn't even blame Ham. Oh no! Instead, he curses one of Ham's *unborn sons*, and all that son's progeny! (Jehovah clearly had no problem with Noah's generational jump over logic, nor over Noah venting his foul hangover on his unborn heirs.)

Noah's kids get busy repopulating the earth. Understandably, this one family, this only remaining family, spoke only one language. That makes things far too easy for everybody, as far as God is concerned, and He sees a huge risk that pooled intelligence and unimpeded communication might make people way too smart (Genesis 11:6). Thus, to establish employment opportunities for future translators, interpreters, departments of linguistics, language schools, negotiators, and probably an awful lot of lawyers and soldiers, God purposely screws up the common language and scatters people all over the earth.

When Abraham appears on the scene a few chapters later, God decides it's time for a new *covenant*, this one being circumcision; every guy who wants to be included among God's people has to have his foreskin lopped off. Why not his left earlobe? Or just get a haircut? Don't ask. (Little boys don't get to ask; it's done to them when they're newly born.)

Anyway, after Abraham unsuccessfully tries to talk God out of slaughtering the entire populations of Sodom and Gomorrah, only a guy named Lot, his wife, and two daughters escape. But as they're escaping, the curious wife turns around to take a peek at what's happening to her former home (God is burning it up), and God in His mercy finds it suitable to turn her into a pillar of salt, after which Lot goes to live in a cave with his daughters, who get him drunk and straddle him to get impregnated and thereby spawn a couple of the peoples God would have fun slaughtering later.

But in the meantime, God commands Abraham to murder his own son as a sacrifice to the God who loves him, just to test whether He's got Abraham where He wants him. How does the demand for blind obedience fit with the concept of free will? How does any of this vile shit fit with anything remotely related to morality?

Although I'd only read halfway through Genesis, the first book in the Bible, I realized that *as a myth* it's an excellent and entertaining piece of literature. But as an alleged fountainhead of Truth and Morality, it's an almost endless source of outrage, an insult to intelligence and decency, a mockery of logic, a bastion of *im*morality. As such, it's also an ancient, historical attempt to enslave the minds of men and women in chains of fear and superstition, and that it's been hugely successful for thousands of years. Now, in the 21st century, people by the billions are still devoting their lives to documents that have no other merits than that they're old. They're documents that generation after generation have been coupled to powerful traditions, without the benefit of evidence, based on warped imaginations, questionable hearsay, faulty translations and convenient revisions over centuries.

What about God explicitly ordering the murder of all the Midians? What about sending His angel of death to slay all the firstborn of every single household in Egypt – when He had the power to slay the bloody Pharaoh instead? It's repugnant to all decency. Jehovah, the *only* God of the Bible, makes Hitler look like a kindergarten teacher!

So had we actually *proved* that there is no god? Of course not! Nobody can ever prove that there *cannot* be one, just as I can never prove that some planet somewhere in the universe doesn't have talking marshmallows that decide the fate of everyone here on Earth. Generally speaking, nobody can *prove* the *non-*existence of anything.

Given the futility of excluding gods nobody's ever heard of (or gods not invented yet), the question "Do you believe in god?" is not properly limited to a yes-or-no answer, but begs a follow-up question: "Which one?" If your reply singles out the God of the Bible (Jehovah), the onus is on *you* to prove he *does* exist. If the Bible is your "evidence", I *can* prove that the Bible itself portrays a god who is bloodthirsty, vindictive, treacherous, murderous, and genocidal. Thus, even if He existed, He would not be worthy of worship. Allah is no better off, nor is Shiva or Osiris or any of the other thousands of gods people have invented. And in terms of those other gods, you too are *already* an atheist.

As far as we were concerned, the *internal* struggle to understand this ancient problem was over. But the *external* struggle – with family and friends, with the assumptions of the vast majority who'd never taken the trouble to get down to the bone on this very fundamental question – was far from over. There would be never-ending questions, challenges, arguments, direct assaults, subtle allusions, penetrating most areas of society and social life. Even in Sweden, one the most secularized countries in the world, there was still a state church (an official religion) until 2000. Tax exemptions for churches are nearly universal, as well as for church-run schools: state-subsidized indoctrination.

The Enlightenment, with the rise of science and humanism, had been backing fundamentalist Christianity further and further into a corner, requiring fundamentalists to make more and more figurative interpretations instead of literal ones in order to make the figuratively barbaric acts of a figuratively psychotic deity less literally outrageous and evil. But I couldn't (and cannot) see how even the most figurative interpretation of the slaying of every firstborn child in an entire country could or can be anything less than a literal atrocity, sadistic mass murder.

Another problem is the basic intellectual dishonesty of "liberal" Evangelical Christians in their unwillingness to define clearly which parts of the Bible they feel should still be read literally nowadays, and which have become figurative. They are even less willing to consider editing out – removing, deleting, expurgating – the most barbaric accounts of Jehovah's dark sides, for a start. Perhaps they fear how thin the "Good Book" would turn out to be if it were *truly* good? (See Thomas Jefferson's attempt.)

The next point of retreat among the new liberals and apologists seemed to be to try to divert all attention from the Old Testament and its embarrassingly voracious god to the new guy in town, Jesus. Indeed, although the New Testament is of highly doubtful authorship and historical veracity, some of the things it claims that Jesus said are *great* things, *revolutionary* things. Jesus was OK, I thought, but he came from a lousy family. I tried holding on to that premise for a while. But it didn't work. We only know Jesus through the Bible, in which Jesus *also* commands us to love and obey all the laws and commandments of Jehovah the Psycho, which means that Jesus was no real improvement after all. Yes, it was great and wonderful that Jesus ranted a lot about helping the poor and the sick and the elderly; I had no problem agreeing with his socialist principles.

I grew up in a country where the word *socialist* was and is mostly used as an accusation or an invective, in addition to being a very misunderstood catchall term for an extremely broad spectrum of sometimes contradictory and incompatible ideologies, from the National Socialism of Hitler's Germany to the Communist Socialism of Stalin and Mao. The socialism I'd experienced in Sweden in the form of Social Democracy offered complete protection of freedom of expression, while also protecting against poverty (even if such protection was at the expense of curbing extreme wealth); equal, universal and free access to good healthcare and care for the elderly; and equal access to free education, all financed by taxes. Where does Jesus fit into this? Read Matthew 25:40-45, in which He basically tells people that if they treat the poor and the sick badly, they're going to be up Shit Creek on Judgment Day – *the way you treat the poorest is the way you treat me*. So how could anyone calling him- or herself a Christian possibly vote Republican – the party for those who cut taxes for the rich, thereby leaving the rest up to individuals, of which there are far too few to be interested in meeting the needs of the poor?!

As good as Jesus efforts were on this issue, however, it doesn't let him off the hook. He talked more about sending people to eternal torture than all the prophets of the Old Testament combined. And yes, it was great that Jesus cured a few lepers. But since He claimed to be one and the same as the Almighty God (with whom *all* things are possible), He *could* have wiped out leprosy itself – and all other diseases – but He didn't. The fact that He could have prevented suffering, and didn't, could defensibly be called criminal negligence, and it makes curing just a few nothing more than a cynical party trick.

Religious life must certainly have been simpler when people believed that the Bible was the literal word of God, period. You either took Jehovah for what He was or you went to hell. By claiming to remove the bloodthirsty Jehovah from the equation, modern Christianity threatens itself with its own irrelevance. *There's this god, but not at all like the biblical Jehovah, who stands for peace and love, but we don't and can't truly know who he is, yet you should believe, but it's all right if you don't, too.* It makes about as much sense to me as the hippy mantra: *it's all cool, man.*

Almost nothing in the contemporaneous literature, apart from the New Testament itself (which was almost certainly not contemporaneous) even mentions the existence of a historical character named Jesus. The Gospels themselves didn't make the cut until around the 4th century, when the leaders of the budding new religion were arguing about what the religion should be and what books should be included in or omitted (or edited or rewritten) from the canon of the New Testament.

Not only were all of those books written decades or centuries after the events they describe, by people who thus could not have been eyewitnesses, they had also been repeatedly transcribed by people with agendas. The Gospels, like the rest of the Bible, are rife with contradictions among themselves – then decided upon by people with vested interests in projecting a business model that would gain them the maximum market share of people eager to find a belief system to latch onto and make themselves subservient to. Thus, even if one accepts the possibility of a historical Jesus, there are no documents written during his lifetime to corroborate it. All the words and deeds attributed to him and his first followers in the New Testament were written long after everyone alive at the time was dead. *None* of it would stand up in court today.

Suppose there were a god, or a Jesus, who is inaccurately represented in the Bible because of erroneous translations or intentionally deceitful editing. Would it not be the responsibility of such a deity to assure that the only story available to mankind about Him was in fact true, 100% accurate? How else could He require the unquestioning faith of every human being? And wouldn't a *benevolent* god find it appalling that people are willing to worship the monster who *is* depicted in the Bible?

Or consider this hypothetical scenario: Suppose there's a God who's testing mankind to see if people are foolish or inherently evil enough to worship a manifestly evil deity – and then He sends everyone who does so to hell? (See

Jesus' parable of the three servants in Matthew 25.) Maybe a hypothetical God gave people brains to see if they would use them to figure out that all the world's alleged deities are totally unfit for worship, and that people need to learn how to be kind and make as much sense of their lives and their universe as they can *on their own*, and that only those who figure that out will be granted access to Paradise? This admittedly doesn't seem likely, but it doesn't seem less likely than the other fairy tales, and nobody can prove this one wrong either.

Nothing sounds quite as silly as *someone else's* religion. Joseph Smith receiving golden tablets from a morony angel in a New York cave? C'mon! Muslims circling some piece of rock in Mecca? Yeah, sure! Hindus and their eight-armed gods? Oh please! Christians and their virgin birth? Whoops, that's us! And why is it only Catholics who have "visions" of Mary, only Hindus of Vishnu?

Most religions, particularly the allegedly monotheistic ones, consider themselves incompatible with all others. (I say "allegedly" because there is some doubt in my mind that the Abrahamic religions *are* monotheistic. Why would their god forbid the worship of any other gods – if they believe there *are* no other gods? It's as silly as commanding someone in Paris not to climb any other Eifel Towers than the Eifel Tower....) If you believe in one god or one version of god, you can't even allow the possibility of someone else's god or version; it's heretical. Each of these mutually exclusive religions claims to be The Right One. Faced with this fact, and with the unbearable fact of Jehovah as the best the Bible has to offer, I found the whole thing extremely doubtful, distasteful, absurd, ludicrous and ultimately a cynical exploitation of people's natural fears and ignorance. Religious people sometimes spoke of an "innate god-consciousness". I began to look for other explanations.

From the things I've read, it seems far more reasonable to me that man has created his gods – thousands of them – in his own image, rather than vice-versa. The grim god of the Bible is a psychopath by the standards of decent people everywhere – at least by today's standards. But today's moral sense is fairly recent; the Manifest Destiny doctrine that encouraged White people to massacre the Indians in America without feeling any moral qualms about it is less than two centuries old (and it still exists in various forms). The enslavement of Black people was written into the US Constitution and wasn't formally banned until the late 19th century. The gross injustices to Black people (and others) continues to this day in the US (and elsewhere). Prior to that, the mistreatment of anyone with whom one was not allied was the rule rather than the exception in human interaction. It was not until the emergence of *humanism* – not religion – that the *im*morality of the Bible and its God began to be driven into the shadows of myths, figurative interpretations, embarrassed logical acrobatics, resigned disengagement, nervous silence, and other backwaters of cornered apologetics.

Getting down to the bare bones of it all, I still could (and can) not state with absolute certainty that there *cannot* be a god, nor that there cannot ever have been one (or 29 of them or 3,009 or 40,010). What I *can* say for certain is that I cannot find the god of the Bible worthy of worship, praise, adoration, or anything but utter contempt. If that particular god were real, He would be even more contemptible if He expected (much less demanded) obedience or subservience based on the awful portrayal of His character in that book, which He has done nothing to correct. Moreover, since no other god has ever stepped forward and offered a portrayal of a being or deity who is even reasonably likeable, it seems to me unlikely that any possible god could give a flying fart about what happens to any of us struggling humans or any other species on this planet or elsewhere.

Jeanette and I had long discussions about all this. They were troubling discussions initially, but mostly for me. Jeanette had already pretty much abandoned belief in God when we first met in October 1964 – despite having been raised in the strong traditions of the Catholic Church (some of which she still retained back then, in certain awkward areas). For her, the emphasis was always on tradition, not on anything remotely like underlying doctrine or dogma; she'd never experienced any of the full-force-feeding to which I'd been subjected.

It's easy enough to understand how the whole religion thing might have gotten started in the dawn of the human race. First, there's natural fear of the unknown – the terror primitive man must have felt in the face of natural phenomena like fiery volcanic eruptions, roaring hurricanes, rumbling earthquakes, inexplicable eclipses, powerful thunder and lightning, awesome auroras – all of which must have scared the shit out of primitive societies and made them turn to anyone who claimed to have an explanation for them, however silly or unfounded the explanation might be. What, then, do you do if you don't have an explanation? You make one up! (Most people *hate* not having answers, even if the answers are wrong.) The rational person may make up an "explanation" in the form of a working hypothesis that fits all available facts – but then changes the hypothesis the moment new facts emerge that don't fit. The irrational person makes up an explanation in the form of Truth which becomes the immutable prerequisite for accepting or forbidding any new information (*"my mind is made up, don't confuse me with facts"*). There was thus a golden opportunity for a few fast-talking storytellers and creative snake-oil merchants to grab power over people's lives – to found religions and invent gods craving appeasement, sacrifices and money, unquestioning worship and money, obedience and more money.

Add to this another "natural" cause of religion: the human predilection for ceremony and tradition, which makes it easy to institutionalize the superstitions and invent whatever god or gods might be needed for an outstanding business launch. The power of traditions seems to prevail in just about every human endeavor and in every culture. Linking tradition to superstition becomes a force so powerful that one might even expect it to be global. (*Psst! By the way, in case you haven't noticed, it is global.*)

Another, still more potent ingredient can account for the nearly universal need to believe: the yearning for immortality. Who has never experienced an almost overwhelming desire to be reunited with a departed loved one, or a wish to deny the finality of a loved one's death – or one's own? Then some self-proclaimed witch doctor or clergyman or shaman or sham-man comes along and says just what you want to hear: "*You can! Just believe this or that, just think this or that way, and just stop asking your damn questions.*" But consider this: the closer to *you* that loved one is – in time or in relationship – the stronger your desire for reunification is likely to be. See your mom or dad again? A beloved sibling or child or spouse? That's normally a highly attractive proposal indeed, devoutly to be wished! Then move away from yourself a notch: a cousin, a not-so-beloved uncle or grandparent, a close friend, a former neighbor or colleague? Sure, why not, but the urgency isn't quite the same. What about reuniting with 2,468 Albanians (*for example*, no disrespect intended!) from the 14th century? Uhhh, well.... Doesn't it come down to how hard it is to accept that somebody as wonderful as *yourself* can just *cease to be*?!

Then people ask, *But where do you go when you die? How can a person's life just end, how can a person simply cease to be?* What makes you think that anyone goes *any*where? Do wasps go somewhere after you smash them? Do bacteria join their ancestors in an afterlife after you've annihilated them with antibiotics? Where does that beautiful, living flame "go" when you blow out a candle? And where were you *before* you were born? Life is a process. A process doesn't go on – or go anywhere – when it's over; it's just over.

Immortality has one more selling point, however: reward and retribution. It's indeed hard to accept that truly good and kind people sometimes endure a lifetime of misfortune and misery, or that truly cruel and evil people prosper in every way their whole life long. How *nice* if everything could be put right in an afterlife! Sorry, dreamer. Nothing is ever going to be true just because it would be nice if it were true. And yet one can never prove the *non*-existence of things. Does that mean that people can believe anything? Yes! That's precisely what they do. *Any*thing! Just look around! But it still doesn't make it true, because truth requires *evidence*, and about gods or afterlives there is none. Truth isn't about majority decisions. For millennia, nearly everybody believed that the earth was flat and that the sun went around it. That didn't make it true. Bertrand Russell offers a reasonable suggestion: "*If a thing is true, you should believe it; if it isn't true, you shouldn't. And if you can't find out whether it is true, you should suspend judgment.*"

The combined *raisons d'être* for religion provide as strong an *emotional* foundation for religion as you could ever want. Does it matter if it's true or not? Don't you dare ask questions like that! Every time I backed John or Al into a corner on something like this, they would say, "*Well, I haven't got the answers to those questions – but I don't need to, since He has the answers, and He will reveal them to me if and when He sees fit.*" One of my brothers once defended his faith by citing a 17th century French philosopher (not an exact quotation): "*Even if there's only a small chance that the Bible is true, I'll believe that, since if it's not, and there's no afterlife, I won't have lost anything.*" Pascal's Wager, a line of reasoning named after its father, gives nothing more than false emotional security to those who need it and don't mind basing their entire lives on what *cannot* be known to be true. It's also contingent on an omnipotent god who demands true devotion and knows people's hearts. Would such a god fall for the claims of people He knows are simply hedging their bets? What the Blaises! What about losing your human dignity?!

The invention of the bloodthirsty Jehovah simply reflects the primitive fears and violence of early Hebrew society, just as the gods of other societies reflect their cultures. What is true in any objective sense is irrelevant to unquestioning belief. Why not just let people be happy following the religions they feel comfortable believing? What's the harm? The answer: most wars, throughout history and right now are inspired, supported and driven by asserting the dominion of one religion over another. Laws that for centuries subjugated women and persecuted homosexuals all came from religions. Real problems *do* arise when people try to pass off as intellectual or rational truth that which they believe because it is emotionally satisfying to them – and then shove those beliefs down other people's throats, because they feel threatened by other people's *un*belief.

The more Jeanette and I talked about all of this, the less troubling it was becoming. I started feeling intimations of liberation from the *anxiety* of faith, the anxiety of realizing that I'd been instructed not only to entertain beliefs, but to embrace them with all my heart, beliefs for which there is no evidence. I could see that only *blind* faith – the willful ignorance of challenges, the denial of doubt, the narcosis of the intellect – would not be full of anxiety, and would allow a person to find "peace" in not knowing. The peace "which passeth all understanding" (Philippians 4:7), however, is the peace that *prohibits* understanding.

My problem was that I couldn't find a leave-your-mind-at-the-door approach satisfactory in any way. *And yet. And yet. Completely* abandoning beliefs that have long been held for purely emotional reasons – beliefs that I was brainwashed into holding since before I was old enough to know anything about what beliefs were, or what holding beliefs meant, beliefs that were simply always *there* – was somehow still an irrational, scary thing, like a phobia: *discredophobia*, the fear of ceasing to believe. Being scared is emotional too.

I knew what I had to do, like when I left Oak Park. Then Norm was in the same boat with me, and now I knew that Bob was also on the brink of another Great Escape with me. Jeanette found it a little odd that Bob and I were making such a fuss about it all. *Why make such a fuss? Why not just walk away from it all, leave it behind?* But she'd never been in our position, and because of that, perhaps she didn't fully comprehend why we saw our position as being on the brink of something both frightening and wonderful. Bob and I were about to abandon the principle of believing anything simply because it could *not* be shown to be *un*true, and instead only believe something *once it is shown to be true* – and then to keep on questioning it.

CHAPTER 3

In this together

Now that trips to see Bob in German-speaking Basel had already become a fixture in our lives, Jeanette decided to take a course in German that autumn. She only needed to work part-time, like me, since our living expenses were so low and our habits so frugal. Besides, she didn't want to fall behind me; I'd already demonstrated a somewhat irritating ability to snap up German words and phrases as if by osmosis, and was totally uninhibited about using several hundred percent of what I knew; I didn't prioritize the importance of correct conjugations over successful communication. Although I certainly made many a native speaker wince a lot (I probably also made some cringe, weep or laugh), I generally managed to make myself understood – my sole practical aim. But Jeanette had a greater, nobler motive for wanting to learn German: she wanted to be able to understand Mozart's *Die Zauberflöte*, as well as and the *Lieder* of Schubert – *Die schöne Müllerin* and other amazing song cycles that Bob introduced us to – and eventually to be able to read the works of Franz Kafka, Günther Grass and other German authors in the original language. She was very ambitious!

The Olympics in Munich began soon after we returned from London. We watched quite a few events on TV, when we were too tired to undertake anything more useful; there was no time difference to contend with either. On September 5th, we heard on the morning news that members of a secular Palestinian movement called Black September broke into the compound of the Israeli Olympic athletes, taking many of them hostage. After unsuccessful negotiations for their release, 11 Israeli athletes were killed during an attempt by special force teams to free them on September 6th.

It was hard to understand why the Palestinians would be so hostile towards the Israelis. I had no clue about it at the time. After all, Israel had only confiscated what was once Palestine and made it their own country – which they claimed was theirs by Divine Right (bloody religion again!) – forcing most of the Palestinians from their homes, lands and livelihoods into miserable refugee camps within the new state of Israel or in neighboring Arab states. And everywhere the Palestinians were driven, they became second-class citizens at best. Why would anyone get upset about a thing like that?

Then three days later, on September 9th, the US lost the final in the men's

Olympic basketball – in the last second of play – to the USSR, of all countries. I was for some weird reason much more upset about that than about the Palestinians. Why?! There was clearly so unfathomably little I knew about the world I lived in, about proportions and priorities, to be able to grasp why the lives, suffering and welfare of an entire people should affect me less than the outcome of a ball game.

Once I thought about it, and could see the parallels between what happened to America's Indians and what was happening to the Palestinians, it finally began to be too obvious even for me to ignore. The blatant injustice, the sanctimonious dispossession, the impotent frustration in the face of overwhelming force, the dehumanizing of the defeated, these were all ingredients in the explosive manifestations of outrage that occurred both at Little Big Horn and in Munich (among other places and times). Does that *excuse* massacre? Certainly not! Does it *explain* massacre? Yes, quite clearly it does! And it seems to me that such a clear explanation *should* point the way towards how to avoid a recurrence, how to understand where the frustration comes from, how to discontinue and rectify the injustice that fuels it. It *should*, but does it?

I hadn't painted anything since June, just before Rosanne's visit. So much had been going on in July and August to make my head spin that I didn't have a chance to concentrate the way I needed to. I did, however, do some sketching, both on paper and on a few canvases. Until now, I worked either by standing a canvas on a table, propping it up against a wall, or by balancing it on a cheap flimsy easel (more like a collapsible music stand) that exasperated me with its wobbliness, or by laying it flat on the floor on newspapers, while I crouched, kneeled, and squirmed around the canvas.

On my birthday, Jeanette surprised me with a proper, robust (and expensive) studio easel. Her loving hint – that she wanted to encourage me to get back to my painting – was none too subtle. I was overwhelmed and overjoyed. The first canvas on my new easel was a motif I'd already sketched a couple of times before. It was a tribute to Bob – who introduced classical music to me, and new depths of it to Jeanette. It's called *The Giver of Music*.[1] The motif comes from Mozart's *Die Zauberflöte* (*The Magic Flute*), which Bob played for us and told us about in considerable Bob-style detail. The opera opens with a snake or dragon

---

1 Painting #19 (see Appendix 2)

threatening to devour the young protagonist, Tamino. Out of this fearsome (although not usually staged that way) opening gushes the most magnificent music, throughout the opera. When we first met Bob in 1970, he'd been told by his doctor a few years earlier that he only had a couple more years left to live. Out of this "death sentence" comes this position of Bob standing in the jaws of death. He brought us music – and so much more, since it turned out that his doctor was wrong.

Following our almost surreal wedding anniversary experience in Świnoujście in '71, Jeanette and I decided to abandon our attempts to celebrate our anniversary in a different country every year, and to return to Switzerland, to Binningen, to Bob again, for our October 8th sixth-anniversary celebration. This time we had no car, so the trip promised to be less dramatic than the one in '70. We took the train both ways.

Since I was free the entire week commencing October 1st (work at the school was pretty slow), while Jeanette had to work mornings every day, we agreed with Bob that I would get a head start by leaving for Basel in the late afternoon on the Sunday, arriving in the late morning on Monday, and Jeanette would leave on Friday afternoon and join us on Saturday. I took a train from the central station in Copenhagen to the same ferry terminal in Rødby we'd driven to two years before. Once the train reached the ferry terminal, it was divided into a couple of sections short enough to fit onboard the ferry. It was then recombined once we got to Puttgarden on the German side.

During the crossing, I headed up to the crowded cafeteria to get a beer to accompany the sandwiches Jeanette made for me for dinner. While looking around for a place to sit, I heard the sounds of English being spoken at a table nearby, turned around and saw three young men conversing. I asked if one of the other chairs at their table was free and they invited me to join them. One of the guys was American, one was English, and the third was Canadian. It turned out that they'd only just met each other by chance as well. After we'd chatted about various things for a while, the American guy suddenly turned to me and said, "You're from England, aren't you?" The Englishman quickly replied, "No, he's not, he's American!" and the Canadian interjected, "C'mon, he's Canadian!" I was grinning broadly during this exchange about my origins, and I'd have to say I was flattered by at least two of their assessments.

The train reached Hamburg in the evening and I had to change there for another old overnight train to Basel, leaving late that evening. My compartment had dark red leather, well-worn seats. There were three places on each side, facing each other, making a total of six seats. I was the first to enter this compartment, so I chose a seat by the window, facing forward. I tried to get some sleep, but the corridor was a bit noisy for a while. People were entering and leaving my compartment, leaving the train at different stops or going out into the corridor for a smoke. The train was jerky. I was missing Jeanette and thinking about the upcoming discussions with Bob – and about the possible regression in the state of his apartment, in addition to all the work that remained to be done from our previous visit.

As the somewhat boring southbound journey consumed the night and northern Germany, and gave me a little sleep, and dawn became morning in the southern half of Germany, I found myself alone in the compartment except for an old Turkish man, sitting opposite me, by the window. I'd been asleep when he entered the compartment. His coat was hanging from a hook by the door. He had a large, gray, elegant mustache and wore tidy but somewhat scruffy clothes. A few attempts in English and my smattering of French and German revealed that he spoke only Turkish, and my Turkish wasn't what it never had been. After a stop somewhere farther south, a German girl joined our compartment and took the middle seat, opposite me, and next to the Turk. (Since the coat hooks by the door already held the Turk's heavy winter coat as well as mine, the middle seat offered the most space.) She made a few comments to me in German that I failed to understand, and I tried English with her, but she knew none. Then she and the old Turk tried to strike up a conversation, but finding no common language there either, we all three sat in silence. The Turk gazed blankly and sadly in the general direction of the window. She was keeping an eye on her coat, which she'd also hung on one of the hooks by the door to the compartment.

It was a magical metaphorical moment; as discreetly as I possibly could, I pulled my sketch pad out of my bag, pulled a pencil out of the pocket of my Harris tweed sport jacket, and pretended to begin writing a letter, occasionally touching pencil to paper in the form of a rough sketch to capture what I perceived to be a striking metaphor of the quintessential isolation and loneliness of Man, the insurmountable barrier to real communication that mutually incomprehensible languages entail, apart from all the other psychological, sociological, political, generational and religious barriers that help to assure and enforce such isolation. I didn't, of course, have any reason to think that the two people sitting opposite me were feeling lonely; what was remarkable to me was how the situation itself became a metaphor of loneliness in my mind, if not in reality.

After finishing my hurried sketch – I didn't want anyone to feel self-conscious – I put my sketch pad away. The Turk got off in Karlsruhe, the German girl in Freiburg, and I eagerly awaited my arrival at the station in Basel, where Bob said he would meet me. It's just that Bob hadn't pointed out – or I'd failed to remember or listen properly – that there were *two* Basel train stations: Basel Badischer Bahnhof (in Germany) and Basel SBB (in Switzerland). I got off at the first; Bob was waiting for me at the second.

When I neither found Bob nor recognized the station from the previous times, I found somebody who could tell me what train to take to get to the right one – and I tried to page Bob there. By the time I arrived at the correct station, Bob was gone, but now I knew exactly what tram to take to Binningen, so I hoped I would arrive at his apartment building before he'd have time to start drowning his sorrows again. It took a while to get him to answer his doorbell (he still had no phone), but after half an hour or so, I was admitted.

I was a little disappointed, but not surprised, to see (and smell) how far the condition of Bob's apartment had regressed in the direction of its former state. However, much of it was cosmetic this time – the staleness was superficial (not deep) stench, and much of the floor was visible. And now I knew how to tackle it.

Bob had only been able to take the Monday off; he had to work the rest of the week and told me I could do with (or to) his apartment whatever I saw fit. *Carte blanche.* I was eager to complete as much as possible of the sorting, tidying and cleaning before Jeanette arrived late Saturday morning. My aim was to see to that during the daytime on the days when Bob was at work.

I wasn't stressed too much about getting started, at least once I finished a perfunctory job to improve kitchen and bathroom hygiene. I cleared a couple of seats for us in the living room and a place on the floor where I would eventually be able to make my futon-less bed for the night. An hour or so of whirlwind activity took care of all that – I was young then!

Bob put on some beautiful classical music while I opened one of the bottles of amazing French wine he'd purchased for the occasion (it might have been a Chateau Margaux – he would eventually serve us several of those – or else something of that caliber). His collection of PX-procured LPs was astounding, and since my last visit he'd purchased a top-of-the-line stereo, as well as a tiny black-and-white TV. Working his way out of his depression also meant a great surge in interest in what was happening in the world, particularly in this year of a growing Watergate scandal amid the enormous US election hoopla and our fear that Nixon would win again. Bob's interest in every detail and every item of breaking news about Watergate was far greater than my own. He seemed to have been hanging on to more emotional ties to the US than I had, in line with his maintained interest in the Meeting (although that never made the breaking news!).

Only after Bob finished venting his disgust with Nixon could we begin catching up on where we stood in terms of our Great Escape from religious superstition. Independently of each other, he'd arrived at nearly identical conclusions to the ones Jeanette and I had been working out after London. And we both realized how much easier it was to let go *together*, because that was another aspect of the attraction of religion that hadn't occurred to me: the role of church membership in securing an individual's *social* safety net.

I'd seen the power of social pressure clearly enough in the Meeting, where the Meeting people were the *only* people in my parents' social circle. Leave the Meeting and you're entirely out in the cold socially too, back to square one! Even though I'd remained something of a loner since leaving my parents' home (more by circumstance than by choice, I always felt), and Bob was closer to being a hermit than most people I'd ever met, there was still a barrier, a threshold, a wall, something that separated the vast majority of Believers (whether hypocritically nominal or rabidly fanatical) from the tiny minority of people who dared to take the position that the entire religion thing was a load of hogwash – ancient and highly popular hogwash, but still hogwash. In our native land, *what* religion you had was not nearly as important as whether you had any religion at all. Uncloseted atheists were not electable. Godlessness was tantamount to lawlessness.

We realized that we were at last putting the fallacies and lies of our upbringing behind us for good, that we were no longer prepared to accept any answers without consciously reserving the right and exercising the duty to question them, a step that meant we were living and thinking freely, no longer on autopilot, prepared to live with doubt and uncertainty and not knowing, even if our unwillingness to believe unfounded things might place certain limitations on our social lives.

Bob could become livid when talking about the tyranny of parents towards their children in forcing them to believe dogma. I didn't like the idea either, but it didn't evoke nearly that level of rage in me. On the other hand, Bob was more concerned than I initially was about not throwing out any babies with the bathwater; he maintained firmly that Handel's *Messiah* and Bach's *Mass in B-Minor* were among the most sublime works of music ever composed, and that the *tunes* of many an old hymn of our twisted childhoods were beautiful, no matter how foolish (and often cruel) the lyrics might be. Many fine old churches were architectural masterpieces; altarpieces by the Great Masters were still great works of art. Even the Bible contained a great deal of wisdom and beauty in there among all the shit.

As far as I know, nobody ever calls a person a fanatic if that person is vehemently opposed to rape or genocide. If the god of the Bible is demonstrably – as in the Bible itself – an advocate and perpetrator of such heinous deeds, is one a fanatic for vehemently opposing worship of him?

We talked as late into the night as Bob's early start for work the next day allowed. Living with uncertainty – the uncertainty of doubt and of having to say "*I don't know*" – is so much harder work than simply swallowing wholesale the beliefs of one's parents or community. But thinking with the autopilot off is also ultimately so much more intellectually gratifying and exciting. It made us postpone sleep until I could no longer allow myself to become an accomplice in what might become Bob's severe sleep deprivation. Before he went to bed, however, I made sure he gave me a key and told me where to find trash bags or where I could buy them. We covered a lot of ground in those first few hours.

The next morning I awoke as Bob was leaving, early, at around half past six. I started by giving the bathroom a much more thorough cleaning, using a razor blade and powerful cleansers to attack the toilet bowl and sink to remove the heavy scaling. I unscrewed the shower head and placed the whole thing in a bowl of ascetic acid to dissolve the lime scaling, so the water wouldn't continue to spray out in all directions except the desired one when taking a shower. Then I scoured the floor before moving on to the next round in the kitchen.

First I removed everything that was spoiled and moldy from the fridge and in the cabinets. That left a deficit of edibles, so I began making a shopping list. The evening before, Bob showed me that he was no longer boiling partially opened cans of food for his dinner, but was trying out some frozen TV dinners. The problem was that the freezing compartment of his fridge was only big enough for one or two such dinners, provided nothing else was kept in there. A further problem with that was that he had to keep ice cream in his freezer. He loved ice cream, which was perfectly understandable to me, but since it meant that all the TV dinners had to be in the fridge instead, they had thawed and were not designed for being kept in that condition, which perhaps explained why mine tasted a bit funny the evening before.

I took a break, and started sorting the carpet of papers on the floor of his living room and bedroom. Among the clothing and garbage and piles of aging newspapers, some porn and some mail, I also came across quite a lot of cash – close to a thousand Swiss francs! – mostly in small bills. That solved the shopping problem, so I took the shopping list and headed down to Migros, just across the tiny Birsig River (more like a creek) from Bob's apartment building. As long as Jeanette and I were going to be at his place, he was going to get some good home cooking, so I bought enough stuff for two dinners, plus a few breakfasts. (His immutable breakfast consisted of a small disposable plastic cup of fruit yoghurt and a glass of juice, nothing more.)

Back at his apartment, I continued sorting papers, taking it upon myself to make stacks of the local daily (*Basler Zeitung*). Most of them were still in their address sleeves. I made other stacks of obvious advertisements and catalogues, and separate stacks of what might be considered personal mail, including numerous bills, all unopened. The dates on many of these things were more than a year old. He had numerous subscriptions to magazines he never read, so I suggested there might be some money to save here, but in most cases the *idea* of being able to read them, even if only in theory, was more important to him than the cost.

Apart from the numerous neat stacks of different kinds of paper on the floor everywhere, the apartment looked amazingly tidy by the time Bob got home from Roche that Tuesday evening. I was in the kitchen preparing some *cordon bleu* I'd found at Migros, to be accompanied by rice, a sauce I'd concocted and a salad of fresh tomatoes. A bottle of wine was already breathing on the countertop. Bob's expression of great pain, anxiety and weariness coming off a day at Roche vanished at the sights and smells that awaited him, and a big smile spread across his face. I knew I'd done the right thing.

We launched straight into our conversation of the evening before, over some wine, during the meal preparation, while he sat in the tiny kitchen to keep me company, then continued our discourse over the meal. Due to the presence of a very large cabinet in the kitchen (mostly containing crates of beer bottles, some empty and some full), there was just enough room for the two of us at the tiny table, with a little help from a laundry basket that could serve as a sideboard. After dinner, I was eager to get some guidelines from him about what I could throw out and what he needed to check first. All newspapers older than a week could go, he said, as well as most of the ads, except for those from Eddie Bauer (a US clothing store), Blackwell's and Foyle's (two London booksellers). I'd separated out a stack of porn magazines, which he took with him into his bedroom. I wouldn't see them again until I tackled that room at his behest during a later visit.

We needed to go through the personal stuff envelope by envelope, but that would have to wait for another evening, since he was pretty exhausted. (So was I.) He perked up a bit, however, when I handed him the stack of cash – but he was somewhat embarrassed when I told him where I'd found it. He told me to keep it and use it for anything I needed to keep this miraculous metamorphosis of his apartment going. I told him I'd already used some of it to buy groceries, and that I intended to buy him a vacuum cleaner. His only alarm about that was that he felt compelled to remind me not to use the vacuum cleaner after 22.00 hours, and not ever on Sundays. I was so pleased to see how the ongoing transformation of his quarters was once again enabling his joy to gain the upper hand on his fatigue – it was now more a struggle with *physical* weariness; his depression had all but disappeared.

In the days that followed, I carried bundle after bundle of newspapers down to the garbage room, and sack after sack of other trash. I went through every pile of personal papers and sorted them by sender. There were not all that many unique senders; many of the bills turned out to be reminders of the unpaid bills in other unopened envelopes. I got him that vacuum cleaner and immediately gave the place its maiden encounter with the wonders of Electrolux.

I also began removing all paper and cardboard from the extremely cluttered passageway, but most of the clutter there was clothing. Bob loved shirts. He had hundreds of them (I seem to recall counting just over 400, plus whatever he had at the laundry at the time). Many were brand-new, unused, but the majority were returns from the dry cleaners, all neatly ironed and folded, then individually wrapped in plastic. They were now placed less neatly on the floor. I tried to fit them all onto the storage shelves in the passageway, but there were just too many. I noticed that he had dozens of white shirts, yet I never saw him wear a white shirt. When I inquired about that, he said that he in fact hated them. Among his many patterned shirts there were duplicates, triplicates, quadruplicates, and numerous other "-plicates". I asked Bob one evening if he wanted to keep them all. He said he would gladly get rid of many of them, including *all* whites and any -plicates above triple, but he didn't like the idea of just throwing them out. I told

Slings and Arrows

him I didn't either, and suggested that I could take them to a charity collection bin I'd seen on one of my outings. He liked that idea, so I bagged them up and hauled them away the next day.

I also found a strange item during the exploration (or excavation) of his passageway. It looked like a fairly large canvas shopping bag, but the sides weren't sewn together, thus making it merely a large rectangular piece of coarse, heavy-duty canvas with a leather handle securely sewn on each of the two short sides. Bob said it was made for gathering firewood. You place the canvas on the ground, lay pieces of firewood across it, then grab the two handles and carry it all home. It was a great idea, but he had no use for it whatsoever (it had never been used) and he said I was welcome to get rid of it. I told him I'd prefer to paint on it, which surprised and pleased him greatly. Free space was beginning to reappear in his apartment, and the ongoing departure of trash, clutter, and dust was clearly lifting Bob's spirits more and more each day.

One evening he handed me his letter opener when we were going to start on the personal mail; in spite of being left-handed, I had the dexterity to open about 20 envelopes to his one. As we were sorting out all the personal papers – letters from me, from his brother Charles, from old friends and acquaintances, correspondence with his lawyer about his divorce, copies of his letters to various editors, bills, receipts, legal documents, his residency in Switzerland, more porn, his taxes, etc – it became clear that his big rolltop desk contained a monstrosity of disorganization. It made him almost break out in a cold sweat just thinking about it. And it simply wouldn't hold any more, which was why the excess ended up on the living room floor. I told him I'd be happy to help to get it all organized, rolltop desk included, and that I *could* help, but that it would take some time – probably on my next trip. Gratitude fairly radiated from his face, and he told me he'd given up hope of ever meeting someone whom he could trust completely and who both could and would be willing to undertake such a Herculean task. But I looked forward to it; in fact, I could hardly wait to get going on it, because I had at last found a true friend, someone I could also trust implicitly, and someone who gladly accepted my help.

My only other *close* friend in the world, my dearest ever, arrived in the late morning on Saturday. I took the tram to meet her while Bob opened a bottle of wine for lunch. Early on Saturday morning, I'd gone over to Migros before Bob was up and got a few of the ingredients Jeanette often liked to use, so we'd at least have enough for Saturday and Sunday evenings. (At that time, almost all shops in Basel closed at 1 PM on Saturday and didn't open again until Monday morning.) I also moved the laundry basket from the kitchen to the bedroom, so I could bring in a small stool from the balcony (after cleaning it up), so all three of us could squeeze into Bob's kitchen, at least for our breakfasts. Bob understood my wish to go and meet Jeanette on my own.

It's hard to describe the joy Jeanette and I both felt in meeting at the station in Basel. For once, she put aside her normal reluctance to display affection publicly; she threw her arms around me and kissed me over and over. On the way back to Bob's, I brought her up to speed on all I'd been up to, and I think she was pretty relieved to know that she wouldn't need to be devoting much time to heavy cleaning work. But I did let her take over the cooking of the evening meals. She was such a willing magician in the kitchen, it would have been stupid of me to interfere with her spells.

The last time the three of us were together at Bob's place, there was so much trash that we scarcely noticed how sparsely furnished it was. Jeanette and I had removed a huge amount, and now that I'd removed so much more during the past week, it became clear, as the three of us were sitting on the living room floor around the low bench that was serving as a dinner table, that there would in fact be room for a sofa, as well as a fairly small dining table – with chairs – and that the teak table (currently covered by and covering mounds of papers and clothing) in Bob's bedroom would be perfect for use in accordance with its original intention: as a coffee table.

Bob liked the idea immediately. More than that, he already knew the perfect place to buy the perfect furniture: La Boutique Danoise, on a street called Aeschenvorstadt in central Basel, just a couple of doors from the Drachen Hotel, where Bob put my parents up less than a year and a half earlier. Bob was madly in love with Danish modern furniture, it turned out. I'd already seen him drooling over similar stuff at Silverberg's in Malmö. We loved it too, but could only drool at it from afar, since it was priced way out of our league. But we certainly had no idea whatsoever that Bob was remotely interested in *acquiring* furniture of any kind, let alone fine furniture or interior design. Nevertheless, we suggested making a little trip there on Monday, and Bob readily agreed.

On Sunday, Bob took us to see the Mariastein Monastery and Shrine up on a cliff outside Basel, to which pilgrims had been coming for something like 600 years. According to legend, a little boy playing near this monastery fell off the cliff and was headed for splattering on a flat rock about 50 meters below – or he would have been splattered there if the Virgin Mary herself hadn't happened to be standing there to intercede and catch him. About 200 years later, in the 16th century, the exact same thing allegedly happened again. I think we were most amazed by the realization that *millions* of children fall to their deaths every year and are *not* caught by any virgins or anyone else. It's almost as if one has to be predisposed to believe something before belief is possible.

Riding with Bob in a car that he was driving tended to be quite an experience as well, especially since his two-horsepower Deux Chevaux, a.k.a. the Citroën 2CV, was an extremely simplified version of a car, kind of like riding in a tin can with a rubber-band engine. Every gear Bob changed to seemed to make it go slower. It was drafty and noisy and didn't like hills. Bob's gifts of concentration didn't always include the task at hand; Jeanette was happy to hide in the back seat.

Then he told us something that made us roar with delight and disbelief, yet touched us deeply: on his way to work in the early morning every working day, he would sing, as loud as he could (which was quite loud in a small car), Sarastro's arias from *Die Zauberflöte*: *O Isis und Osiris* and *In diesen heil'gen Hallen*. To our astonishment, he had a good, rich baritone voice, and he sang them beautifully, with great feeling. But he laughed when he explained some lines from *In diesen heil'gen Hallen*, in which Sarastro, the leader of some mystical Brotherhood, explains that the Brotherhood welcomes and embraces *all* men, but if you don't like their teachings, you don't deserve to be called a man ("*Wen solche Lehren nicht erfreun, Verdienet nicht, ein Mensch zu sein*"), and are thus presumably to be reviled. That codicil sounded all too familiar, as in "God loves everybody" followed by "if you don't love Him, he'll send you to hell." What a guy!

On Monday, in the early afternoon (it should have been morning, but when Bob was on vacation, he slept in, so Jeanette and I continued sorting and tidying the rest of the apartment), we all took the tram into town and visited La Boutique Danoise. Bob was like a boy in a candy store. I'd made some notes of measurements so he wouldn't fall for something that wouldn't fit, or reject something he loved for fear that it wouldn't.

He fell for a very beautiful but tastefully simple three-seat teak-framed sofa, and was smiling (synonymous with drooling in this context) wide-eyed at the samples of the upholstery that could be ordered for the cushions. He eagerly selected a coarsely woven woolen fabric in a few autumnal yellow-orange parts of the spectrum. Muted colors, especially autumnal ones, were his favorites for the home (and to a large extent clothing as well). Then he suddenly began to have doubts about making the purchase (and adding other much-needed furnishings to his apartment), and whether there would be room for it, but I quickly checked the length and width and told him it would fit perfectly along the wall – or would fit well in several other arrangements. He decided to go for it, and was disappointed it wasn't available for delivery the same day (with his custom upholstery). His mind wasn't ready for a dining set yet. I didn't push him; once delivered, the sofa (with the coffee table from his bedroom) would allow at least two of us to move up from the floor for dinners, and someday it might even present him with opportunities to invite others to *his* place for a change. And since the cushions could easily be placed on the floor, it would make a welcome change for Jeanette and me from our nights on the hard, non-futon floor.

We also found him a bedside wall-mounted lamp, the kind that can be swung to any angle and extended to reach just about any reading position. It didn't take a lot of convincing for Bob to welcome this improvement on the bedside flashlight he'd been using for years for his bedtime reading! Next, he wanted a new TV – a color TV this time. Bob did nothing by halves; he'd already researched the market for the latest TVs and concluded that Sony's Trinitron technology was the best available, and that's what he was going to have. He was not, however, going to shop around for the best buy. In connection with his latest stereo purchase, he'd come to trust a shopkeeper named Marcel Hagen, and where electronics were concerned, nobody else would ever do after that. Hagen had done Bob a big favor – and himself a bigger one, as it would turn out – by personally bringing all the stereo components home to Bob from his shop on Spalenring Street and hooking them all up, so now Hagen could charge Bob pretty much whatever Hagen wanted for a color TV.

We made several day-trips by car during our remaining days together, one to the Black Forest, where we took the breathtaking Schwarzwaldhochstrasse, and followed the entire length of that scenic route, where the trees at the higher altitudes were beginning to turn and display the most glorious colors. One of the things that made the outing so breathtaking was the real uncertainty as to whether a 2CV could make the climb with three adults aboard. White knuckles were in evidence, especially with Bob driving on the downgrades.

We also visited Alsace, focusing on the amazing town of Colmar and its many old half-timbered buildings, charming little winding streets and wonderful restaurants. We were glad that Bob decided to leave the exploration of the nearby Vosges Mountains for a later trip (in a car with a more powerful engine and me driving).

Jeanette and I didn't leave Basel until Monday, October 16th, so we spent the entire weekend with Bob. Besides, we were making more progress every day in establishing order where chaos once reigned. The satisfaction and pleasure our efforts were producing were written all over Bob's face and made every drop of our sweat a source of joy for us too. The results this time seemed to have achieved enough momentum to assure that the task would no longer be Sisyphean; some regression could be expected, but Bob said he was now looking forward to coming *home* to his apartment for the first time ever.

Almost as soon as we got home to Malmö, I hurried out to the artists' supply store and bought stretchers. A set of stretchers 50 by 80 centimeters would be perfect for Bob's canvas firewood bag. I already had a sketch for it. An idea from another recent sketch called for a much bigger set of stretchers – by far the biggest painting I'd ever painted – 130 by 130 centimeters. I couldn't wait to get going, even though I had to work full-time every day at the language school that first week after our return to Malmö.

I found the coarse canvas of the firewood carrier intriguing. When the carrier was laid out, I saw powerful symbolism in the handles, one at each end, suggesting to me the different – often contradictory – internal impulses and external influences that can pull a person in different or opposite directions. The sketch I used was a face with eyes that see everything and nothing. The overall expression is of bewilderment (*What's happening to me?*). I call this painting *A Face*.[2] [*I gave this painting to Bob – he got his firewood carrier back. After Bob died in 1999, I gave it to his nephew Dan.*] I put no frame around this one and hung it by the top leather handle, on an ornate hook I purchased for the purpose in Basel. I completed it just a few days after getting home from Switzerland.

My next painting was the big one (for me), both literally and figuratively, and probably my most complex in terms of color symbolism. It was also my first attempt to tackle the theme of great loneliness, isolation, and the difficulty of breaking through, surmounting or circumventing communication barriers between people. In this case, the loneliness of the central figure is unmitigated by

---

2   Painting #20 (see Appendix 2)

being in the presence of others – smackdab in the middle of a dozen others, to be precise – yet having no contact with them whatsoever.

Surrounding the central figure are four groups of three figures each. The only color shared by all four groups is green – a color that is missing in the central figure. The central figure is composed of pastel forms of red, orange, blue and violet. Each of the four groups includes all four of these colors but one; they are all incomplete relative to each other as well. And none of the four groups includes brown, which the central figure does include (in pastel form). The background consists of greens (which all four groups have, but not the central figure) and browns (which is only found in the central figure).

The color groupings of all 13 figures are intended to underline their interrelatedness and interdependence, despite their rejection of it, which is another way of saying that they need each other if only they'd look around and see it. The central figure is larger than any of the others, and his mouth is wide open in a full-throated cry of distress, unheard. The painting is called *A Cry*.[3]

I worked with unprecedented (for me) intensity on this one, almost around the clock for something like 10 days, with Jeanette cheering me on, seeing I had nourishment, encouraging me to sleep a little now and then, shielding me from distractions, caressing me when I needed that too. I finished it on November 1st, then nearly collapsed, drained.

It turned out that the outside world hadn't ceased to exist in 1972 after all. Anti-war demonstrations in the US were reaching 100,000 participants. Yet despite the burgeoning Watergate scandal and the continuing official government lies about what was really happening to America's interference of Vietnam's civil war, Nixon won the election by a landslide, one of the biggest margins of victory ever in a presidential election. *What did that say about American voters?!* Jeanette and I shook our heads in anger, dismay and disbelief. And we were terribly glad we no longer lived there.

Following Nixon's re-election in November 1972, he incomprehensively and mendaciously declared that the US had been victorious and began withdrawing US ground troops from Vietnam, in early 1973. Almost simultaneously, the North Vietnamese and Viet Cong began launching a counter-offensive. By 1975, when the final withdrawal of troops was complete, South Vietnam had fallen.

---

3   Painting #21 (See Appendix 2)

The entire war had been for *naught*. It accomplished nothing at all, beyond what war is best at: killing.

During the duration of US involvement in Vietnam, between 1964 and 1975, the US had had some 2.7 million troops serving in Vietnam (part of the 9 million on active duty during this period). At its peak, there were about 550,000 US troops in Vietnam at the same time.

And what did that 11-year-long party cost? In money, hundreds of billions of dollars. But in human lives, the cost was so much greater! If we start with American lives (which is usually where Americans like to start, isn't it?), close to 60,000 US troops were killed and around 150,000 wounded – but that figure doesn't include countless thousands with no visible injuries, but whose lives were shattered, homes wrecked, peace of mind gone, perhaps irretrievably. Among the North Vietnamese and Viet Cong, over a million dead, which proves that "we won", doesn't it?! And the more than 600,000 civilian dead don't count for much, because they weren't *our* civilians. Needless to say (except that it's not, so I'll say it) I've never regretted for a single minute that I turned down my invitation to join that party.

Nor had the world outside the US ceased to exist in late 1972, even though little of the news made it above the radar of "my fellow Americans": thousands were killed in earthquakes in Turkey, Iraq and Nicaragua; a seemingly endless string of deadly internecine battles raged on in Northern Ireland's sectarian war between Catholics and Protestants. Little things like that.

In other news from the outside world, Mom wrote to say that FBI had stopped by my parents' home in Oak Park to ask questions about me. It was close to two and a half years since I officially became a fugitive for disobeying my order to report for military service, so my first thoughts were that the Feds wanted to ascertain whether I'd slipped back into the country so they could nab me. It gave me a creepy feeling. But then another possible explanation occurred to me: my high-flying brother Al was getting into all kinds of assignments – both for Boeing and for various government agencies – for which he undoubtedly required some pretty advanced security clearance, and with him having a fugitive left-leaning brother living in "Communist" Sweden, investigations were to be expected. (Years later, Al told me that some of his neighbors told him that they'd also had visits from FBI agents asking about Al's comings and goings – and that these agents were actually wearing trenchcoats! For real!)

Late that fall we began to notice a significant increase in the number of empty apartments in our stairway. When a neighbor moved out an apartment, the vacancy was no longer being filled by a new tenant, and now nearly half of the 10 apartments at Vårgatan 4A were empty. And yet, as far as we could figure out, the housing shortage in Malmö remained a problem. Another mildly disturbing change was that our monthly rent, which we'd been paying to the postal account of a person in Malmö whom we presumed was the building owner, was now going to a building administration company in Landskrona instead. And there was no longer any caretaker living in one of the apartments in our stairway. We guessed that the current landlord was aiming to conduct a high-cost, comprehensive revamping of the block so that he could jack up the rents and make many times more money. Although they lacked the authority to evict existing tenants – like us – they had no obligation to accept new ones.

That autumn, Jeanette showed nearly imperceptible signs of increased moodiness. I didn't notice (or didn't dare to notice) such signs at the time; writing *Hindsights* more than four decades later had enabled me to connect some dots. Changes in Jeanette's temperament were becoming more abrupt and less predictable, as though she were flying and had inadvertently switched off her autopilot and begun slowly drifting (not veering) off course. As autumn progressed, these moods occasionally exploded into outbursts of extreme, inexplicable and hysterical sexual jealousy, usually lasting several hours. She picked nearly anyone she could think of to designate as the object of my supposed unbridled lust. My first reaction was incredulity, then I tried to laugh it off because it seemed so out-of-the-blue ridiculous to me, but she would keep hacking away at me with unfounded accusations until she provoked me into frustrated anger – how could I *prove* that I *hadn't* done something?! Although I kept my temper under control, the fact that I could be provoked repeatedly eventually made me feel sick with guilt.

Fortunately, such outbursts didn't occur too often, and once they subsided, she always looked confused, like something had happened to her that she couldn't control or understand. Then we always made up. When we talked it over, she told me that when she was a child she often provoked her parents and siblings in much the same way (although not involving the sexual jealousy part) until she received their "recognition" that she was troublesome and bad. Yet each time she directed an attack on me, I failed to see through the "game" she was playing, thinking it really *was* directed against me instead of against herself.

In mid-November, a special package arrived for us from Bob: a superb recording of Handel's *Messiah*. The sheer musical beauty of it lifted us like few things ever had. When Jeanette came home from work to find me painting each day, she asked me if she should use the headphones, or if I also wanted to hear the music while painting; I found the music tremendously inspiring. In fact, as long as Jeanette was there, there was music. And inspiration.

The motif for my next painting, the penultimate one for 1972, was superficially a still life, consisting of half a loaf of bread and a half-full bottle of wine, with a half-empty glass of wine next to it. I call it *Memory of a Friend*,[4] based partly on the *Rubiyat* ("*A loaf of bread, a jug of wine and thou...*"), but also on the concept of the Communion (or – as my family's Meeting friends called it – the breaking of bread). What struck me for the first time was the incongruity and contradiction of the wine with the ban on alcohol enforced by nearly all the religious fundamentalists I'd ever heard of. It seemed clear to me that in the biblical tale, Jesus picked two of the most ordinary, everyday things by which to be remembered; bread and wine were probably found on every table every day in biblical times (potable water was very often scarce and inferior); these were hardly unusual things, but those ignorant fundamentalists decided that wine must be banned in all other contexts!

My final painting of the year was *Smile*,[5] which was also the first of my paintings where I consciously emphasized teeth to illustrate intense, rampant, raging emotion. Sometime during the summer, I'd visited a dentist, Gunnar Johansson, for the first time since coming to Sweden. He had a part-time practice near Dalaplan in Malmö. He was also a professor of forensic odontology (the branch of dental science that enables investigators to identify bodies through dental records, etc). When he heard that I worked as an English teacher, he immediately asked if he could possibly have some private lessons with me. Naturally, much of our English conversation was related to his work. I was fascinated to hear about the time he helped the police catch a burglar who couldn't resist sinking his teeth into a block of cheese in the home of someone he was burgling. My encounters with Professor Gunnar were making me teeth-conscious.

Jeanette and I had to resign ourselves to the fact that Bob wouldn't be spending

---

4   Painting #22 (see Appendix 2)

5   Painting #23 (- " -)

the Christmas of 1972 with us either; he'd again succumbed to pressure from Tante Lore to spend Christmas with her family in Garmisch. We didn't mind too much, however, since we had some catching up of our own to do.

We bought a reel-to-reel tape deck, with seven-inch reels on which we could record numerous LPs and listen to uninterrupted music for hours at a time, without needing to break concentration to change records. This became my new working mode when painting: the whole *Messiah*, the whole Bach's *Mass in B-Minor* and dozens of *Cantatas* (Concentus Musicus Vienna, original instruments, Nikolas Harnoncourt), Mendelssohn's *Elijah*, Bach's *Brandenburg Concertos*, and others. Except in the cold months or when we had visitors, I usually didn't bother to dress before starting to paint.

Ever since the dam burst on my painting, with *Introduction to Music* at Easter 1972, there was a continually rising level of intensity and passion in my work that was being simultaneously pushed and pulled by Jeanette's urging me to paint on one hand and my growing love of classical music on the other. Which force was doing the pushing and which was doing the pulling was impossible to say. One thing is clear: painting was the most consuming and difficult artistic work I would ever undertake (with the exception of writing *Hindsights*). Inconsequently, some people expressed the unfounded conclusion, on hearing that just because I had no particular interest in selling my work, that painting must therefore be something I did as a "hobby" or "for relaxation". I refrained from telling them how such statements made me struggle with simultaneous impulses to laugh in their faces and to strangle them.

On the whole, 1972 was a wonderful and harmonious year for us. We were both working part-time, in addition to which I was painting full-time and Jeanette was studying; ours was mostly a simple life, with very low income but very few expenses. And although Jeanette was still subject to (or subjected to) moodiness, her temper outbreaks were rare. We were happy just being together, happy to be alive together.

CHAPTER 4

Glacial flow

Glaciers form over centuries in places where snow accumulates year by year faster than it melts, like at high altitudes or in Polar regions. The build-up of snow gradually becomes more compact, heavier, transforming into extremely dense ice. Eventually, if glaciers are located on some kind of slope, even a slight slope, they may lose their grip on the underlying surface and begin to flow, usually imperceptibly to the eye, perhaps only a millimeter or two per hour. But under certain circumstances they can lurch and surge at speeds more than a thousand times faster. If the glacier is moving across an uneven substrate, it can also crack and form deep crevasses. And at the edge of a glacier, where the flow has borne it inexorably towards the sea or a lake, the glacier can "calve", with enormous chunks suddenly breaking off in loud and dramatic crashes, forming icebergs, while the movement of the rest of the glacier remains nearly undetectable.

In researching this book in late 2016, attempting to maintain my no-holds-barred honesty, I have repeatedly experienced the phenomenon of how writing about one or two clear memories can trigger or activate dozens more. Most of these I've been able to confirm through external sources. In searching for such sources, I stumbled across a few notes and notations my Jeanette made, papers filed away in dusty folders, binders and boxes, remaining there for decades. I'd read a few of these things – the few she chose to show me just after she wrote them – but of course I never made any connections to possibly perilous mental conditions of whose existence or to what extent I was blithely unaware or couldn't bear (didn't dare) to see.

Being a blind husband, I perhaps presumed they came from her imagination rather than her inner world, or perhaps I was too frightened to face their potentially devastating implications, the imperceptible movement of the unstoppable glacier. Among the things I would later discover that she'd written and that I'd never seen or read before, were things that were too painful for me to face before or at the time I lost her, things I now realize were significant and or might have been, things that I *might* have seen as foreboding. There were cracks and crevasses I'm certain I never saw among the things I *did* see, things that might have been perceivable all along – *if I'd had a different perspective* – things that now re-break my heart.

Glacial flow

1973 began undramatically enough, except that the US stopped issuing draft orders and the Watergate scandal was swelling like an infected boil in the American psyche. I had full-time teaching work for the first two weeks. Jeanette had her part-time work, and resumed her German class. I began to notice (at the time?) that she made tiny stick-figure cartoons of a frowning or crying girl in her pocket memo calendar on the dates her period began. She never mentioned to me any particular pain or discomfort at those times, but perhaps if I'd been more alert....

Another strange (to me) thing around this time was that Jeanette began making fairly regular (perhaps once every two months) visits to a beauty clinic in the NK department store building downtown in order to have facial hair removed from her upper lip. I'd never even noticed that she had any hair there, and when she pointed it out to me, it seemed so insignificant and far-fetched that I couldn't help wondering what the fuss was about. Yet it caused *her* great distress. She was hyper-sensitive about it. (Or was it that I was hypo-sensitive or insensitive?) Just how insecure did it make her? I never asked myself such questions at the time. That I can ask them now, decades later, is presumably due to the "benefit" of hindsight.

When Bob told us in early December that he'd received delivery of his new sofa, he said he was delighted with it, but was kind of overwhelmed by the task of arranging things in his living room in a way that would enable him to fully benefit from all the advantages a sofa could offer. So I decided to take 10 days off and take the train down to Switzerland (arriving on Saturday, January 13th) to help him. I also wanted to deliver two paintings – *The Face* and *The Giver of Music* – as a surprise, and for all his generosity with the scores of expertly selected LPs he'd given us, and just because we loved him.

He flatly refused to allow me to give him both paintings. He insisted on paying me for one of them, although considering the amount he forced me to take for it, he might as well have been buying four (not that I gave much of a damn about that ephemeral thing called "market value"). We both realized we were in danger of turning giving into a game of one-upmanship. We resolved it like we did everything else we'd been able to resolve: by discussing it rationally. Our friendship had reached a level of absolute trust; we knew that neither of us would ever dream of exploiting the other.

It was immediately obvious to me that the arrival of the sofa threatened to overturn the new order in Bob's living room. Although he saw it as a huge problem, it took me just a few hours that Saturday afternoon to achieve a furniture arrangement – including the teak coffee table from his bedroom – that he was delighted with. And the additional paintings on the walls made both him and the room glow.

We spent Saturday evening and most of Sunday talking and sipping an old Glenfarclas single-malt whiskey. He reminded me that he'd given me *carte blanche* to go through, sort out, and help achieve order among his most personal papers in his bedroom as well. I hoped to get through all of them during the coming week, when I would be on my own. I told him I thought it would be best if I were not too drastic about throwing things out, since I'd learned enough about him to know that while many such papers might have been totally lacking in any *practical* value for him for many decades, there might be those that could still have high *personal* value for him. As long as they could be arranged and ordered in such a way that he could easily find them (perhaps with not too many duplicates), I suggested that we keep them, since those criteria alone would decimate the height of the unsorted mountains. He was delighted with my suggestion, and told me we should also take a look in his basement locker.

I'd forgotten about that extra stash of paper and "memorabilia". I knew he had a small storage cubicle down there, where he kept the detergent for his laundry days twice a month. He could only use one of those two days, the one day a month that his laundry day fell on a Saturday and he wasn't at work. I asked him why he didn't find out whether he could switch that day with somebody else; there were probably at least 20-30 housewives in the building who might have preferred a weekday to a weekend anyway, so as to keep their weekends laundry-free for family activities, but Bob suddenly switched to his all-formal Swiss mode and couldn't begin to imagine how he would go about approaching any of these unknown ladies with such a bold suggestion, or how he would formulate the highly formal and duly proper letter of request – and where he might find the most appropriate stationery to write it on!

I repressed a deep sigh and suggested that he simply tape a notice on the wall in the laundry room offering to trade his weekday laundry days for weekend laundry days to anyone who might be interested, and include his name and apartment number. He claimed that house rules wouldn't permit him to put up any signs. I suggested he ask the caretaker (who assigned the laundry days), but Bob felt he'd be overstepping some unseen boundaries and somehow cause his delicately constructed amicable relationship with the caretaker to topple.

I'd met the caretaker several times on my many forays to the garbage room; he was a young, friendly, helpful and informal guy, very easy-going and down-to-earth. I was certain he'd be more than glad to help Bob out with that and all manner of other things. But I also understood that for whatever reason, Bob ultimately had to be Bob, and in the area of practical matters, he would always perceive simple solutions as challenges for him to figure out to how to imbue them with the greatest possible complexity. The ultimate lesson wouldn't change: when Bob was really and truly opposed to a change in his routines, no change would be made.

The basement cubicles in Bob's building were like wooden cages, about three square meters, with walls made of vertical wooden slats about 4 cm apart, thus allowing circulation of air as well as easy visual inspection. Most of them were extremely tidy. Bob's was loaded with cartons, in stacks covering most of the floor space and heights nearly reaching the low (fortunately) ceiling. The cartons were mostly filled with old papers: from and about his military days; receipts from just about every purchase he'd ever made in the US, Germany, France and Switzerland; impersonal letters from people he neither knew any longer nor wanted to; newspapers, catalogues, brochures and magazines, including old copies of *Playboy*, which he still purchased, nowadays in both English and German. One of the many somewhat unexpected (by me) facets of Bob's personality was that he was a secret admirer of Hugh Hefner as the ultimate Man about Town, Man of the World, someone suave who exuded a debonair style that Bob was apparently captivated by, especially while he lived near Orléans, the polar opposite of his Swiss-formal obstacle-seeker mentality.

The sight of this huge extra cache of papers waiting patiently to be sorted by me totally annihilated my ambitious plans to complete the task of achieving order among all Bob's papers during the course of my current stay. (Since this particular glacier was being continually replenished, my work on this would continue for decades, although requiring steadily decreasing effort.) I would finish what I could by Friday afternoon, and we would have Friday evening and Saturday morning for relaxing. But on Saturday morning, Bob wanted us to go into town some hours before the departure of my train, so he could buy a magnificent, complete version of *The Magic Flute* (conducted by George Solti, with Hermann Prey as Papageno) for Jeanette, as thanks for her letting him have the benefit of my assistance for a week – a gift from my patron to my muse.

I came back home to what would have been week after week of full-time work if I hadn't talked with Hamadi about my situation before Christmas. I told him that I couldn't handle all the English teaching now that his school was becoming so successful, and that he would have to find someone who could relieve me by assuming part of the load. Somehow he got in touch with an Englishman named Rob, who came over to Malmö to work at Interspråk in the beginning of 1973. Rob said he was under the impression that he'd be working full-time, a fair assumption to make for anyone seeking a job.

Rob was from Cambridge (the town); his higher education, in Scandinavian studies, came from a university in Newcastle, where he met and married Chris, whose father was English (by surname and nationality), and whose mother was Danish. Chris came to Sweden with Rob, but commuted by hovercraft to Copenhagen, where she worked as a translator at the British Embassy. They found a small and cheap apartment in an old building above a furniture store on Lundavägen, only about 50 meters from our apartment.

Rob seemed to be a nice guy. He was skinny (almost gaunt), and had a fairly long and scraggly red beard. The mustache part of his beard largely hid his mouth, which might have contributed to the difficulties we had in understanding him. Many of his pupils told me they found it nearly impossible. It wasn't a question of his accent; it was that he failed to enunciate, so that when he spoke, it sounded like his words had a hard time making it past his teeth, and the mustache nearly eliminated any last chance of support through lip-reading.

Chris, on the other hand, spoke clearly and impeccably, but she wasn't the one teaching. She was clearly highly intelligent. Her qualifications for the job at the British Embassy in Copenhagen not only included the fact that she was totally bilingual (like her Danish mother), but she had a university degree in Scandinavian studies as well. Jeanette and I had the two of them over for dinner soon after their arrival, and we discovered that all four of us enjoyed a little tennis now and then, so we decided to play an hour of mixed doubles on Sundays once the spring weather permitted outdoor play. They seemed to be much more active socially than we were.

Within the first four days after I returned home from Switzerland, Jeanette and I listened to *Die Zauberflöte*, in its entirety, twice. I had plenty of teaching work during the coming weeks, but I defined "plenty" as part-time. We couldn't afford for me not to work at all, but working mornings, then painting in the afternoons and evenings (and sometimes into the night) was not a problem for me. It quickly became a problem for Rob, however; when Hamadi had only one booking for an English course during a given week, Rob had to share the light teaching duties with me, and he had *not* been looking for part-time work. [Actually, I'm making a mistake saying that I *worked* part-time. I was *gainfully employed* part-time, but I was also *working* full-time at painting, so I was actually *working* 150% of full-time. Even though I wasn't making any money at it, it was hard work all the same.]

My first painting of 1973 was *Love*,[6] one-half of a planned pair with *Hate*,[7] three paintings later. The juxtaposition of these two reveals polarities and parallels of emotion which, in spite of being generally thought of as opposites, have something in common: great intensity.

I'd been reflecting on how many things in life can change totally by changing just one ingredient, and how many opposites have key things in common, or how the right combinations of two dangerous things can render both of them harmless, like when powerful hydrochloric acid is combined with equal parts of caustic lye, resulting in harmless salt and water (HCl + NaOH → NaCl + H_2O). The small shifts in the relative positions of the two people in *Hate* and *Love* change the situation from one emotion to the other; in fact, love changes everything.

I was so immersed in the intensity of painting *Love* that I had to back off a little before proceeding to *Hate*. I took another idea from one of my sketches, dealing with *A Choice of Illusions*.[8] In this painting, a man has two choices or ways to ignore or protect himself from acknowledging or facing the void behind him: cut flowers or wine. Both are escapes; neither offers more reality than the void itself.

My other interim painting between *Love* and *Hate* also deals with strong emotions, this time jealousy and envy. It again uses a lot of teeth to amplify the intensity. I call it *Green-Eyed People*.[9]

There are several huge differences between *Love* and *Hate*. The two figures are totally separated by the void in *Hate*; in *Love*, they are joined by an embrace. Both paintings reveal a ravenous intensity of feeling, but in *Hate* they direct

---

6 Painting #24 (see Appendix 2)
7 Painting #27 (- " -)
8 Painting #25 (- " -)
9 Painting #26 (- " -)

sharp points at each other, but flat surfaces in *Love*. Most importantly, in *Hate* they have unequal stature, aligning their jaws to enable them to rip into each other; while in *Love*, they're on the same level, their jaws will not interlock and instead their lips will meet. Finally, *Love* is predominantly warm reds, while *Hate* is mainly cold blues. [*I by no means allude to how Americans use these colors in their political spectrum, contrary to most of the world – and even to their own earlier usage!*]

After *Hate*, I had to do one more painting in this burst of emotional intensity, carrying the grinding of envy into an eruption of hate. If envy seethes beneath the surface, with the void neatly suppressed, it seemed to me that competition – blind, pointless competition to be first, to win at all costs – would be the eruption. The figures in this painting are all aggressively battling each other to claw their way forward, over each other, yet they only see each other, not where they are heading: to the void. The prize is meaningless, the reward is emptiness, but they don't care, as long as they get there first.

When I was a kid, I struggled to be more competitive, urged on primarily by my brother Al, who in turn was undoubtedly well trained and spurred by our mom, and by a society that preached winning. Choice quotes from prominent sports figures, such as "*The only good loser is a loser,*" or "*Winning isn't everything – it's the only thing!*" underscored this top priority. Unsubtly encouraged to think in this way, I did. It came quite naturally to me. But as I learned to recognize that "natural" doesn't necessarily mean or even imply "good", I consciously struggled (with mixed success) to resist my competitive impulses, because I didn't like the person I became when I became competitive. Painting *Competition*[10] was my attempt to deal with it.

Almost at the same pace as we were upgrading our apartment, the building that housed it continued to deteriorate, but we scarcely noticed the degradation around us; we were too happy with the improvements we were making in our own little world.

Many of my pupils (and a few others, although most of the Swedes I'd ever engaged in any real conversations with were my pupils) used to ask me if I was a typical American. On the face of it, I told them, I couldn't be; typical Americans live in America, for a start. But apart from that obvious difference, there were

---

10 Painting #28 (see Appendix 2)

other aspects. One was that I'd *never* felt like a *typical* American even when I lived there. In my childhood I hadn't been *allowed* to be a typical American, to do the things typical Americans do, however much I may have wanted to. I was constantly being admonished and commanded to see myself as *in* the world, not *of* the world. I was warped by my parents' and the Meeting's *apartheid* policies.

After I left my parental home, and almost as soon as I arrived in San Francisco, my country began indicating that they wanted to send boys like me off to Vietnam to fight their stupid and horribly unjust war. As a result, I became one of a small and atypically American minority of my peers who fled the country to avoid participating in that war in any way. Typical Americans were churchgoers; I was not, not any longer. Typical Americans at least believed in god; I no longer did even that. Typical Americans firmly believed that their country was the greatest in the world; since I no longer defined "greatest" as "most powerful" or "richest", I was again atypical. And typical Americans refer to the USA as "*our*" country, not "*their*" country – as I nowadays found myself doing most of the time (except when the US basketball team played the Russians in the Olympic final in Munich or in the hockey final at Lake Placid).

But nor was I by any means a Swede. Swedes were so much more formal than I would ever be or aspire to be. That was certainly true during my early years in Sweden, but since then they have changed more in this respect than I have. Was Swedish formality shaped by the language, such as having a choice between formal and informal forms of "you", or did the language usage reflect the inherent cultural formality? [*Sweden, too, has changed in this respect; the formal usage has gradually disappeared in the last few decades.*]

One day we decided to look for an ottoman to match our black leather sofa, but neither IKEA nor Domus Interiör had them, so we went across the street to the furniture store on Lundavägen (Rob and Chris's landlords) to have a look. They had nothing like it on display, but they let us study their catalogues, where we found what we were looking for. The price seemed affordable, so we said we'd like to order one. The middle-aged lady who took our order asked me (in Swedish, of course), "*Would Mr Erisman like the leather to be glossy or matte?*" I quickly swung around to look behind me, thinking she thought I was ordering on behalf of some namesake of mine who was standing behind me. "I'm Mr Erisman!" I exclaimed. "*Yes, I understand that,*" she replied, briefly closing her eyes as she summoned her patience, "*and what type of black leather would Mr Erisman like?*"

During the first year or so in our apartment building, when it was full of tenants, one of them had a little girl of around seven years of age. One day when I was returning home and hurrying up the stairs two at a time, she was on her way down. When we met, she *curtsied*! Nobody had ever curtsied at me, to me, for me before, and I nearly burst out laughing, having found it both amusing and bizarre. But when I told Elsa about it, she said it was quite normal.

It was also quite normal back in the early 1970s for older men to wear hats, and to tip or raise them as they passed each other in the street. [*I began wearing a hat or cap when I reached my late 60s in order to protect my nearly bald head from sunburn or chill.*] Although it seemed old-fashioned to me, I didn't think too much about it. Then one day I saw two elderly behatted gentlemen approaching each other along Lundavägen. When they were about 10 meters apart, they looked up and eyed each other blankly. When they were level with each other, the recognition phase came. And just *after* they'd already passed each other, each one lifted his hat, *with their backs to each other*! I stared in amazement and thought that someday I'd have to paint that absurd and melancholic metaphor of non-communication (but I never did).

Back in the 1970s, it was still very unusual (although not unknown) to see or hear overt expressions of emotion – laughter, anger, crying, shouting, excitement, passion – in public places in Sweden, *except* when the emotional extrovert in question was sufficiently inebriated to let go of the reins. Displaying emotions was almost like a breathalyzer. Indeed, Sweden's parliamentary protocol forbade "outbursts" in excess of properly restrained and muted applause in those hallowed chambers. (A typical session in the House of Commons in London is *raucous* by comparison!) Several times, while waiting in line to buy some wine at *Systembolaget*, I momentarily forgot what country I was in. When I attempted to start a casual conversation with a person standing near me, that person might react by sniffing audibly and ostentatiously in my direction. Then I realized that in early 1970s Sweden, only insobriety would render a person so uncouth as to address a complete stranger. [*I should again point out that Sweden has changed considerably in this respect since the 1970s.*]

At first, Swedes seemed to me to be much more tradition-bound than Americans, as though every social situation had to be approached with the formality of a wedding. Then I began to wonder whether it was just because American traditions and the American way of doing things came to me more automatically than I realized. Was I more American than I thought? Is everything a person does automatically "right", while everyone else and everything *they* do is automatically "weird"? But on paper, *any*thing done automatically is more likely to be *a*moral, since morality requires a choice, doesn't it? And being bound by tradition is seldom a conscious choice, and is rarely challenged; it becomes automatic before people are even aware that they are bound by it. It only *begins* to become a choice when a person accepts that whatever action it concerns could legitimately be done otherwise, but this may not be realized until after frequent encounters (or collisions) with other peoples' traditions.

Once when I was out for a walk with one of my male pupils, I noticed that from time to time he'd suddenly make a little skipping movement. At first I thought he'd tripped on something; our conversation continued unbroken. When it happened again, I thought he might have a bum leg. After the third or fourth time, when I'd been observing his gait more closely and realized that it had nothing to do with his leg, I stopped walking and asked him why he was skipping now and then. (I wasn't challenging him; I was truly curious.) He hadn't been fully aware of it, he explained. He presumed that it came from his military training to walk in step. I told him that when he was speaking English, he wasn't required to walk in step. He laughed and said he understood. Then, after about 10 meters, it happened again, automatically, and I immediately took a couple of looooong strides, followed by a couple of exaggeratedly short ones, while he looked like he was tap-dancing to try to get back in step with me – until he realized what I was doing, and he stopped and laughed again. But still it continued; he couldn't help himself. (Nor could I help exaggerating my responses, which soon approached John Cleese's in the *Monty Python* "Silly Walks" sketch. The same thing happened with dozens of my middle-aged male pupils over the years.

Most Swedish strangers I met seemed at first stiff, formal and reserved to me, yet most of the Swedes I'd had the time to get to know were open and friendly (although still a bit shy). That didn't make a lot of sense, so I developed a theory: that Americans have very thin outermost shells, while Swedes have thick outermost ones, by which I mean that it's so much easier to start friendly social conversations with American strangers than with Swedish strangers. However, once you get beyond the outermost shell to the friendly acquaintance layer, Swedes are no more difficult than Americans. And getting beyond the inner shell to the innermost core layer of true friendship is usually going to be difficult no matter where you are.

Americans are thus often deceived by the thickness of Swedes' outermost shells, thinking them reserved or even arrogant when it's usually a question of mere shyness, while Swedes are often deceived by how thin Americans' outermost shells are, thinking that true friendship is closer at hand than it really is. Some of my pupils would tell me how incredibly friendly the Americans they'd met were, how they'd heard their entire life stories while sitting next to them in an airport or on a train. Then I asked if they knew their names. When they realized that no names and addresses were ever exchanged, they also realized they'd been mistaken in thinking that because they'd reached that inner shell within 15 seconds, they were already well on their way to the core.

I also asked them why, if Americans were so goddamn friendly, helpful and hospitable, are there far more Americans sleeping rough, on the streets, impoverished, than in Sweden? My own theory is that Americans like to show off their material success to strangers and foreigners (at least those they perceive as peers). But move into their neighborhood and you're just part of the competition.

Henry Carlsson was one of those highly formal, extremely proper Swedish gentlemen, and however unlikely or incongruous it might have seemed, I was his favorite teacher and he was my favorite supplier of building materials, and we were favorite tennis partners, and we soon became good friends. Jeanette and I were often dinner guests at the lovely home of Henry and Elsa near Jägersro, and they were dinner guests at our humble apartment on Vårgatan, despite the fact that our conversations were always somewhat reserved and guarded, and seldom controversial.

On one such occasion, in early 1973, Elsa expressed how distraught she was by the rumors she'd been reading in the gossip magazines about a budding romance between Sweden's crown prince and "some Brazilian girl" he'd met when she was working as a hostess at the Olympics in Munich the previous autumn. *"Why can't he find a nice princess somewhere in Europe instead of that Brazilian Silvia?!"* she moaned. But when their engagement was announced three years later, Elsa was overjoyed that the crown prince had found *"that lovely German girl, Silvia"*!

One thing that continued to dumbfound me about Sweden was how a country that was more democratic than any other I knew, as well as more secular and more egalitarian, could still have an official state church and still cling to a monarchy?! It was true that the king no longer had any official power, but royalty had plenty of tax-funded privilege – and the majority of Swedish people seemed content that it should be so. Even though the former aristocracy had nothing left but their inherited wealth and a few historical titles (mere mementos, discarded vestiges of authoritarian rule), many if not most Swedes remained a bit in awe of their venerable names. The ruling Social Democratic party had had abolishment of the monarchy in their charter for decades, but never acted on it even when they had a majority government. And the gossip magazine industry continues to thrive.

After the flurry and fury of emotions of *Hate* and *Competition*, I felt I needed to work with other concepts for a while, which I did both stylistically and thematically in *Pipe and Bottle*.[11] I used a still-life motif similar to my first painting, but with a palette-knife technique, and a broader, brighter color spectrum. I also included the void, peeking out in numerous places from behind it all.

For the next canvas I used the same technique as in *Pipe and Bottle*, but this time on a canvas as big as *A Cry*, and I reintroduced a little toothed emotion. (I used a canvas I'd already painted on but quickly became dissatisfied with, so I'd scraped it and painted over it.) The title is *Man Reading a Book*,[12] a tribute to the joys of literature – the passion, the feeling, the complete world. I included an aquarium with two orange fish. (Jeanette and I had just bought an aquarium and some fish, including a few red platys, which were more orange than red.)

On April 8th, Picasso died. A number of people were saying that my paintings reminded them of Picasso's. While I could agree that the similarities were greater than the similarities to Rembrandt, and while I might have been flattered by any comparison between my own work and Pablo's, I felt that those who made the strong connections understood neither Picasso, nor cubism, nor my work. But I certainly admired Picasso's tremendous sense of adventure, evolving in multiple directions whenever he felt like it. I admired his breathtaking talent in whatever he chose to do – and he chose to do many things that only became "popular" long after *he* chose to do them, not because they were already trendy. I admired his prodigious output: tens of thousands of paintings plus graphics and sculptures in all kinds of media. And I admired his political courage against fascism, raging against injustice, and fearlessness in letting the impact of his art speak with an increasingly loud voice. Jeanette and I mourned his death together.

The motif of my next painting was taken directly from my studio. A house plant has turned inwards from the pale light of a distant winter sun towards the lamp, and flourishes. The metaphor I was working with here was the notion that

---

11 Painting #29 (see Appendix 2)

12 Painting #30 (-"-)

if the old creeds and mythologies proved empty, a person can create his or her own light; life needn't "mean" anything beyond the meaning we give it, the very living of it. This insight was probably pre-verbal in me. It would take some time – and a couple of cataclysms – to fully bring it to my consciousness. I call the painting *Sun, Plant and Lamp*.[13]

We were thrilled that we managed to persuade Bob to spend more than three weeks – April 13th to May 5th – with us in connection with the Easter holidays, when I wouldn't be having much work at the school and Jeanette could get some extra days off. She was also working enough extra hours to earn even more free time during Bob's stay.

As usual, we had much to talk about and Bob was overwhelmed by the paintings I'd done since his previous visit. He was also now totally consumed by Watergate, so we weren't "allowed" to miss a newscast; Bob didn't want to miss *anything* of this drama that was unfolding daily. Ever since the discovery of the burglary of the Democratic Party offices in June 1972, and the subsequent unravelling of the burglars' ties to the Nixon White House, Bob was on red alert. And ever since books on the subject began pouring out in 1972, Bob was purchasing and devouring them by the dozen.

Jeanette and I had long been appalled by everything Nixon represented, and were of course astonished by the brazenness of this scandal, but not as surprised as Bob seemed to be. It was fun – and worthwhile – discussing the affair with Bob because he, as usual, was so well-read on the subject. It was also history in the making, right then and there; in fact, on April 30th, during the latter half of Bob's stay, Nixon formally and officially accepted responsibility – but not blame! – for the whole thing. Yet "Tricky Dick" still wasn't going anywhere.

We'd given religion the heave-ho the previous fall, but Bob and I both wanted to avail ourselves of the supporting arguments, despite the realization that one can never prove the *non*-existence of anything. (Jeanette said there were far too many crazy ideas out there, and too little time, for her to have to feel compelled to defend all her non-beliefs – how sensible!) Bob was reading more and more of Bertrand Russell, and finding his works to be a goldmine of sound, rational thinking. Bob quoted him with increasing frequency, and began giving me copies of Russell's works. I examined them with the same critical eye I used on

---

13 Painting #31 (see Appendix 2)

the books Al sent me by Francis Schaeffer, but Russell knew his logic and didn't make foolish claims of certainty: *"The trouble with the world is that the stupid are cocksure and the intelligent are full of doubt."*

Bob and I never aimed to think alike as such, but we were mostly interested in the same subjects, in testing the validity of mostly the same propositions, in calling received wisdom into question, and in honing and refining the things we tentatively came to regard as most plausible or least implausible. And since we used each other as sounding boards, it is perhaps not surprising that our working hypotheses about life and the universe gradually came to resemble each other's to an ever-greater degree. We didn't insist on – or respond well to – claims of Final Answers and Truth without overwhelming evidence. The freedom to question was always so much more important.

During Bob's visit, I started and completed another painting, called *Loneliness*.[14] Every detail suggests emptiness and entrapment. Like *Loneliness*, loneliness has precious little to do with solitude. The background, the room, converges on an empty corner. Outside the window is the void. The door has no handle. The man's bowl, plate and glass are empty. He is curled up on himself.

Our outings with Bob whenever he came to visit us always tended to include several favorite stores. One was the Gleerups bookstore in Lund, nearly across the street from the old 12th-century cathedral. Here Bob claimed he could count on finding more books of interest to him in English than anywhere else he'd seen in Europe apart from London: books on philosophy, cosmology, political issues, biology, the works of John Fowles, Bertrand Russell (he sometimes found a few he didn't already have) and others. Another of Bob's musts was the Silverbergs furniture store in Malmö. And then there were the record stores, mostly for our benefit. On this trip he probably bought us another 15-20 LPs, among the most important of which was the exquisite *Mass in B-Minor* by Johan Sebastian Bach.

When Bob first introduced me to classical music, I couldn't have distinguished Mozart from Wagner, or Handel from Tchaikovsky, and I couldn't imagine how Bob had no problem doing so. I could play a track from one of the records and ask him to identify the composer. He would do so instantly. I asked him how he knew, and he simply said, *"Because nobody else wrote that kind of music!"*, and as he did so, his one eyebrow shot halfway up his forehead and he broke into a broad, mischievous, gleeful grin. But now, listening to Bach two years later, I was

---

14 Painting #32 (see Appendix 2)

beginning to understand what he meant.

While with us, Bob unexpectedly began growing long sideburns. He was clearly feeling very different –much better – inside. Were the sideburns some kind of manifestation of that? Opportunities that he was in the habit of transforming into impossibilities, like obtaining Swiss citizenship, were being reconsidered! He'd been living in Switzerland for well over the 10-year residency requirement, but hadn't yet made any move towards applying. Why? Because he'd felt that his medical condition would not only bar him from citizenship, but would also open a can of worms that might jeopardize his permission to remain in the country at all. Now he was beginning to see things differently. I laughed with delight when I heard this, and told him that he was "in danger of becoming an optimist!"

My next painting, however, was of the old Bob, the deeply melancholic Bob, the summation of a lot of feelings he'd had and that I had observed about him. It depicts an old man, balding, staring with tired, narrow red eyes into space, smoking his meerschaum pipe, sitting at a table with his hands loosely folded in front of him. The smoke from his pipe is all that separates or shields his gaze from the void. This painting, which I call *Old Man with a Pipe*[15] (Bob loved this painting and bought it from me), was the first of four consecutive paintings with a format of 46 by 65 centimeters. Bob saw this painting as a milestone for him – a reminder of where he'd been, but was no longer.

At some point in the late spring, we received a letter from Poland. Krzysztof wrote that he and his girlfriend (I can't remember her name, so I'll call her Jolanta) would very much like to come to Sweden to visit us for a couple of weeks in the summer. We'd kept up correspondence with our young Polish friend since saying goodbye in Copenhagen in August 1969, when Jeanette and I disembarked from the *Stefan Batóry*. They had to plan a possible trip to Sweden months in advance, he explained; getting permission to leave Poland was no easy matter, a subject we'd discussed in some detail during the voyage.

First they would have to go to the police and apply for a passport, stating with whom they would be staying, for how long, why, as well as many invasive questions. Then they would be called for interviews, both individually and together. After that, if they got tentative approval, Jeanette and I would have to visit the Polish consulate in Malmö to fill out forms, including a pledge to defray

---

15 Painting #33 (see Appendix 2)

all their costs while they were in Sweden. Then Krzysztof and Jolanta *might* be issued passports and, if so, they would be eligible to apply for Swedish tourist visas. If all went well, they could then come. We needed to allow enough time to accomplish all this, so we suggested August 11th to 26th. And Krzysztof was going to bring me lots of Polish canvas as payment for the math books I paid Al to acquire and send to me so that I could send them on to Krzysztof.

My next painting was the first to tackle the god myth head-on, my Genesis revelation from the fall. It's also a small painting with a jungle-like garden setting of numerous shades of green. In a bright clearing off to the right, almost like a bower, a naked man and woman are standing, smiling innocently, while reaching out blindly for a couple of pieces of golden fruit on a branch in front of them. Beneath the branch is the head of a frowning serpent, facing the couple, also with an unseeing eye. The coiling body of the serpent extends upwards, to the top of the painting where it is being firmly held – like a marionette – by a cold blue grinning figure (with plenty of pointed teeth) in the void at the top of the painting, seeing clearly, and sardonically enjoying himself. I was working out the equation: If there were a god who created everything, he would thus have to have created evil as well. So guess who the real villain would be if that were true? To me the answer was now so obvious that it became hard to understand why so many people still refused to see it. I didn't find it possible to be subtle. The painting is called *Eden*.[16]

I wanted to try something more figurative in the next painting (in the same format). The style is thus a considerable deviation from my previous work. It depicts a man buried up to his neck in the bed of a body of shallow water, but deep enough to keep his head submerged. Although he is pale, there is no reason to suppose he is dead. Rather, the "underwater" symbolism is of the sub-conscious – that which we can come to learn about only by great effort, but are not necessarily empowered to change anyway. The man is, in fact, powerless to act; he can only observe. His eyes see, but there is a look of resignation – not acceptance – on his face. There are a couple of small aquarium-type fish swimming around him. The only void is along the top of the painting, above the slightly troubled surface of the water. The title is *The Underwater Man*.[17] Bob also bought this one.

---

16 Painting #34 (see Appendix 2)

17 Painting #35 (- " -)

The last of the paintings I did in this particular format was originally intended to be a preliminary study for a much bigger work (never undertaken) later in the year, on the theme of "the four horsemen of the Apocalypse". It's based on the sixth chapter of *Revelation*, the last book in the Bible, in which God, calling himself the Lamb yet behaving more like a hyena, opens a book sealed with seven seals, bringing ever-greater destruction and terror to the world, and ending with "the great day of his [*sic*] wrath". The first four seals release four different-colored horses, the second of which is red.[18] Sweet guy.

Jeanette and I were playing tennis (mixed doubles) with Rob and Chris fairly often now that balmier May weather was here. The fish in our aquarium were even producing babies. We soon discovered that we had to buy a cage for the little ones to prevent the other fish (parents included) from eating them up within minutes of birth.

At the end of May we took the ferry over to Travemünde and a train on to Lübeck for an enjoyable weekend break. Jeanette was working part-time, studying German, creating culinary delights, and being my enthusiastic muse. I was working part-time and painting full-time. The glacier seemed to be standing still.

---

18 Painting #36 (see Appendix 2)

CHAPTER 5

Lurches and surges

As we were entering a chilly June and longing for beautiful and balmy summer days, Jeanette and I began to get itchy feet and found ourselves a cheap charter flight to Paris for a whole week, June 9th to 16th. It would be Jeanette's second visit to the French capital (the first was with her brother in the summer of '65) and my first ever. We were fairly bursting with anticipation. Our budget hotel, the Picardy, was situated diagonally across the Rue de Dunkerque from Gare du Nord, the big train station in northern Paris. The Picardy was adequate, and we were not aware of having to share our room with anything having more than two legs, nor anyone else with two legs other than ourselves.

We did all the touristy things (it turns out that there are legitimate reasons why tourists find tourist attractions attractive): the Eiffel Tower, the Louvre, the Museum of Modern Art, the Luxembourg Gardens, the Left Bank, Notre Dame, Montmartre and Sacré-Cœur, l'Arc de Triomphe, the Champs Élysées, Fontainbleu and many more. Spectacular as they were in themselves, they were also good orientation points for our experience of other aspects of Paris.

We found our hotel to be ideally situated for explorations. Numerous nearly parallel streets radiated south from the Gare du Nord area towards most of the aforementioned tourist attractions, so we left by one street in the morning, came back by a parallel one in the evening, left by a third the following morning and so on. It took only a day to discover the strong tendency in that part of the city for shops of the same kind to be conglomerated on the same street: butcher after butcher on one street, florist after florist on the next, one street full of wine merchants, the next full of leather goods, on and on like that. Fortunately, we both enjoyed walking and had the legs and feet for it.

We also discovered that Paris attracts more than tourists. We were lucky enough to be overwhelmed by a performance of Handel's *Messiah* in the Notre Dame cathedral, as well as a sterling performance of Hugo Wolf's *lieder*, with the world-class baritone Dietrich Fischer-Dieskow at Salle Pleyel, accompanied by Daniel Barenboim – a brilliant performance topped off by five encores.

We took a walk beyond the Île de la Cité and found the smaller Île Saint-Louis, a charming, tranquil oasis in the heart of the bustling metropolis. When darkness was falling, we looked up to see a bright sphere of light on the horizon, which turned out not to be the full moon rising, but the amazing dome of Sacré-Cœur. The only big disappointment for Jeanette was that the huge food market, Les Halles, had been demolished since her previous visit in 1965. But there were plenty of local bistros that made our mouths water and our waistlines bulge, even though we couldn't afford any of the fancier restaurants that made French cuisine famous.

We'd scarcely returned to Malmö before we booked our next trip, to see Bob in Binningen, from June 30th to July 15th. We found that it wouldn't cost us a lot more to fly via Zürich than to go by train. Our time together with Bob was too precious to be wasted on a long train ride (it took two extra days, and it felt longer each time, once all the views became familiar). From Zürich, there was just a short train trip to Basel, where Bob met us.

Bob was more absorbed by Nixon and Watergate than ever, but now there was an added scandal in the making. Nixon's loathsome right-wing vice-president, Spiro T. Agnew (his real name!), was the target of increasing media and political attention. (Perhaps intended to deflect attention from Nixon's role in Watergate?) Agnew had long been under investigation for charges of bribery, extortion and kickback during his years in high-level politics in Maryland, but now there were charges of tax fraud, charges recent enough not to be covered by any statutes of limitations. (Remember what they finally put Al Capone away for?) Bob's passion for the ongoing events in the US was, of course, rather contagious, although our interest never came close to Bob's consuming level.

A couple of days before our trip to Switzerland, we received a letter from Mom saying that Dad was "feeling better" from something in his chest. We hadn't even heard he'd been feeling ill. The letter also announced that Dad was going to be taking "one last job" for Link-Belt – six months or so in Pittsburgh! – before retiring. This also came as a big surprise, because we hadn't realized that Dad would be retiring already (he was only 61). It was unclear to us what they would do with Grandma when they moved to Pittsburgh. She not only lived with them but was entirely dependent on them (she had advanced muscular dystrophy). I'd heard that my parents had been considering some vague plans to pull up from Oak Park after Dad's retirement some day and build a new home in the countryside outside Knoxville, Illinois, together with Ralph and Maxine. Was this part of that move? Would they move back to Oak Park after the Pittsburgh job, or move directly to Knoxville? I had a lot of questions, but they were all soon to be irrelevant.

We had a lovely time helping Bob with additional home furnishings. We sorted out carton after carton of papers from his basement cubicle, freeing up a lot of space. A flash of spatial inspiration led me to measure the elephant of an ugly cabinet that had always been hogging so much space in his kitchen, to see whether it could be fit in the basement cubicle. It turned out to fit perfectly, with not more than a centimeter or two to spare, and it could swallow nearly all of Bob's remaining cartons. So I emptied the bottle crates from it and put them with the others on the balcony. Then I moved it, with Bob's amazed approval and Jeanette's help, and we somehow squeezed it into the basement cubicle. Suddenly the kitchen felt almost spacious; the three of us could sit there without feeling like we were in 4th-class seats on a 12-hour flight.

We took a day trip to the beautiful medieval walled town of Solothurn, not far from the hamlet where my great-great-great-great-great-grandfather Melchior Ehrismann was born and lived until he emigrated from Switzerland (or a region that was to become part of Switzerland) to America (or to the British colonies that were to become part of America) in the early 1700s.

Bob was noticeably feebler, physically, since we last saw him a few months earlier, but he never surrendered the wheel of his 2CV to me. We made several extended explorations of the streets of central Basel together, took the tram to the Markplatz or the Barfüsserplatz, and from there we headed out to a variety of destinations within Bob's walking distance.

At some point I became aware – I have no idea how long it took me to reach that point – that when we were listening to beautiful music, particularly piano music, Bob's fingers would be moving, flowing, almost pounding over some invisible and inaudible keyboard, and that he was completely absorbed, in another world. My persistent questions eventually led him to reveal that he was once quite an accomplished pianist. He even revealed that Schubert's outrageously beautiful song *An die Musik* regularly afforded him the most rapturous solace and joy, and that he sang it to/for himself in many a gray hour, in solitude. But for some reason I didn't understand and barely noticed, Bob was finding it increasingly difficult to manage long, handwritten letters – something that had long been a favorite pastime of his. Typing wasn't optimal either; he was still using a manual typewriter, usually with carbon paper, a bit of an ordeal for hands that had lost their agility.

A few days before our return to Malmö, we received a letter from Mom, addressed to us in care of Bob, informing us that Dad had been diagnosed with Hodgkin's disease. We didn't know what it was or implied, but Bob did, and he turned pale. Mom went on to say that it was in the early stages, that the doctor said not to worry because it was treatable, and that Dad would soon be coming home. We – Jeanette and I – were predisposed to believe that, so to speak.

We discussed my dad's illness back and forth with Bob during our remaining days in Binningen. Bob brought his medical training (rather than his predispositions) to bear on what we'd heard, and he was much more alarmed. By the time we left, I was determined to write a letter specifically to Dad the day after we got home, July 15th. Since Mom had always handled nearly all the correspondence (Dad occasionally added a few lines, at most), it felt strange to be writing directly to Dad.

I told him how much I'd always loved him, how much he meant to me, in spite of our verbal battles and the differences that played such a villainous role in my adolescence. It felt awful that I couldn't just drop everything and jump on a plane, but I knew I would face almost certain arrest the instant I arrived on American soil. I told him I just wanted him to understand what a wonderful Dad I thought he'd always been. I was crying as I wrote it, and Jeanette was crying with me. I mailed it special delivery on July 16th. It took two days to arrive.

On Wednesday, July 18th, we got a phone call from the West Suburban Hospital in Oak Park. *Dad had died a few hours before*, just a couple of hours *before* my letter arrived. I thought I would dissolve where I stood. Jeanette saw the look on my face; I told her, and she collapsed on our bed. The glacier lurched.

We hadn't even known that Dad was *seriously* ill until a couple of days before he died. According to John, Dad suffered and was in terrible shape the day before (possibly more from the treatment than the disease). The funeral was held just two days later. Although I might have wanted to be there to lend support to Mom, it was probably just as well that the Selective Service made that impossible. (OK, I had a role in making it impossible by having refused to obey their orders.) I would not have been able to stomach what I was certain they would be saying: that Dad went "home", to "be with the Lord", praise the Lord, God is love, blah, blah, blah. It would have made me either furious or sick to my stomach, and my reactions wouldn't have given a lot of comfort to anyone.

We took Dad's death hard, Jeanette perhaps even more profoundly than me.

Lurches and surges

It was the first death of anyone close to either of us since Jeanette lost her only real girlfriend, Marie, when she was thirteen. I knew that she loved my dad, but I didn't foresee that she would react so forcefully. She said she was so scared – of losing *me*. It was difficult to calm her, so difficult that it probably became easier for her to hide her fear than to deal with it, but I couldn't see that then.

I was trying to avoid confrontation with Mom, which was why I did nothing to refute Mom's view of Dad being in some blissful afterlife, the "pie in the sky when you die" that they'd been doing everything to avoid going to. To me, the conclusion was inescapable that if her god, who was always in control of everything, really existed, then he would thus have allowed – or *caused* – Dad's suffering! Yet He was somehow supposed to be the epitome of goodness and love?!

But even though I let Mom get away with her religious rantings for a while, so to speak, I was not about to grant the same temporary permit to my brothers or anyone else. Thus, when John wrote me a letter with similar religious clichés to those Mom used, I took him to task about the "merciful god" he was peddling. His reply was remarkable: "*I have the feeling that I must defend something that you seem to delight in putting down.*" He didn't mention *his* delight in repeatedly trying to foist his indefensible, irrational, fairy-tale views on me. I'd have been content to keep my ideas to myself if he'd done likewise, but apparently he just couldn't resist the urge.

It was odd, sad, perverse, foreign and heart-rending addressing letters just to Mom; it made Dad's death so palpable.

I'd always found it weird – *wrong* – that most married American women tended to efface their own identity on marrying, by adopting "Mrs John Smith" instead of "Mrs Mary Smith". Mom had always done that. Even her personal return address labels showed "Mrs Maurice Erisman". Although I endeavored not to be bound by custom and tradition unless there was good reason to do so, here was an opportunity to restore a little of Mom's identity to her, so I began addressing all the letters I sent to her to "Mrs Francys Erisman". I later pointed it out to her, and told her why, and she adopted it too.

But in the months after Dad died, Mom was confused, trying to go on, pretending life was "normal" without Dad, which it couldn't be until the long lonely passage of time redefined the word for her. Yet four days after Dad's death she even sent Jeanette some birthday money, apologizing for not sending a proper gift, which only made it seem all the more unreal. John sent us a photo of Dad in his coffin that seemed perverse to me – it wasn't Dad, it was some goddamn corpse. Dad and I hadn't had much direct contact for years, so why did I miss him so much now? And what was happening to Jeanette?

On August 6th (19 days after Dad died), Mom received a piece of mail: the Selective Service had sent an impersonal form letter to me – to Mom's address – announcing that my draft order of June 1970 was *cancelled*. Mom didn't understand what it was when it arrived at her place, she just forwarded it, and it didn't reach us until August 14th. It contained no explanation about why, nothing about the implications or possible consequences of this potentially huge decision, or whether there would be any further actions from them, or what such actions might be.

At the top of the single sheet of paper was printed "*SELECTIVE SERVICE SYSTEM – NOTICE OF CANCELLATION*". Below it was printed the date and my Selective Service number, then my former Oak Park address, after which the form began: "*Your: (x in box indicates which)*", followed by three boxes, each one the continuation of the sentence beginning with "Your". The middle box was ticked and read: "*order to report for induction (SSS form 252) issued by this local board on*", followed by the stamp "*Jun 19 1970*", and continuing with "*has been canceled.*" [!!!!] At the bottom there was a further pre-printed text: "*Please continue to keep your local board advised of any change in your status.*" Beneath that, there was a signature: "*(Mrs) Linda D. Hutcherson*". That was it.

The timing of this notice felt to us like the bitterest of ironies. If there were anybody running this show (whether a god or a head of the Selective Service), he or she or they must certainly enjoy making a mess of things. Jeanette said that Dad's death made her even more convinced than before that she didn't want children. We'd been highly skeptical about parenthood from the time we stopped considering it a matter of social and biological course and realized that we had a choice. And since Jeanette strongly rejected parenthood for herself, and she was enough for me, I'd always readily agreed.

The subjects of my discussions with Jeanette often wound up in my paintings. People try to superimpose a purpose and meaning onto the uncaring void of the universe, preferring to live with that illusion instead of finding the only provable purpose and meaning as something that comes from within ourselves, what we bring to it, what we give it, what we imbue it with. I'd assumed that we both held this view from the same perspective, but would later come to realize that that was not necessarily the case. My perspective was one of detached philosophical theory, translatable into daily life where it seemed to be suitable. Jeanette's perspective was one of personal emotional involvement.

When Mom forwarded the draft cancellation notice (it didn't reach us until August 14th), she also enclosed a poem in Swedish by Esaias Tegnér, written in 1810, called *Det eviga* (The Eternal). Mom received this poem from a Swedish-speaking Meeting friend who found it beautiful, so Mom asked us for a translation. Why on earth would she ask us and not the selfsame Swedish-speaking friend who gave it to her?! There was only one plausible explanation: it was a ploy, yet another example of Mom's "subtle" way of pushing her agenda (*ahem!*). After all, she must have thought, how could "the eternal" *not* be one of *her* messages?

But she got this one quite wrong. As Jeanette was working on the translation, she looked up and said to me, "Hey, take a look, this one's really good!" It turned out to be a secular poem, one that took a strong position against the negativity of war and violence, instead promoting the positive – and eternal – values of compassion and humility: and no religion in sight. Mom expressed her great disappointment in the poem once Jeanette's translation enabled her to understand it. Jeanette wrote back, with far greater veiled sarcasm than I understood at the time: "*Hope you were not saddened by the poem. If we had known you would not have liked it we naturally would not have returned it. Excuse our lack of understanding.*"

We couldn't dismiss the possibility that the draft cancellation might be another kind of ploy – a trap – that the SSS knew about Dad's death and wanted to lure me back to the States in my grief, there to nab me and throw me in Federal prison. Mom and my brothers and various others were also wary of that possibility. Could they cancel an order but still make me criminally liable for having disobeyed it when it was issued? Why did they send it to Mom and not to me, considering the fact that they'd sent the draft order to me in Sweden in the first place, at the same address, and that I'd always informed them of changes of address? Were there other charges lurking somewhere, like breaches of Article 58616, section 2703B, paragraph 97? The timing would certainly have been the perfect set-up for a trap. But that didn't mean there was one.

Bob continued to amaze and surprise us. In early August, he grew tired of his pokey, rattling beige Deux Chevaux and traded it in on the last thing in the world we might have guessed: a used yellow Lancia sports car!

Slings and Arrows

On August 11th, our friend Krzysztof arrived, along with his girlfriend Jolanta, as well as a 150 cm-wide roll of fine canvas. The roll was 50 *meters* long! He insisted that he hadn't paid more for it than I paid Al for his math books. To say I was thrilled would be like calling steam slightly warmer than ice. It was great to see Krzysztof. He still had that boyish face and much of the timidity that dominated everything he said on the boat. Thankfully, he now seemed less anxious.

But he told us that when he'd gone for the interview to apply for his passport at the police station, they asked him, "*What did your friend say to you when he phoned you from* Świnoujście *in October 1971?*" I was dumbfounded. That had been a *domestic* phone call, after all, not even from outside the iron bloody curtain! I'd always naively thought that such things only happened in spy movies. So presumably they'd been opening and reading our mail exchanges as well. Now that we were safely face to face in Sweden, we set about devising an intricate system of folding the thin letter paper we'd been using, multiple times, using odd angles and folding sequences, and creasing each fold in both directions so that it would not be apparent after unfolding it in what direction to refold it. Then we agreed that if the first letter of the second line in the second paragraph of the subsequent reply were a consonant, it would indicate that the letter had arrived with folds intact. If it were a vowel, it meant that the letter had been opened and the folding sequence was altered. (In all our subsequent correspondence, the letter in question was a vowel.)

Both Krzysztof and Jolanta seemed well aware of the severe limitations on their freedom in Poland: the limited freedom of expression, the constant fear of unexplained detention, the barriers to free travel, the material privations. They even lacked the freedom to protest or debate what they didn't like about the autocratic actions and corruption of their government. And yet they seemed willing to endure all of it. For what? Were they, too, indoctrinated, brainwashed?

I thought about the similarities to my own indoctrination. I'd managed to escape; my brothers and most of those Meeting people hadn't – *nor did they want to*. I suddenly understood what Bertrand Russell was talking about when he claimed that Communism was just another religion, something requiring blind, unquestioning fealty to unfounded and fallacious beliefs. Or conversely, that religions are just other forms of ideology, and that ideologies tend to be most convincing to the vast majority if they prohibit questioning *and* if they *lack* a rational foundation. When I told Bob about these thoughts, he chuckled and said that I had one more thing in common with Russell.

Something else, something far more pernicious and inexplicable, was going on right under my nose during the two weeks our visitors from Poland spent with us. We'd never met Jolanta before, nor had we seen a picture of her. She hardly spoke any English, so Krzysztof had to interpret nearly everything. Jolanta seemed young and immature. She was possibly under 20, and was excruciatingly skinny. She didn't look well. Krzysztof apparently saw something attractive in her that got lost in translation from Polish; I couldn't see it at all. But the scary thing was that for some reason I can never hope to understand, Jeanette became outrageously and inexplicably *jealous*!

Her jealousy affected and infected everything she did and said when she and I were alone – she retained the mask of the gracious hostess when we were not alone – and gave me intense grief that I was less able to hide, which Jeanette perhaps mistook for an admission of guilt, confirmation that I was secretly attracted to Jolanta. This came within a few days of their arrival and remained throughout their visit and beyond, poisoning our time together, making everything awkward. I was at a total loss to figure out what to do about it; *you can't prove that kind of negative*.

Looking back at the younger me from the older me's perspective, I've often wondered whether I failed to see what might have lain beneath the surface of Jeanette's jealousy. (The Swedish word for jealousy – *svartsjuka* – is so much better at describing the condition; the Swedish word literally means "black disease", and jealousy really *is* a disease.) Was there a possible connection to Dad's death, which hit Jeanette so hard, and which caused her to express her *angst* about losing me? Was death only one of the possible ways she feared I might leave her? As if I ever could or would!! In hindsight, I think the most likely explanation was her own insecurity, a deep self-loathing (instilled as a child?). Nor did it occur to me that the glacier might have surged – again.

On August 20th, nearly a week before the departure of our guests, Jeanette's German class resumed, but it was only for a few hours a couple of evenings a week. Our trip to Paris aroused her interest in learning French as well, so after our guests returned to Poland, Jeanette found a beginner's course that she also attended for a while.

In her German studies, Jeanette constantly struggled with her lack of self-confidence. After every exam she took or every paper she submitted, she would come home convinced of utter failure. And when it turned out, as it usually did, that her grades were among the highest, she seemed impatient and annoyed, as if frustrated by her own success. It seemed to be part of the same pattern that kept appearing in her work. She was always sure she was going to be fired from her jobs for incompetence, no matter how much her bosses tried to convince her that she was as close to indispensable as anyone could be.

I was hoping that things would return to normal again after that disastrous visit from Krzysztof and Jolanta, and most of the time they *were* normal. But "normal" now had a somewhat altered definition, one in which Jeanette's almost imperceptibly increasing moodiness started including hints of hypochondria, with slightly greater mood swings than before, and more virulent outbursts of jealousy and temper – but they seldom lasted more than an hour or two. The brevity of these moods, outbursts and bouts suggested that they were not in any way rational, not like a long-term nagging fear or suspicion based on anything external. I told myself that it was all "*just in her mind*" in order not to have to think about anything frightening that I wouldn't know how to handle. But is there ever any "*just*" about what goes on in a person's mind…?

I mentioned none of this to anyone. I felt it might make it much worse for Jeanette if I did – that if she found out I'd told someone else, she'd become even harder on herself, in the way she described her conviction that her parents always saw her as a nuisance and a burden. I didn't want to contribute to that in any way. The one person I might have confided to in this was Bob, but I also feared that it would cause him to view Jeanette less favorably, perhaps even negatively, and I knew that he was somebody, to a certain extent like me, who tended to wear his heart on his sleeve. Was I wrong in keeping this from him? That was a question I would keep coming back to for years, yet another road not taken.

In any event, I kept it all to myself, hoping it would just blow over, perhaps hoping that the shock of Dad's death would wear off and that Jeanette's increased moodiness would wear off with it. It was just a phase, wasn't it? (There's that "*just*" again….) Once in a while, Jeanette would complain of some internal pain. I would immediately ask her about the exact location, how long she'd had it, whether she'd strained herself, whether it hurt more now than an hour ago, and whether she would agree to see a doctor about it. We seldom got as far as that last question before she abruptly put a halt to the subject, saying things like, "*No, it's all right now, it's nothing, it's gone, it's just in my mind.*" I wanted – I *really wanted* – to believe that "*just*" part, and so I did, not realizing that the mind can be the

Lurches and surges

worst place of all to allow things to fester. There's no "*just*" about it!

At the same time, Jeanette and I were already eagerly discussing the whole new situation brought about by my apparent draft cancellation. We were nearly certain that it changed nothing regarding our determination to remain in Sweden. Maybe if we'd come to Sweden when we did, but knowing that we'd be free to return as little as four years later, we might never have bothered learning Swedish, might never have focused on making a new life for ourselves in Sweden, might never have done anything but tread water. We might simply have been counting down the days until our return. Who knows? *There's no control group for the individual human life.*

But as much as we wanted to continue with our lives and our future in Sweden (I reassured Bob on this point), we were just as eager to *visit* the US again, to see what had become and was becoming of our fatherland in our absence: the protests against the War in Vietnam were now reflecting the majority view; the Watergate scandal was still in full bloom; Agnew's position was hanging by a thread; and even though Nixon was still President, everything we'd been reading about or watching on TV suggested that a lot of people were wishing they'd voted for someone else in 1968 too.

So we started playing around with ideas for a trip to the States in the summer of '74. We'd have a lot of family members to visit and geography to cover, with Mom in Oak Park, John in LA, Al in Seattle, and Jeanette's entire family still in San Francisco. It would take time and careful planning. It had to be as convenient as possible for everyone involved.

The sudden availability of an almost unlimited amount of good canvas gave me a real kick to start tackling some further things I'd been reading in the Bible that were troubling me. My parents had been telling me my whole life that the Bible was the unerring Word of God, that everything in it was factual, and that it had all the answers we needed (but we absolutely should avoid asking questions). This was the unwavering position of the Meeting. Even though most other so-called Christian denominations (at least in America, and as far as I knew elsewhere) were not inclined to insist on literal interpretations of *everything*, most of them still held that the Bible was the cornerstone of morality for all times, and that the Bible represented Eternal Truth and the Word of God. (Wasn't it hard to preach absolute relativism?)

I remembered that it disturbed me as a kid to read that King Solomon had something like 700 wives and another 300 or so "concubines". What the hell is a concubine? I understood it to be some other kind of wife, a second-class version. It turned out that a concubine was more like a rich man's sex slave. And yet the Meeting excommunicated people for sex outside of "wedlock". What about the Bible condoning slavery – *ownership* of another human being? Can anyone help me with the Biblical absolute-morality math here?

Getting back to Abraham, I read (using my brain this time around) that Abraham also had a few wives. One of them, Keturah (not terribly famous), bore him half a dozen sons (not terribly famous either), and presumably some daughters (not even worth mentioning). It was only Sarah's firstborn son, Isaac, who counted, and who would inherit everything. Actually, the Bible says that Ishmael was Abraham's firstborn, but he was born to Abraham's servant, not his wife, so he didn't count. (Islam has a completely different take on this, but I'll leave that for somebody else to write about.)

It was this highly "moral" firstborn birthright principle (I don't *think* I found this grossly unfair only because I was my parents' *last* born!) that was at work in the tale of Isaac's twin sons, Esau and Jacob. Isaac loved his firstborn, Esau, while Jacob was the favorite of their mother, Rebekah. Whenever the story about Adam's and Eve's first two kids came up in the Meeting, it was always emphasized that God respected Abel the shepherd's offering of a sheep because God's holiness required blood to be shed, while God had no respect for Cain the gardener's offering of the fruit of the ground (not bloody enough?). That little *non sequitur* of God requiring a blood sacrifice was never explained, but it certainly offers compelling evidence of bloodthirstiness. After all, *He* made all the rules!

With Esau and Jacob it was the other way around. Esau was the hunter, and brought home the bacon (and other meat), while Jacob puttered around the garden and delivered his veggies to mommy. But now God had moved the goalposts – without telling anyone; He wasn't respecting the blood-shedder this time, but He had no problem with mommy and smooth-skinned Jacob conspiring deceitfully behind Isaac's and Esau's backs to cheat hairy Esau out of his birthright. In the extremely far-fetched plot, the hairy elder brother returns empty-handed from his frustratingly unsuccessful hunting one day, and he's starving. Jacob has connived with his mother to get Esau to sign over his birthright in exchange for some lentil soup – Esau's alternative being to die of starvation. After Esau, faint with hunger, has signed on the dotted line, Jacob and

Mommy go on to lie and deceive Papa Isaac into thinking that Jacob is Esau, so the now-conveniently-blind Isaac will bestow his blessing upon Jacob, thus sealing the deal on the now-transferred birthright. For this, Jacob is rewarded well, and Esau is made destitute. That's the sort of uplifting story that makes the Bible a true bastion of morality in our society, isn't it? In my painting, *Esau Eating*,[19] Jacob and Rebekah are hiding in the background watching the desperate Esau eating his soup while they laugh at the success of their plot. Outside is the barren field and the void.

I was about to go on with another Biblical motif when I got a call from Per-Olof Börjeson. He was planning to stage an exhibition on the theme of Watergate, prioritizing works by American artists, and wanted to know if I would be interested in contributing something. Since it was a subject that engaged and enraged me, particularly through Bob, I said I'd see what I could come up with. This turned out to be the only painting I ever did "on assignment" (in a manner of speaking). In this fairly small painting, I used a table as a "divider", as I did in a couple of other paintings. Above the table is a stalwart public figure, backed by flags (Nixon and Agnew were outstanding models of America's current moral turpitude). Before him are faceless members of the Public – foolish, undiscerning, easily conned by the flag-waving going on in front of them. Under the table (literally and figuratively) is where the wheeling and dealing is going on, with prying eyes, sharply pointed planes and a hand wielding a dagger. The dominant colors, both above and below the table, are oranges, blues and violets. And the void pops up everywhere. I call it *Public Image*.[20]

The flow of my work was overpowering and energizing me. Ideas were springing up in my head like a pot of popcorn in which the oil has reached the perfect temperature and the popping kernels are lifting the lid off the pot. Jeanette was glowing, Bob was astounded. It felt more real than anything I'd ever experienced – and yet totally unreal.

---

19 Painting #37 (see Appendix 2)
20 Painting #38 (- " -)

Slings and Arrows

CHAPTER 6

Grasping and grappling

The autumn of 1973 was a time of grappling and turmoil in many part of the world that left a lot of people grasping after meaning. Although far too many Americans seemed to have little interest in anything happening outside the US (unless US interests were deeply involved), American actions continued to impact the world, just as world events would profoundly affect the US. For those who shared with me the view that Winston Churchill was right on target when he so cleverly defined the value of democracy ("the worst possible form of government, apart from all the other forms"), the news – that the democratically elected and forward-thinking government of Salvador Allende in Chile had just been overthrown by a military coup backed and/or orchestrated by the CIA, that Allende had been assassinated, and that the Pinochet dictatorship had been installed – was bitter. *Chile con carnage*. Unfortunately, it wasn't all that new or unique; my fatherland frequently authorized itself to interfere with and overthrow democracies, while the majority of its voters and stay-at-homers seemed unperturbed by the flagrant hypocrisy at the root of it.

Mom was understandably finding it very hard to cope with a new life without Dad, with cooking for just one (or at least one less), and with the many long hours of nearness that suddenly became frighteningly empty. Her lifelong training and indoctrination to believe that Dad must now be in some sort of paradise, running around some mansion in the sky maybe playing a harp, counting the stars in his crown, and singing His praises for all eternity, somehow failed to assuage her sudden and profound loneliness.

After *Public Image*, I could hardly wait to get back on the Biblical track, to something of utmost importance to me. My brothers were continuing to send me Christian apologist arguments, and every time I backed them into a corner (which was becoming embarrassingly easy to do), they would retreat behind their ultimate argument-stoppers: "*I don't have the answer to that, but the Lord does, and He will reveal it to me when He sees fit;*" or "*That part of the Bible isn't meant to be taken literally.*" It used to disgust me, because it was a total abnegation of reason and decency. When they employed excuses like that, they as became impenetrable as high-grade armor or Teflon – or as elusive as greased eels.

I had to do what I could to break through and show them what they were so insistent on ignoring. I thought that the means, the crowbar, would have to come from the Bible itself. It would be one of my largest paintings, but first I needed to paint a study – a small thematic foretaste of that projected painting – before moving on to grapple with the real thing, my watershed, my water*barn*.

In the pre-study, there are soft, rounded forms of dead and dying people, defenseless, covering the foreground. A lone figure remains standing, trying frantically to protect his head from the reign (and rain) of terror from above, symbolized by the jagged projections from the upper left-hand corner. Everything else is the void. I call this pre-study *The Victims*.[21]

I no sooner finished it than I launched into my disturbing milestone, my *Guernica* (cf. Picasso's powerful political painting manifesto against the Nazi bombing of the eponymous Basque town in Spain in 1937). I had a different axe to grind: I was taking on Jehovah. It marks my achievement of escape velocity, the final realization of the impossibility of believing in a *good* god (which makes the notion of worshiping a god at all either irrelevant or immoral).

The motif comes from the Bible again, the fourth book, *Numbers*, chapter 31. Jehovah orders the Israelites to completely annihilate the Midianites, so they go out and slaughter every last adult male, but take the women and children as prisoners – thereby disobeying Jehovah's order to fulfill the genocide. For this disobedience, Jehovah becomes "wroth" and has Moses tell the Israelites what they have to do to appease Him:

> *Now therefore kill every male among the little ones, and kill every woman that hath known man by lying with him.*
> *But all the women children, that have not known a man by lying with him, keep alive for yourselves.*
>
> (Numbers 31:17-18)

I'd read this many times before. It doesn't seem like it should have been hard to understand how grotesquely psychopathic it is. But somehow it hadn't registered. All the little boys are being slaughtered at the explicit command of God himself! All the non-virgin women are being raped and slaughtered! The virgins – the ones whose fathers, mothers, and brothers had just been slaughtered? Keep them

---

21 Painting #39 (see Appendix 2)

alive for yourselves! Fuck them and rape them! And all this is to please that ultimate arbiter of morality: Jehovah, the god who loves you. *Hallefuckinglujah*!

In my painting we thus have the slaughter of the boys on a slope upwards to the right; their contorted bodies are being sliced and impaled by viciously grinning blue soldiers in a psychopathic, murderous frenzy. Other boys are already dead or wailing and terrified. On the left, up another slope, the girls are being led away or slaughtered or raped (one might presume they weren't all that willing to become sex partners of the slaughterers of their families…) by additional sardonically grinning blue soldiers. Between the two slopes is the confluence of two rivers of blood. Presiding over this awful carnage is the blue-robed, reverently sanctimonious figure of Moses, blessing the whole scene with sanctimoniously closed eyes. Over his shoulder, and in command of it all, is the madly, sardonically grinning purple figure of Jehovah, against the background of the void. I call the painting *The Midian Children*.[22]

The crux of this Biblical story for me was that it doesn't matter whether one interprets the Bible literally or figuratively. Either way, it's abominable! The actions are those of a sadistic maniac, the biblical god who here demonstrates that He has nothing whatsoever to do with goodness, righteousness, kindness, compassion, justice, mercy – none of the qualities I believed in and believe to be worth aspiring to attain, however short of His glory I fell.

My choice of blue for the soldiers and Moses was informed by a movie Jeanette and I saw a couple of years earlier, called *Soldier Blue*. We loved going to the movies, and before we learned Swedish, we tended to go to see almost any English-language movie in Malmö (Sweden used original soundtracks – no dubbing), which means we weren't terribly discriminate. The title song, sung by Buffy Sainte-Marie, a Canadian Indian, was now a popular anti-war song, and the movie was supposed to be some kind of paraphrase of the Mỹ Lai massacre in Vietnam, set as a Western.

The story didn't get to me during the first part of the film, even though the opening titles stated that it was based on a true story. It rang no bells. There was this nasty Indian-hating Colonel Iverson, and much later there were these Indians living peacefully by a riverside, abiding by their peace treaty with the American Government. As Iverson's soldiers began riding towards the village, with bloodlust in their eyes, a huge bell suddenly rang piercingly clear in my

---

22 Painting #40 (see Appendix 2, for god's sake!)

head: *they changed the names for the movie!* "Colonel Iverson" was the real-life Colonel Chivington, the psychopathic sonofabitch who led his men to slaughter the entire peaceful encampment of the Sand Creek Cheyenne, the same story that made me ill and left me weeping when I read it in the Horace Mann school library when I was a kid of 10 or 11. The story that had haunted me ever since. I sat there, *knowing* what was about to happen onscreen, unable to move. After the movie was over, Jeanette and I had to walk around Stortorget for a couple of hours. The awful slaughter was the same type of thing my country's soldiers committed in Vietnam. The ghastly carnage was the same thing that the god my family worshipped commanded to be done to the Midian children. *No* difference in the viciousness and brutality, *no* difference in the unspeakable immorality. "*Suffer little children to come unto me*"?! Why don't they get how perverse and hypocritical that sounds?!

To me, it was the most important painting I'd ever done. I realized that it most emphatically placed me outside the category of painters who aspire to please their audiences, to rub people the right way, to offer them lovely wall decorations. This was a painting that would and should shake people up, provided they could be bothered to try to grasp what was going on. Jeanette was with me all the way on it, cheering me on, urging me on; she may have understood it fully before I did, and perhaps even better than I did. I started it on September 11th and finished it, exhausted, on October 2nd.

Even though I was teaching part-time at Interspråk, I was still able to paint full-time; I had Jeanette's full support and she was always with me while I painted, whether she was at home or not. When she was physically at home too, we sometimes talked or we chatted the whole time, sometimes she was just there in the room with me. And sometimes we did other things.

When I was particularly wrapped up in a painting, and Jeanette could tell I was growing weary despite my eagerness to keep going, she would sometimes put on Beethoven's 5th piano concerto (Bob had given us all five, in a superb recording with the Russian pianist Emil Gilels and conducted by George Szell). The first movement got my pulse going, racing with exhilaration. Then, in the second movement, the Adagio, my ears and head and heart were immersed in the most sublime, serene, sensual beauty. (I've never been able to hear that movement with dry eyes, or without thinking of Bob.) The end of the movement morphs into tension, building into wild excitement that bursts and explodes in a celebration of life: the Rondo Allegro third movement. I would be invigorated, charged, unable to sit or stand still, full of passion for life and my work and my love of my muse. (Dear reader: *Listen* to it! The whole concerto, in the right order, banishing all distractions. Let it happen to you!)

In mid-September, we saw in the paper that the Tuesday evening concert at the theater on September 25th was going to feature none other than Emil Gilels himself, playing Beethoven's third piano concerto. Our recordings of Gilels playing all of Beethoven's piano concertos were among our absolute favorites, so we immediately cycled to the theater to get tickets. We got seats in the third row, in full view of the pianist. We were just a few seats too far to the right to get a view of the keyboard, but we got his face instead.

We listened to our recording of it five times in the days preceding the concert. It was a great recording, but it didn't come close to the experience of being there, seeing him, the full house, hearing, seeing, and feeling the live sound. The *Concertmeister* saw that the orchestra was properly tuned up and ready to go. The conductor appeared and was given a round of polite applause. Only after the audience was completely silent did Mr Gilels appear. He was short and stocky, with an extremely stern, almost fierce, countenance. He sat down firmly at the piano and glared at it as if to inform it that it had no choice but to do the will of his thick fingers. Then his hands took flight in a blur of perfect clarity (it's probably impossible to play Beethoven's third piano concerto well if one's hands remain on the runway). But the clarity, the emotion, the yearning and fury, the energy and desire he put into it took us to a completely new height in musical experience.

We'd been to a number of Tuesday evening concerts at the theater, many of them pretty good, several excellent, a few outstanding. Back then, Swedish audiences tended to be reserved in their applause, almost always quickly falling into clapping in unison (which reminded me of sports audiences trying to encourage their team to score) for 15-30 seconds before falling silent and heading for the exits. Not this time. Everyone seemed to be as electrified and transported as we were: clapping wildly, stomping, soaring to their feet, cheering like they never wanted to stop, couldn't stop. (A few decades later, unfortunately, standing ovations suffered from galloping inflation in Malmö and became the rule rather than the exception, even for mediocre performances.) Mr Gilels even did two encores, short pieces by Bach and Rachmaninov, if I remember correctly.

Perhaps the intensity of Beethoven rubbed off on my painting of *The Midian*

Children. It felt like I'd never painted – or done anything – with that level of intensity before. Also during my work on it, Börjeson phoned again about his Watergate exhibition, and I told him I'd done a painting I thought would be suitable. He asked if I could submit two, and I told him I could. There were, in fact, a couple of other subjects more inspiring to me than Watergate and Richard Bloody Nixon, so I decided I'd simply let him exhibit *Green-Eyed People* as well; thematically it fit well enough with *Public Image*. And Gunnar Johansson, my odontologist-dentist-pupil, asked if I'd be willing to exhibit a few paintings at the Dental College in Malmö, so I said sure, if for no other reason than to deflect occasional accusations that I was hiding my work.

After *The Midian Children*, Jeanette and I both needed a break, so we took another extended weekend trip to Travemünde to celebrate our anniversary (on the Monday). This time we brought our bicycles along for a beautiful 20-kilometer ride through woods and open fields to Lübeck. Two days after our anniversary, eight days after I finished *The Midian Children*, Agnew resigned from the vice-presidency. Shortly after, Gerald Ford was appointed to be the new vice president. With Nixon's own position increasingly under fire, there was a chance that Ford might become the first-ever US President never elected to the presidency or the vice-presidency.

Mom was naturally still overwhelmed with grief at times, confused by the endless paperwork to settle Dad's estate, and dealing with grave uncertainty about her future as a widow. She and Dad had been planning to build a house on a big plot of land in the middle of a field outside Knoxville. Ralph and Maxine were going to build a similar house next door, some 300 meters down the road. My aunt and uncle told Mom that they were going through with their plans, but where did that leave Mom? And she was the one who had Grandma – Ralph's mother – to care for. She was hoping that her sister might agree to build a duplex, but that didn't seem to be what they were after, so Mom was "losing heart" about a move to Knoxville, and decided to postpone every thought of a move "for the time being". We offered to paint the garage and the basement of the house in Oak Park for her when we visited in the summer, to ease her burden just a little.

Mom continued her irritating predilection for telling Meeting people we didn't know to look us up whenever they visited Sweden or Denmark. When she wrote to enquire whether somebody named Paul Robinson had been in touch, I replied, honestly, "We haven't heard from Paul Robinson, and frankly

I haven't any idea who he is." Jeanette's responses to such things tended to be more diplomatic than mine (which probably comes as no surprise to anyone who knows me).

Henry Carlsson did a little research on our behalf and came to the conclusion that a major renovation of our building was the most likely explanation for the non-replacement of tenants, which we might have welcomed – it would mean central heating and no more drafty windows – if the rent didn't go through the ceiling, which we feared was probable, and Henry knew was certain. Maybe it was time to start looking look for other options?

Jeanette heard from Rosanne that their mother, Rose, had been taken to the hospital "with a heart spasm that caused damage to her heart." Jeanette reacted with enormous agitation and anxiety, which she tried to suppress. Why wouldn't she show it, let it out? My dad's death was still painfully fresh; Rose's condition was yet another reminder of her mortality, of ours, or everyone's. Of course we both *knew* very well that nobody gets out of here alive, but knowing that and being able to deal with it emotionally are not the same thing. How does one face the fact of inevitable death without resigning oneself to it? Not an easy question. (And deluding oneself that there's "pie in the sky when you die" doesn't amount to facing anything).

On October 6th, Egypt and Syria launched an offensive to regain the land Israel stole from them in the Six-Day War of 1967. The land in question – the so-called occupied territories of Sinai and the Golan Heights – thus resulted in a new war variously called the Arab-Israeli War of 1973, the October War, the Yom Kippur War, and the Ramadan War. This one lasted a few weeks, but again caused untold suffering and destruction. Most of the Western press said it started when the Arabs invaded Israel, not that they invaded their own occupied territories that Israel had seized from them, a mere semantic (or Semitic?) problem if one's own home isn't involved. We followed the TV coverage with alarm, and I made some sketches.

The same evening the war broke out, Jeanette and I were invited to a dinner party at Hamadi's apartment. Jeanette and I were getting dressed up to go, and I put on a somewhat dressy shirt and a sport coat. I liked wearing sport coats (except in the summer when it was too warm) because of all the pockets to put my pipe paraphernalia in: two pipes, a tobacco pouch, a few pipe cleaners, a lighter or matches, and a tamper. I always carried a pocket memo calendar and a pencil as well.

Then, by force of habit, I began putting on a tie that evening. I hated ties – not the way they looked, but due to my personal discomfort from having something squeezing at my throat. I suddenly stopped, in the middle of tying it, looked up at Jeanette and said with a sigh, *"Do you think the others will be wearing ties?"* She said she thought they probably would, so I resumed the tying procedure.

Then I stopped again. I thought to myself, *"What if every other guy who'll be there this evening is at this very moment asking his wife the exact same question, and the only reason any of us end up wearing a tie is that we're assuming that all of the others will be wearing ties? Should I ask about the color of the underwear they're wearing, so I can do likewise?! What are we, <u>sheep</u>?!"* I yanked my tie off, and Jeanette looked at me with surprise. I told her what I'd been thinking, and she laughed, saying I'd probably be the only one without a tie. *"As if that ever made a difference!"* I laughed back. *"Besides, I'll bet at least half of those there won't be wearing ties."* She wondered how I could suppose such a thing. I smiled and said, *"<u>You're</u> not…!"*

When we got to the party, I was indeed the only *guy* without a tie – for the first five minutes. Within 10 minutes fewer than half of the guys were still wearing theirs, and by the end of the party, only one still had his on. Centuries of men had been enduring discomfort, all because some 17th century Croatians wore some kind of neck scarf (Croat → cravat) when they served as the Royal Guard of King Louis XIII during the 30 Years' War, and Louis decided to declare it fashionable, *de rigueur* – and *de riguer mortis* to independent thinking. *Ba-aa-ah!* (I should point out that I find many ties beautiful and that I have no objections whatsoever to others' wearing ties. I do have strong objections to being *coerced* into wearing anything I personally find uncomfortable when it serves no other purpose that to conform to others' sense of fashion, style, taste, propriety, or decorum. Live and let live! How hard is that? Sheesh!)

Bob arrived on October 13th for a three-week stay. So monumentally much had happened since our last meeting: Dad was dead, Krzysztof and Jolanta had come and gone (although we barely mentioned that), I painted *The Midian Children*, the Watergate scandal was snowballing, Vice-President Agnew had resigned, the war in the Middle East was roaring, and the US announced cessation of all its war activities in Indochina. And it was still only mid-October! No wonder that fall felt like a time of turmoil! We not only had a tremendous amount to talk about with Bob. History was happening as we spoke. In early October, the Nobel

Committee in Oslo committed an effrontery to decency by awarding Henry Kissinger (Nixon's new Secretary of State) half of the Nobel *Peace* Prize. Perhaps in response, or as a solace, Bob bought us an excellent interpretation of Verdi's *Requiem*.

One of the repercussions of that awful October War in the Middle East (and to US involvement in it) came on October 16th, when the Arab oil-producing countries within OPEC placed an embargo on oil, cutting production drastically, thereby sending oil prices soaring by 70% overnight. The "oil crisis" was upon us – a major upheaval of the global economy. In Sweden, our heating bill suddenly doubled. Gasoline rationing was introduced, and although we had no car, everyone was affected. In one of the soundest responses possible, Sweden began revising building codes, calling for significant increases in thermal insulation to cut energy consumption (and oil dependency) drastically.

I continued to paint (oil paints use linseed oil, not petroleum!), moving from confrontational and controversial biblical themes to deal with responses – or the *absence* of responses – to them, apart from Jeanette and Bob. So in my next painting I was in a way getting back to the theme of isolation. It depicts a compact "hedge" of conforming people who are not looking at each other. In spite of their proximity, they appear to have no contact. Neither are they looking at the row of red tulips along the bottom edge, forming the counterpole to the void along the top edge. I call it *Garden Visions*,[23] although if I'd been painting a couple of decades later I might have used the term "comfort zone" as the title. If people don't react to a painting like *The Midian Children* with horror or outrage at the story and immorality it portrays, can they *ever* be shaken out of complacency? What would it take?

In my next painting, *Boxes*,[24] I took my battle against superficiality a step further. There are six boxes floating in the air above green rolling hills (or the waves of a green sea). The boxes are roughly cubes, but with only four sides – like a four-walled house with no floor or roof. Each visible outer surface has the upper torso and head of a red man, all of them positioned so as to be unable to see any others. Even though the overlapping planes of the figures might otherwise make them seem three-dimensional, their placement on the outer surfaces of the boxes makes them flat, two-dimensional, superficial.

---

23 Painting #41 (see Appendix 2)

24 Painting #42 (- " -)

I was feeling a lot of outrage, not least from feeling all the outrage Jeanette was feeling about wars, death, illness, jealousy, and all that suffocating superficiality and complacency and conformity, and nobody wanting or daring to think, to voice an opinion, to take a stand, to speak out (or at least up) about injustice, to abandon greed and try compassion instead, to abandon the chains of religion and superstition and wake up instead.

My next painting – *Outrage*[25] – is raw emotion coming right out of the canvas at the viewer. A lone figure occupies the center of the painting, from the bottom and almost to the top. His crying or roaring expression is one of anger, pain and disgust – outrage! – and his eyes are glaring and unevenly contorted. His mouth is wide open, with his sharp teeth showing. Behind him are two rows of skyline silhouettes. Behind them are the last rays of twilight beneath a bank of clouds, above and beyond which is the void.

During Bob's visit, Jeanette displayed a level of moodiness that she hadn't shown in Bob's presence before. He didn't say anything about it to either of us, but it may have altered something in how he viewed her – or me. Whatever new impressions he may have formed were probably not mollified by the unusually formal letter she sent him in mid-November after his return to Binningen. And her moodiness continued to grow.[26]

Although I had to increase my teaching load after Bob's departure to make up for all the time I'd taken off, I continued to paint almost unabated. After *Outrage*, the next one was a small painting, and a complete departure from my previous work. It was based on some of my doodling – a disproportionately large man sitting on a tiny stool. The room is blue and green, he is yellow and green, all very harmonious. His eyes are vacant abstractions, yet give the impression that he's looking out the window at the void. He is clasping his arms to himself, defensively hugging himself, as if for self-preservation. His legs, however, are comfortably crossed, as though he is relaxed, unperturbed by the view. The figure of the man

---

25 Painting #43 (see Appendix 2)

26 During my research for this book, on 23rd February 2016, I found a scrap of paper written by Jeanette on the back of an old BTP calendar page for 23rd November 1973, among Jeanette's notes: *"Vectoral psychotherapy, Wolman, B.B. Schizophrenia. Hypervectorial (deteriorate). (1) He becomes capable of correct perception of reality; (2) His emotions are balanced; (3) He is soundly adjusted. 'Love helps normal growth and hate poisons it.' Vectorosis praecox."*

Slings and Arrows

is possibly the only figure I ever painted that could lend support to an argument in favor of a Picasso influence. It's called *Sitting at the Window*.[27]

My final painting of 1973 (making a total of 22), *Regret*,[28] was a stylistic return to paintings like *Man Reading a Book*, and was also from a series of sketches I'd made of the human face torn by regret. Here again, I felt like dabbling a bit with the palette knife. The colors are warm enough, but the regret is intense; the man is squeezing his eyes shut in a look of agony.

In early December, Al told us that Nancy was pregnant. The baby was due in May, meaning conception in August. Mom mentioned that she found it "inappropriate" – it was "too soon" after Dad's death. I challenged her on that, asking whether she thought that Dad would have objected in the slightest. She backed down – at least in what she communicated to us for a while.

Airline routes changed in our favor, so Jeanette and I were able to take our first-ever direct flight from Copenhagen to the new (for us) and newly extended Basel-Mulhouse airport for a two-week stay with Bob starting on December 15th. Bob met us at the airport, which occupied an enclave situated in France, with a fenced-in highway corridor to Switzerland to obviate the need for extra border crossings. (The negotiations required to complete this bi-national airport took more than three decades!)

It was our first look at Bob's new Lancia. It seated two comfortably, three in a pinch (Jeanette endured a lot of pinching). However much it might have been able to perform like a sports car, Bob drove it in the same way he always drove his Deux Chevaux – the choice between slow and slower. But at least he could now choose his speed on the hills. (I never got to try that car out either.)

Bob had to work during our first week there, so Jeanette and I divided our time by continuing the work of fixing up and cleaning his place – to his delight – and visiting museums. He was relieved that we weren't working all the time. During our second week, we went with Bob to hear some beautiful Bach cantatas at Martinskirche, and took some slow drives around the countryside in the Lancia. Jeanette was feeling more and more at home in Bob's kitchen, and made us both a turkey dinner and a duck dinner (absolutely delicious).

The better Bob seemed to be getting mentally, the weaker he seemed to be

---

27 Painting #44 (see Appendix 2)
28 Painting #45 (- " -)

growing physically, but he said that everything was OK and not to worry about him. Each time we met and asked him how he was doing, he would reply with a quote from Gilbert & Sullivan's *H.M.S. Pinafore*: "*I am in reasonable health and happy to see you all once more.*" Since he seemed so confident in his newfound emotional stability, who were we to argue?

On one of our excursions into the countryside, Bob began talking about buying an old watermill or some such place, for me to rebuild into a home for him and a place for frequent long visits from us. Had he not been the one driving, I would have thought he'd been drinking. But I went along with it, thinking he'd been reminiscing about his cabin in the woods in his last years in the US, or about the old villa he'd rented near Orléans. I told him I'd be glad to do everything I could to make it happen, even though I couldn't at all see how he would benefit from the far greater isolation he claimed to be seeking when he was becoming so much weaker. But I said nothing about that.

Jeanette seemed to be gaining some confidence in using her German – more in reading and listening than in speaking. During one of our days of sorting Bob's papers, she either couldn't resist the temptation to see what the correspondence from this famous Tante Lore could be all about, or perhaps she just wanted to read a German text that wasn't written by a professional, so she began reading one of Tante Lore's letters to Bob. She reacted suddenly, powerfully and adversely to a turn of phrase, apparently in response to something Bob had written, in which Tante Lore referred to Jeanette as "*diese Frau*" ("this woman"). Jeanette interpreted this formulation – probably correctly – to mean that Bob had written something negative about her. (He undoubtedly wrote numerous positive things as well, but negatives tend to stand out and win every time insecurity is part of the equation.) We returned home on December 30th.

I knew I'd have a lot of painting time in January, and 1974 had scarcely begun before I found the motif for my next big work – from a sketch I made after watching a newscast from the Golan Heights during the October War. The scene was from a family gathering at a cemetery in a Syrian village. The family's son, killed in the war, was being buried *in absentia* (his body hadn't been recovered or recoverable). At the bottom of the painting are three grieving women: the mother, grandmother and sister of the victim. Lacking penises, they are of course not allowed inside the cemetery wall (in conformance with the comforting teachings of Islam). They are standing outside it, distraught. In the middle of the painting are the father and brothers. Having penises, they are allowed inside the cemetery, where they are standing around the dead son's/brother's grave, praying with hands cupped upwards, the Islamic gesture symbolizing receiving gratefully whatever Allah choses to dump on them. Their prayer, according to the TV report, was "*Thank you Allah, for allowing my son to go to his reward with glory.*" This prayer is inscribed, in Arabic (Hamadi helped me with it) on one of the tombstones. The graves are all elevated rather than excavated, apparently in keeping with the local custom, perhaps necessitated by the local stony ground. The naked, twisted, ugly, bleeding, disproportionately large corpse of the son is seen up in the barren hills in the background, as well as superimposed over the cemetery. The inverted figure of the laughing deity (recognizable from *The Midian Children*), in the void, surveys the scene with satisfaction. I call it *The Funeral*.[29]

The next painting, another of my personal favorites, stems from the sketch I made of the old Turkish man and the young German woman I encountered on my train trip to Basel in 1972. It's called *Train Compartment*.[30] The two figures are predominantly blue, with his blues in the direction of violet and hers in the direction of green. Light is entering from the window to the far left, and ends with their blue coats hanging up to the far right. The seats are shades of red. There's a kind of divider between them, an armrest of the mind. The void runs along the top of the painting. Before I started painting this one, I made a new sketch, abstracting into overlapping planes the original sketch I made on the train.

My final painting of January 1974 is called *Empty City*,[31] loosely inspired by musing about Paris. A clean, empty river flows through a city that is also empty except for the shadow of a figure standing with head hung low in the gap between two rows of nearly identical empty houses. The doors are red and inviting, but the angles are such that we can only glimpse two of them. The bridges, closely spaced, would seem to invite easy transfluvial access, but there is nobody in sight, except for a shadow. Behind the rows of houses is the ever-present void.

I had a feeling that Jeanette inexplicably tended to become moodier and less stable when I wasn't painting. She was so eager to help, to keep me going, and

---

29 Painting #46 (see Appendix 2)
30 Painting #47 (- " -); the significance of the sketch is described further in chapter 3, above.
31 Painting #48 (- " -)

Grasping and grappling

she took it upon herself to start stretching canvases for me so I could keep my brushes warm. I seldom needed to scrape my palette nowadays, and although I was getting pretty tired, I had to keep going. I wanted to undertake a series of small, identically sized paintings, almost like a large-scale "sketch pad", just to see what I could do with it. When I went to the artists' supply store to buy the stretchers, I was thinking of something like ten 40 x 60 cm paintings, but they didn't have close to that amount of stretchers in those sizes that day, so I ended up buying enough for nine 39 x 55 canvases.

On the last evening of January we went to the theater to see a performance of *The Magic Flute* and were disappointed with what they'd done with it (or to it). It didn't start well; the conductor made the overture sound like a dirge. Also, it was in Swedish – we preferred the original German (we knew the translation of the libretto well enough) – and the singers were definitely not of the world-class caliber we'd become used to from our fabulous recording. We were most likely a bit spoiled.

Our plans for an extensive trip to the US in the summer were taking shape, and we were now talking specific dates with our families. We planned to spend a total of five whole weeks there, which seemed like a minimum for fitting in a reasonable amount of time with each of those we had to visit. We had mixed emotions – both excitement and dread – with a little fear of the SSS thrown in for good measure.

A letter from Bob, in which he lavished Jeanette with praise of her cooking, was just what she needed to hear from him after her surreptitious reading of the "*diese Frau*" letter – of which Bob was unaware. I just hoped things would get back to *normal*. I also had another building project underway: to wall up one half of the big double doorway between our entry and our bedroom and turn the other half into a bookcase-door that wouldn't look like a door from the entry, but could be opened. But I didn't want a fake; I wanted to be able to fill it with actual books, not just dummy spines. It would therefore require a wheel at the free end to support the considerable weight. But I couldn't spend too much time on it; I had to get back to painting. And I probably needed to be teaching a bit more to bring in some cash.

The first of my nine 39 x 55s was a different approach to loneliness: the lack of completion and fulfillment in the form of what is ostensibly a somewhat joking still-life, which I call *Still Life with Fruit*.³² There's an armchair with only one arm, a pair of glasses with only one lens and only the lower half of a set of dentures. There's also an apple and a banana, each in two distinct yet conjoined halves. The only "group" is a bunch of grapes. The room has a door out to the void. But there's still life – with fruit.

The idea for the next one, *The Club*,³³ came from watching a TV production of a Dorothy Sayers murder mystery, *The Unpleasantness at the Bellona Club*, which shows stuffy old fat cats, cold blue, sitting around in big, stuffy leather armchairs at their stuffy club, against the background of the void. The gents are keeping an eye on each other, but making no contact, each is keeping to his own defined territory – loneliness despite proximity. I placed each of them at the top of separate flights of warm reddish stairs, which don't converge, so even if they descended them, it would not enable them to meet.

Many a time I'd observed Bob coming home from work. He'd slump into a seat and just sit there for a while, as if he'd climbed all the way home, and the air and energy had gone out of him. Even though he sometimes liked the work he did well enough, the things around it – the endless intrigues, piques and office politics – tended to make each day a thing he dreaded. Thus he greatly looked forward to coming home, but was too exhausted to do anything about it once he arrived. *Exhaustion*³⁴ depicts this uphill battle to get home. The "primary" view of the man's face – in profile suggests his exasperation and general "fed-upness", while the "secondary", face-front view, is more like total bewilderment and mental chaos.

The loneliness of disappointment is the loneliness of *Having waited…*.³⁵ In the background, he, cold blue, is standing in a doorway, head drooping, arms hanging in resignation at his sides. She didn't show up or call (the phone is disconnected anyway). He's already drunk most of the wine himself. The room is distorted, but is illuminated through the half-empty bottle. A bright yellow tulip lies there, not in a vase, so it will soon wither.

Staying on the same general theme, *The Late Guest*³⁶ shows a green-gray

---

32 Painting #49 (see Appendix 2)
33 Painting #50 (- " -) ; Al often said he wanted to buy this one, but never made me an offer….
34 Painting #51 (- " -)
35 Painting #52 (- " -)
36 Painting #53 (- " -)

dejected man sitting at a table, watching an empty doorway – also the void – in the background. His right hand supports his heavy head. The planes that comprise the floor can be seen as an obstacle course that makes entry to the room more difficult. Superimposed on the floor beneath the table, a pale corpse is laid out – the guest who hasn't shown up because he is dead, "late" in both senses of the word.

It's not always possible to choose what one will remember. Memories can well up unsolicited out of one's brain like the birth of Athena. Those that are irrepressible are almost by definition undesirable – things one is ashamed of having done (or not having done). The red person in the foreground of *The Irrepressible Memory*[37] is being haunted by such a memory, personified as a threatening figure rising up behind him. Yet he remains calm, patiently waiting for it to recede again.

By the end of February, I'd completed six of the nine 39 x 55s. I was on fire, and Jeanette loved every one of them and every minute I was painting them. At the same time, now that our plans for a summer trip to the US were becoming more concrete and real, our agitation was on the rise. Would I *really* be safe? How could we be certain that no trickery was involved? Mom's fears were also growing, but were still under control at this point.

I asked Mom some months before if she could try to get in touch with Ken Keisling, the Meeting guy who bought my seventh painting (*Hands*) back in 1964, and ask him to send me a high-resolution photo of the painting. All I had was a Polaroid photo – not the best quality. Ken and I hadn't been in touch for nearly a decade; I was even prepared to buy it back from him. I wanted to improve my catalogue, not only by adding the new paintings, but by having decent photos of all the older ones as well. Bob had an extra copy of my catalogue; he was so proud of it that he guarded it jealously, apparently refusing to let any visitors look at it – the exact opposite of my wishes.

Our correspondence with my parents had become relatively sparse prior to Dad's death. Mom was the only one who wrote from their side, and nearly every letter contained mildly nauseating levels of her religious clichés, so there was less and less to respond to. Our lives were incomprehensibly foreign to them, but they asked few questions and sought no explanations.

---

37 Painting #54 (see Appendix 2)

In the year or so following Dad's death, we wrote frequently, both Jeanette and I, as our only safe way of offering Mom support. There were still lots of clichés in her letters, but there were many factors that affected her desire for real communication favorably: Dad's pain, his death, her loneliness and confusion, her seemingly endless struggles to get through the red tape of Dad's estate, her sudden need to deal with the daunting practical tasks that Dad had so effortlessly performed, and our active disinterest in responding to her expressions of superstition. The effect of our somewhat improved communication was multiplied by the prospect of seeing each other in June.

While I was painting, almost frantically, Jeanette was stretching more canvases for me, and supplying me with beautiful music, delightful food, and the warmest of all possible hugs and affection, whenever she perceived that I might need any or all of them.

I used to cycle through Kungsparken on my way to work at the language school. Near the statue of *Pegasus* (by Carl Milles), there was a broad clearing lined with trees and benches. One day when the autumn leaves were particularly beautiful, I saw a solitary person sitting on one of the benches, lost in thought, looking lonely. In my painting *Autumn in the Park*,[38] the warm colors of the leaves (although they are dead or dying) is contrasted by the cold colors of the man (although he is alive). The array of color in the treetops almost shields out the void.

One of the issues I'd been debating in discussions (mostly written) with my brothers was why a good God wouldn't just haul everybody off to Paradise, preferably without a life of misery preceding it. Who was there to stop Him from doing the right thing? The pathetic answer I usually got was that He didn't want the eternal praise of those who didn't *choose* to follow Him; that's why He gave us Free Will. I wanted to illustrate a starting position for this monstrously stupid notion by asking if they knew of any parent who would allow their child the free will of playing on a 50th-storey balcony with no railing? No sane, loving parent would allow their child to make that wrong and irrevocable a choice! At this point it hadn't yet occurred to me to ask whether (if free will were the prerequisite for the validation of praise) people in paradise would retain their free will – and could thus at some point in eternity slip up and make the wrong choice and be sent to hell after all? "'Eternal security'? Sorry, fella, you forgot to

---

38 Painting #55 (see Appendix 2)

read the fine print!"

For *Man in a Waterfall*,[39] I challenged that supposition further by metaphorically asking what options – what free will – a person might have who finds himself falling down a cascade? He can see everything around him quite clearly, he knows where he is and where he is going. But he can do absolutely nothing about it. The water contorts his torso (one leg is twisted back behind his head). But does he fear the water as much as the void?

For the final painting in my 39 x 55 series, *Writing a Letter*,[40] I was thinking of how stunned I was when I wrote my last, futile letter to Dad. I could hardly tell him that his good, merciful and compassionate God had in His wisdom chosen to make him suffer, to make Mom suffer, to make all of us suffer – for no goddamn good reason at all. A left-handed guy is sitting at a writing desk, staring off to one side, trying to find what to say, something. Anything? The stationery is well illuminated by the lamp, but no words come. Behind him is an empty doorway – and the void. The envelope seemed like a good place to sign the painting.

Returning to more random painting sizes, my next one shows three figures, all looking straight at the viewer, expressing different forms of surprise: the surprise of the green figure (against a red background) is in the direction of alarm or horror; the violet figure (against a yellow background) shows general astonishment; and the orange figure (against a blue background) is covering his mouth with his hand to hide or suppress his feelings – could it be a laugh, a scream or a yawn? The other two could be talking, arguing or singing, but none of the three appears to be communicating with any of the others. Outside the two small windows is the void. Have they all just discovered that there's nothing but a void outside and they've turned their backs on it? The title is *Imagine Our Surprise.*[41]

I wrote to Mom on March 17th that we hoped she could come to spend some time with us the following spring, "for as long as you like – the whole summer?" My relationship – *our* relationship – with Mom was out-of-the-ballpark weird. When you love someone boundlessly, and that someone is always judging you, disapproving of nearly everything you do or think, suffering (or pretending to

---

39 Painting #56 (see Appendix 2)
40 Painting #57 (- " -)
41 Painting #58 (- " -)

suffer) anytime you drop your guard and be yourself, anytime you deviate from *her* indefensible and ignorant positions, how do you handle it? How do you survive on a playing field that will never be level?

The next day, on March 18th, OPEC ended the oil embargo and the world breathed a sigh of relief, but some element of fear remained; they'd done it once and could do it again. The world was *too bloody dependent* on oil, but too few were committed to reducing that dependency!

Two days later, Jeanette came home from work pretty excited and agitated. Her boss told her that he was planning to start up a branch office in Khorramshahr, a key port city in southern Iran, close to the Persian Gulf and to the Iraqi and Kuwaiti borders. He said he might want Jeanette to be in charge of setting up the new office there, and to stay until things were up and running, for a period of six to eight weeks starting in early August, after we got back from the States. I, by the way, could come along for the ride (and spend all my time painting). He said we'd get to live in a comfortable house near the Persian Gulf. It was a totally unforeseen idea, out of the blue – exciting, scary, exotic and completely unknown – pretty much in that order.

We immediately plunged into finding out things about Iran that we'd never known before: that Iranians were not Arabs, although they were Muslims (we were still unaware that Islam comes in many discordant and often violently opposing versions, pretty much like Christianity, Judaism and other religions); that their language was an Indo-European language (like English, Swedish and languages from India to Iceland) called Farsi, based on Ancient Persian. Farsi uses the Arabic alphabet, but is otherwise linguistically unrelated to Arabic (which is a non-Indo-European Semitic language related to Hebrew); that the country once had a democratically elected prime minister, Mohammad Mosaddegh, until the democracy-touting Yanks and Brits overthrew his democracy in 1951 and handed all power to the Shah; that "Shah" means "king", as in "check" (in chess). And "check mate", literally means "the king is dead", when the chess game is over. We learned that the Shah had modernized and secularized Iran, enfranchised women and allowed non-Muslims to hold public office. BUT (why does there always have to be a *but*?) he autocratically crushed his opponents in doing so; that the climate in southern Iran, where it was nearly all desert and oil, was hot as hell (as high as 50°C). We also knew that Iran/Persia had beautiful carpets; but that was pretty much *all* we knew before this possible adventure.

As the plans for our US trip were progressing, we got a letter from Jeanette's

Grasping and grappling

mom, stating their generous intention to give us $1000 towards our trip. I shamelessly informed Mom of this, and she immediately matched the Minihanes' contribution, so our strained finances were rescued. We were trying to save as much as we could, especially since we realized that we might have to find another place to live (and most likely a much more expensive one) at some point in the not-too-distant future, given the intentional neglect and deteriorating state of our apartment building.

At the end of March, I asked Mom to phone my draft board – they'd now moved from Forest Park to Berwyn – to make sure it would be OK for me to visit the US, to confirm that there was no risk of prosecution, and to put it all in writing. Paranoia was rising, the way people with vertigo feel panic rising as they know they are approaching the edge of a cliff, even though they can't see it (or even though their information about the cliff was false). But contacting the SSS made Mom very nervous too. Jeanette told her not to bother – I had my draft cancellation papers, and we would bring them along.

Every once in a great while, there's a person who comes along with whom you have instant chemistry and rapport, even without words. Stig Svensson, my full-time pupil from the Swedish chemical company Perstorp, was such a person. He could hardly speak a word of English on Monday morning, yet he could converse with me in English, barely but incredibly, by Thursday afternoon. He was jovial and avuncular, exuding sincerity, humor and cheer. I wrote all new words for him in his notebook, and he absorbed them like blotting paper. (I learned to write upside-down directly in my pupils' notebooks, to be able to teach one-on-one more efficiently and effectively. I also made charts and tables of key conjugations, and little illustrations of important words that lent themselves to pictorial definitions.)

One of Perstorp's businesses was decorative laminate, where Stig was employed. (Since Perstorp was Sweden's biggest producer of laminate, it came to be known as *Perstorpsplatta* in Sweden, just like Formica was the household word for decorative laminate in the US.) Stig's work was soon to become largely international, with a lot of overseas travel, so he needed English badly – and quickly. Even within the first four days, he learned enough English to explain to me (with the help of some body language and sketches) how decorative laminate is made. "*You take paper, many pieces, special paper in chemicals to be wet. Thick laminate, many papers, on top, more and more on top. Then you take the picture paper – the pretty paper – also with chemical in it, impregnate, on top of all of them. And one more paper, harder, to protect. And then you put all into a press, very hot, and the chemicals make the paper to be plastic, so you can have it in your kitchen, to work on! Worktops, yes!*" Try learning how to express *that* in a new language in less than four days!

Then he asked me if I had other sketches on paper – not the ones I'd made for his notes – and would I like him to take a couple of those sketches and turn them into decorative laminates, just to see what it would be like? This was *not* about reproduction – the original sketch would simply replace the décor paper and become part of the laminate itself. So on Friday, I brought two or three of my sketches from home and turned them over to him. He said it might take a while before they could fit my drawings into the schedule for the small press they used for experimenting with new patterns and techniques. I said I wasn't in a hurry.

Our approaching trip had Jeanette and me grappling with thoughts about Dad and his death, as well as Mom and her drastically altered world. Jeanette was talking a lot about death itself – how sudden it could be, how random, unfair, how difficult to understand and final it was. She spoke of Death with simultaneous fascination, fear and contempt. I tried to capture the image of what I saw in her mind with my next painting, *Shifting Void*.[42] It was an attempt to deal with grief in general, and Dad's death in particular, more directly. The person in the bed has just died. The only one of those gathered who doesn't have his or her back to the dead person (and the void) is the grieving woman seated by the bedside, but she has covered her face in grief. The others seem mostly inconvenienced.

The long winter darkness was now behind us, and for a time (six months) the vernal equinox turned us Northerners into the Earth's more illuminated ones, Mom struggled her way past her lonely 61st birthday, and the longed-for signs of spring were frustratingly slow to reveal themselves. We found ourselves wondering whether there would ever be a year without some new trauma or upheaval in our lives: "*No news is good news.*" At least it was never dull.

---

42 Painting #59 (see Appendix 2)

CHAPTER 7

The missing tapes

Since Bob hadn't felt physically able to come up to see us for our now-traditional Easter get-together, Jeanette and I flew down to Basel on April 6th, the day after my week with Stig, for a week of sensational music and conversation. Bob seemed kind of confused by all our travel plans – the US and now also the possibility of Iran – and seemed to be both delighted and a little resentful, even though neither trip, nor both, would affect the normal frequency of our meetings with him. He resurrected his notion of a watermill conversion a couple of times, but he seemed to realize that it was never going to be even slightly feasible, particularly since he hadn't found anything remotely like a candidate for such a conversion (nor had he taken any steps to look for one).

In recent months, perhaps since the beginning of the year and because of his increasing difficulty in writing (he was still using a manual typewriter), Bob would phone us on a Sunday evening instead of writing responses to our letters. The Sunday Night Phone Call from Bob was soon to become a wonderful institution that would go on for many years. On the first or second day of our visit, Bob wanted us to listen to a cassette tape he'd received in lieu of a letter from his brother Charles, with whom Bob had a sporadic, strained, in-spite-of-everything, loving relationship. Bob didn't quite know what to do about responding to this tape, so we bought him a couple of blank cassette tapes and a microphone, and then showed him how to work them so he could send a reply in kind.

Then it occurred to us that it could be a great approach for us as well – not only to supplement our letters, but to decimate the phone bills, especially Bob's. Bob wanted to rush out and buy us a cassette recorder too, but we said we'd get one at home so we'd be able to take it back to a local store if a problem arose.

One place Bob wanted to visit in town during our stay was a special liquor store, Paul Ullrich AG, on Schneidergasse, just a block off the Markplatz, where he bought a bottle of Chateau Laffite Rothschild and another of Chateau Mouton Rothschild, as well as two fantastic cognacs (Hennessey Extra *and* Martell Extra). Bob said he'd always been curious to try them and wanted to do so with us. They were outrageously expensive, but that didn't stop him. We then visited the exclusive glassware store, just around the corner on the Markplatz, where Jeanette and I bought him three cut-crystal wine glasses, as might befit

Slings and Arrows

such auspicious wines. (Bob's selection of wine glasses was depleted, but he did have some excellent brandy snifters.) Then we went home to Binningen, listened to great music, drank great wine, enjoyed Jeanette's great cooking, sampled the super Cognacs, and conversed until well past midnight, until we were too sleepy to continue.

Bob's shaky health was not improved by the problems he was having at work. He was burdened by Theiss[43] and the backbiting of office politics. I asked him whether he'd looked into Swiss citizenship yet, but he still hadn't gotten around to it. I knew he had a nagging fear that someday there would be a referendum in which the enigmatic Swiss voters would decide to cast all foreigners out of the country. I suggested that *that* ought to be reason enough to do something about becoming a citizen.

Most of the world's democracies are representational democracies. The people elect representatives whose duty it is to immerse themselves in the details of every issue, to propose laws and to vote on them, thereby achieving governance roughly in accordance with the will of the people. If these representatives do otherwise, they will (in theory) not be re-elected and the people will have the right to vote for those who better achieve what the voters want. Elections are normally held at two-to-six-year intervals, depending on the country. Once in a while, a country with a representational democracy may hold a referendum, i.e. dabble in direct democracy, whereby a particular issue is decided directly by the voters, rather than by their elected representatives. In Switzerland, however, referendums (Latinate purists call them *referenda*; the last syllable is pronounced *duh*) – hundreds of them every year, on the national as well as the cantonal levels – decide just about everything. This is because Switzerland is primarily a semi-direct democracy, and secondarily a representational one. Such a democracy requires an electorate that is (in theory) exceptionally well-informed on every issue, and that they are not too fickle.

In the late 1960s or early 70s, the canton of Basel Stadt held a referendum to build a new opera house to replace the existing one that was in appalling shape. The people voted yes, and work got under way, swiftly and efficiently, as one might expect of the Swiss. Within a few years, a majestic new theater and opera house had been built close to the old one, which was still standing – and

---

43 Bob's boss; see Book 3 (*No Traveller Returns*), chapter 6.

operating. Before the new opera house could be opened for use, there had to be a new referendum to approve the operating budget of the new music palace. The people voted no. There were several new referendums on the same issue over the next couple of years, and the people kept voting no. Ultimately they must have realized what a bad return they were getting on their investment of public funds, so at last they voted yes, and the new building could finally open its doors to the public and to theatrical and musical performances.

Issues concerning immigration kept coming up in Swiss referendums, every year, each one traumatizing Bob. It wasn't as though the Swiss could be unflinchingly relied on to faithfully uphold democratic and humane ideals in every last one of these referendums. After all, it wasn't until a referendum in 1971 that women were finally allowed to vote in Federal elections nation-wide! It took longer on the Cantonal level. Federal courts finally forced Appenzell to grant women the vote in 1990! That's why we were concerned about Bob getting citizenship, and that's why Bob was afraid of applying.

Jeanette wrote to Bob how nice – and important – it was to have a "safety net", pointing out that she and I had our respective families, whom we felt, despite our differences, that we could turn to if anything happened. *"And we also have you, Bob, and want you to feel the same about us. You could come and stay with us, not as a guest, but as a member of our family, or even better: as our friend. We want you to have that feeling of security, that you could turn to us, because we would enjoy being turned to."*

Towards the end of our stay, we finally focused our attention on Bob's balcony. He said he loved to be out there when the weather was decent. The views from the 13th floor were fantastic – all the way to downtown Basel and beyond to the Vosges Mountains in France in one direction, and up the fertile Swiss valley in the other. Storks and large hawks would occasionally fly past at eye level. We got Bob a little table to put out there, a comfortable lounge chair for reading and napping, and even some pots with pansies and a dwarf Japanese maple tree. He was fairly bursting with pride.

The first thing I did on the Monday after we got home was to buy a cassette player and a couple of blank tapes and begin recording our first tape-letter to Bob. (During the time we were exchanging letter-tapes with Bob, I unfortunately treated the tapes as disposables and recorded over his to make my next ones. I thus found myself with almost no tapes from him when researching this book, but he'd saved a few of ours.) We soon found it harder to talk into a machine for an hour than to converse for an hour. It took Jeanette and me nearly a week to fill one tape. I also went to Börjeson's to pick up my "Watergate" paintings, but he asked me to wait because he'd arranged an additional exhibition in Odense (Denmark).

There were some problems with Jeanette's boss; three of her colleagues felt they had to quit. Was something going there on that would affect the Iran deal? We were rapidly becoming accustomed to the idea of going there, and saw it as a great adventure.

There was a good letter from John waiting for us on our return from Switzerland. He'd taken it upon himself to check with the FBI on my behalf. They told him I was in the clear – no warrant had been sworn out for my arrest – but my paranoia remained largely intact. Mom also mounted the courage to check with my draft board. They said that after my draft order was cancelled, my file had been destroyed, so there was no risk of arrest or complications. But they advised her to check further with the attorney-general's office, who also confirmed that there was nothing to fear. So the proverbial coast seemed to be clear, although I didn't feel I'd be able to breathe easily until we were back home in Sweden.

My crazy aunt Marion wrote to her congressman, Carlos Moorhead, asking him to double-check. She also got the all-clear, as well as a more detailed account of why. I had indeed been indicted, Moorhead wrote her, but the US Attorney found that the SSS had made some procedural errors in handling my case, so my indictment was dismissed. The SSS then had no option but to cancel the induction order. To top it off, my file was destroyed. "*He is, indeed, 'home free,'*" Moorhead wrote. My paranoia was still smoldering, but no longer blazing.

During our absence in Binningen, our water heater broke down (heavy scaling on the immersed heating coil) and we were back to sponge baths. But the weather turned warmer, so we were no longer shivering in our apartment (which could get really *cold* in the winter!). Henry again helped us by sending someone around to fix the water heater, almost free of charge. The plumbing contractor who took care of it happened to have Henry's company as a major client, serving all their building complexes, so it was a drop in the ocean for them, and Henry would get a few free English lessons from me and everyone would be happy. The cold apartment, however, wasn't possible to fix. There was nothing to do about the howling absence of central heating and thermal insulation. (Adding enough electrical heaters to keep the chill out would have either blown our fuses or our budget, or both.)

We *liked* our apartment, and the four flights of stairs were no problem for our young legs, although we could see that they were getting to be pretty strenuous for Bob. And our building was a source of increasing anxiety; it was deteriorating, and no maintenance at all was being performed. When we complained to the caretaker (who lived in the adjacent building), we were told that he'd heard something about modernization plans, but no action was being taken. He had almost no direct contact with the landlord – and no budget or mandate for undertaking any but the most urgent repairs.

There was no lock on the door between our stairway and the street; there were no longer any families or even couples among the other tenants. In fact, there were no tenants at all on the first two floors, where the windows in the doors were broken, and the doors left ajar. There were only two other tenants in the building; they seemed to be drunks who were taking advantage of the dirt-cheap rent in order to have a place to drink. [*Sweden had almost no drug problem at that time.*] Even scarier was the fact that we sometimes heard sounds of people moving around in the stairwell below us and the attic above us at night; there was no carousing, but it made us uneasy about burglaries or even fires. The absentee landlord didn't seem to mind only 30% occupancy. Our only conclusion was that the landlord was simply waiting for the last tenant to move out voluntarily – Swedish laws prevented landlords from evicting tenants without just cause, but didn't require them to find new tenants – so they could undertake a total renovation of the building and jack up the rents to levels we would be unable to afford. (Maybe they were hiring people to prowl the attic at night to scare us out?!)

So we felt that we would have to start looking for other alternatives as soon as we got back from the States. Besides, we were beginning to feel a bit cramped. With all my paintings (and many more to come, we hoped), we were running out of wall space to hang them on. Another couple of rooms – a bigger studio and a dedicated guest room (primarily for Bob) would be great. A new place would also have to be centrally located (no car – walking distance), preferably in an old building with high ceilings (at least for my studio). But, we told Bob, we wouldn't want anything that would involve major renovation. Some fixing up would be fine, but nothing structural. And the rent would have to be low. "*Maybe we're dreamers?*" I asked Bob, profoundly and rhetorically. "*But I suppose you have to have a dream if you want any to come true!*"

The Garden of Euphoria,[44] my next painting, bears some resemblance to the previous year's *Garden Visions*, with its floral setting and people not looking at each other. In my new painting, the people are in a jungle created by the potted plants from which they sprout. They are all in various states of oblivion, or euphoria, a much easier approach to reality than dealing with it.

By the time we made our second tape for Bob a week or two later, Jeanette's boss told her that the tentative move to Iran was no longer a question of 6-8 weeks' duration, but one of 2-3 *years*. Jeanette told her boss it was out of the question for us; shortly after, the whole Iranian deal fell through. We were relieved, not disappointed. The more we found out about what life in Khorramshahr would be like, the more it felt like something to be endured, not enjoyed. It would have been a question of oilfields and a huge petroleum industry in a desert oven setting, without culture (what did we know?) or escape. We'd grown far too accustomed to freedom to find anything attractive about living in an autocracy. (For instance, what kind of trouble would a painting like *The Funeral* have gotten me into there?!) But the *idea* of moving to Iran for a short time had been fun while it lasted.

Recent phone conversations with Bob revealed that Theiss was treating him with great hostility, and Bob's health was being affected: he was "flat on his back". We argued for and encouraged him to take a leave of absence, spend it with us, and break a vicious circle. "*Our time and friendship with you has brought a whole different dimension to our lives, making Europe a bigger and less foreign place,*" I said, and Jeanette added "*We hold you very dearly.*" But he still said he didn't seem to know the *real* cause of the state of his health. I urged him to find out.

Bob mentioned having received a *long* letter (more than 20 pages) from a guy named Charlie Bowerman, an old friend from Rochester, with whom Bob had had no contact since he left the US. The letter indicated that Bowerman was now a real right-winger. Bob was disturbed about the letter and its implications and wanted my input on his analysis. Bob felt that the guy's conservativism seemed to be based on pessimism and callousness; pessimism because it implied that only the older world order was worth hanging onto, callousness because of the lack of empathy for the poor. In Bob's view, not wanting to face reality – at least the reality of the disadvantaged – was an ostrich attitude towards life. I fully agreed

---

44 Painting #60 (see Appendix 2)

and was delighted to note how directly Bob's analysis reflected the turnaround he'd been making in his life, not only from nihilism and depression to a lust for life, but also from his former political conservatism to the value of having a society that protects the disadvantaged.

Sometime in the first half of May, Börjeson phoned me again. He wanted to offer me the use of a whole floor or room of his gallery, to set up my very own exhibition, taking my own risks! I still turned him down. I was so intensely into painting that I had no time to think about organizing any exhibitions. Besides, I was by now even more skeptical about selling – and Jeanette was downright averse. But Bob was buying; *he* was my patron.

Our mid-May weather was balmy, and we could keep our balcony door open. I made shutters for our bedroom windows. Shades and curtains weren't enough to achieve darkness at 4.30 in the morning when the Scandinavian summer sun hit them.

In researching this book, I discovered a few missing tapes (some 42 years after they were recorded!) that were as astounding for me as Nixon's "missing tapes" were for the Watergate investigators. One side of a tape we sent to Bob on May 24th was largely devoted to a long, wistful, sometimes barely coherent, deeply melancholic meandering monologue by Jeanette, a further development of an issue she raised with Bob during one of our visits to Binningen. I don't remember that original discussion (I might not have been present for it), but Jeanette had clearly mulled over it a great deal. Her musings on tape were spoken slowly, painstakingly, as if each word were being weighed. She sounded like she was trying to recall an almost-forgotten dream, far away, almost lost, as if she were a patient lying in a hospital bed having recently woken up after major surgery. Almost every sentence "trailed off" as if she'd almost forgotten she was holding a microphone; few ended as clear assertions. (Jeanette's voice, which I hadn't heard in decades when I listened to the tape, sounded strikingly similar to the wistful moments of Andie MacDowell in the closing part of the film *Four Weddings and a Funeral.*)

> *I wanted to say that I was thinking about something I asked you while in Basel. It wasn't the last time, though. It had something to do with knowing the difference between reality and unreality. And I would like to take advantage of your good ear, and your friendship, to comment, even though it pertains only to me.*

Reality to me is the basics for living: food, shelter from nature's vengeances. Aside from the necessities for survival, I think that reality is a relative question, or is connected with – for example – my construction (mentally and physically), my exposures, my handicaps and limitations, my values. It has to do for the most part with me. I don't know, though, if having such a definition of reality doesn't eliminate the word 'reality' or the question of having to accept or not accept reality as such. I think I'm extremely realistic, when it comes to my circumstances, and that which I'm confronted with and how I deal with it. It is my form of reality. I don't think, other than the basic needs, that there is a set of standard rules for reality. I'm not sure why the question of reality or unreality ever came up? It seems so unimportant! Reality now seems to be an awareness of that which I set up as principles, rules for me to base my decisions on, that which I'm able to account for. I'm not certain that I have the right or that I'm correct in saying that some other person is unrealistic. Because now I think that it's, as I said, a relative question, and the realities available for me aren't realities to another, and vice-versa. If I could get by this question, I would get closer – or hope to get closer – to accepting myself and handling my void.

If I could try, and succeed, in knowing something basic about myself, I might be able to accept others. If I were to want to. Or at least the acceptance of realizing that this type of contact that's necessary, according to how I think now, will eventually be proven unnecessary – not so much for distaste or dislike of contact, but for disinterest. Boredom! It's not a question of disliking people personally, it's a question of disliking their choice of illusions, their methods and interpretations of life and ways of living. It's uncomfortable!

I don't disagree with them, I only, I'm not – what I mean is, I don't judge them to be wrong in their choices or decisions; they're not my choices and decisions. And it's that which makes it uncomfortable. I'm interested in knowing the person who is going to occupy my grave. And I find contact of the type or nature we have extremely distracting and frustrating. It has so little to do with....

I don't know if other people have this problem, but I find it unbearable not being able to understand myself, and yet I find myself – not myself personally, but my person as an individual, fascinating. Interesting. I mean, can you tell me why I cry? I know there are tear ducts, but what sets them off? And why do I laugh? Why don't I? Why are there prejudices against crying? What is the reason? Why is it an 'exposure of weakness', from what I've heard? I don't think it so anymore. I'm just awfully curious as to why, though. Just think: the tears running down your face! And seeing – the drops! Such things are beautiful to me – it's life! It's fascinating! It's not anything at all to condemn or to feel uncomfortable about. I have to admit I do sometimes, but when you really think seriously about it – and clearly – I don't think there is any reason.

These are the realities that I would like to live with – and want – but how do you keep them, and retain them? I think it might be possible if you can get to know – if I can get to know – myself. And thereby I think I could get to know – [deep sigh] – you! Stan! Everyone! Not 'know'; the knowledge which brings understanding – an awareness of it, not a need for it. A choice of it. I know this is a question of choosing your illusions, and I would choose such an illusion if I knew how to acquire it. I would be willing to work for it if I knew the direction to take. I'll try, though, even if I'm continually confused. It doesn't make much difference; I don't have anything else to do anyway, and I prefer that which interests me. I think I would probably be a better person for Stan too, and a better friend to you.

Maybe I wouldn't be so selfish if I knew myself. I would like to be naturally helpful, without having first to consider. I almost feel as if I were, and feel as if there's something else in the way. Well, that's going to be the case. At least I have two very human individuals to think about – Stan and you – as an encouragement.

And now I'm hungry.

Bob had apparently responded to what she'd said in a way she didn't agree with, but she didn't feel like pursuing it further. She wrote, "I want to thank you for accepting and understanding a nuance of my character. I could easily contradict everything you said (I know myself *fairly* well), but I think it would be senseless, and I just want to thank you again."

I'd recorded my message to Bob the other side of this same tape, but I had no memory of hearing the side Jeanette recorded – not until researching for this book (I repeat myself, but I was *really* astounded!). In hindsight, I have to wonder whether Bob listened carefully, or at all, to Jeanette's meandering thoughts, since he never related anything pertaining to them to me (perhaps he assumed I'd already listened to it), much less spoken to me of any concerns he had about them. I find it doubtful that any reader of this book can fully imagine the chills it gave me to hear that tape – her voice – for the first time in March 2016.

In our next tape exchange with Binningen, Bob solicited my views on the outcome of the French presidential elections on May 19th, in which the conservative Valéry Giscard d'Estaing defeated the socialist candidate François Mitterrand. Bob preferred the former because he was a "strong man", which Bob felt that France and Southern Europe needed. I countered that if Mitterrand only had a Socialist parliament behind him, he could certainly be as strong:

Let's look at the core differences between the goals of conservatives and socialists – not so much their arguments per se, but the actions they translate into, the results they entail for the governed.

The conservatives' or right-wingers' criticism of the left usually boils down to criticism of the taxes that limit the opulence of the wealthy, placing limitations on their 'right' to exploit. When it appears that there might be a leftist government coming, they rush all of their capital out of the country, fearing they will have to limit themselves to three Mercedes instead of five, and only two Learjets instead of seven. The socialists, the left-wingers, on the other hand, nearly always see to it that they also represent the people living in squalor, and make policies to provide opportunities whereby a decent living standard for everybody takes precedence over the 'right' to opulence, resulting in the eradication of squalor. I'd take the latter, any day.

My example many be a bit extreme, but not very. Perhaps Giscard d'Estaing doesn't quite represent the five-Mercedes crowd, only the five-Citroën crowd. Mitterrand seems to me to be on the other side, where the right to exploit is replaced by the right to decent living conditions, decent working conditions, education available for everyone who wants it and is willing to work for it. I actually haven't got anything against opulence, as long as it's not at the expense of someone else living in squalor. It's like Gandhi reportedly told the British Viceroy, when the latter hauled Gandhi before him in exasperation about British inability to deal with Gandhi's non-violent non-cooperation that was breaking the back of the British Empire. 'I suppose if you could have your way, you'd also do away with first class on the trains?!' the Viceroy roared. 'No,' smiled Gandhi, 'I'd do away with second class.'

As far as I'm concerned, as long as you've got the squalor, you've got to limit the opulence. And I don't see Giscard d'Estaing representing a policy that will do anything in this area; or if he does, it will be to increase the opulence of the opulent, with the claim that by so doing, the others will somehow be dragged upwards – the old capitalist con job – but people in need always get left behind. And unless you can assure the absence of squalor (which purely capitalistic societies make no provision for), I don't find it acceptable.

On May 20th, Jeanette and I took a late-afternoon ferry over to Copenhagen to go to a concert at the Tivoli Gardens. On the program were two Mozart piano concertos, the 25th and 26th, both of which we knew fairly well by this time. As a special treat, the soloist was Daniel Barenboim, whom we saw in Paris the year before. Also on the program was Mozart's 38th symphony, with Barenboim conducting. A week later we were back for another Tivoli concert, this time with Wilhelm Kempf playing a delightful selection of Beethoven piano sonatas.

There was so much music in our lives now, with Jeanette orchestrating our daily exposure to it, and it was acting like a turbocharger on my painting.

I completed three more during the month before our June 20th departure for the US. The first of these, *At the Pub*,[45] shows a small crowd in an atmosphere conducive to contact, yet they have no contact with each other. The only one who might be looking at anyone else is the one on the far left, and he is physically separated from the rest.

Bob's long letter from his old friend Bowerman – in combination with my anticipated forthcoming meetings with a few people I hadn't met since moving to Sweden and even earlier – made me think of some scenes I'd witnessed or experienced involving people who'd grown apart without realizing it, and then suddenly meeting. Initially they assume or hope they might pick up where they'd left off, only to realize seconds later that they have no wish to do so or to meet at all. *The Unexpected Meeting of Long-Lost Friends*[46] tries to capture this feeling. Even before they start talking, the two figures become painfully aware that they have nothing to say to each other; their meeting is an instant embarrassment. Perhaps they remember that they didn't even really like each other, or perhaps they've simply drifted apart.

Following up on this general theme, the title of *Residential Area*[47] implies that people live there, but no one is in sight. The houses are warm but empty. Stairways lead to and from nothing.

Bob told us that he managed to talk his way into getting a new and greatly improved job situation at Roche. Back when he started working for the company, he had an office in Basel, before being transferred to the company's facility in Grenzach, across the Rhine in Germany. In Basel, Bob had been able to smoke his pipe at work and explore central Basel each day on his lunch hour. None of that was possible in Grenzach, which also gave him a longer commute, plus red tape as a US citizen residing in Switzerland and officially working in Germany. It also meant crossing the border twice a day. But with the new situation, he would be working half the time in Basel again – and have Basel as the official base for his work. He was delighted; it showed in his voice, which rang with a whole new

---

45 Painting #61 (see Appendix 2)
46 Painting #62 (- " -)
47 Painting #63 (- " -)

vitality. Jeanette commented that *"it's good that you've started putting your boss in his place once in a while. Tell him off!"*

On the phone one Sunday evening, Bob told us that he'd been invited to dinner at the home of some acquaintances. He'd had a few such invitations in the past, but always nervously declined, so I asked if he'd accepted this one, and he enthusiastically shot back, "*Of course!*" – as if he'd always (or ever) been accepting invitations (apart from ours) with pleasurable anticipation.

On June 6th, Mom wrote that it was 10 years to the day since my departure for San Francisco with Norm. (It occurred to me that nearly five of those years had been in Sweden!) She mentioned that she was still a little upset about the timing of Amy's birth a couple of weeks earlier, as if she felt that Al and Nancy should have realized that Al was supposed to abstain from bumping his body against Nancy for an undisclosed period of time. (She stopped short of actually saying that she would tell them when it was OK!)

I wasn't looking forward to visiting Dad's grave while in Oak Park, not because I had a problem with it *per se*, but because I knew that Mom would be along – and almost certainly Ralph and Maxine – and that they would most likely make each other feel "obligated" (or entitled, or both) to turn the situation into an opportunity for preaching at Jeanette and me. (Breathing, whether in or out, or both, apparently also constituted such an opportunity as well.) I would feel obliged to shut up for Mom's sake, something I wouldn't have done for anyone else.

A couple of months beforehand, I'd written to Carroll Anderson[48] to tell him we'd be coming to visit the US, and would like to meet him, and that I was looking forward to taking a better photo of my painting. He replied that he no longer had it up. I replied that I'd like to buy it back or at least get good photos of it. He replied without photos, but told me he would "retrieve" it from his son's college dorm room, but didn't say he'd sell it. I hoped so. We could phone from Oak Park about the details.

Jeanette worked full-time during the last month before our trip, and her boss gave her a 1000-kronor bonus. I was effervescently excited about the trip the day before. American money felt funny to me now, almost unreal – the pennies, nickels, dimes and quarters, as well as bills of different denominations yet of the same size and color. And it felt funny that it felt funny.

---

48 cf. *Natural Shocks*, chapter 10; and *The Undiscovered Country*, chapters 4 and 9.

We were carrying two suitcases filled with presents, with one collapsible suitcase inside each, and almost no extra clothing for ourselves. Clothes were so much cheaper in the US; we had the extra suitcases in order to bring four suitcases home with us, stuffed with new clothes, foods, California wines etc.

Commenting on our imminent trip, Jeanette wrote to Bob, *"We've received very welcoming letters from everyone, but it's a little scary. I don't know what to expect. It will be fun to come back home to Sweden. Yes, this is now our home."*

CHAPTER 8

Testing the water

When I was a child, "home" for me was wherever my parents lived, which in turn was probably wherever *they* felt at home, even though they frequently claimed (when they were in their religious mode) that their only *true* home was in heaven, a place they'd never been and had absolutely no certainty of ever going to, despite their claims to the contrary. For me, in my childhood, home would have been Glendale (California) and Oak Park (Illinois). I think there were times – long periods, even – when my mom had to struggle a bit to feel at home in Oak Park. I think home remained Des Moines for her for quite a while after she got married. She said she never felt at home in Dallas, and I think she wanted home to remain Glendale for some time after we moved back to Oak Park.

When I left my parental home in 1964 at the age of 18 years and nine months, home for me almost instantly became wherever I lived, wherever I kept my stuff, wherever there was a door for which I had the key and not just a copy of it. Initially, for the first week or so in San Francisco, I was only moving *from* things – from strangulating restrictions, from suffocating indoctrination, from imprisoning pressures. At that point, the only things I was moving *to* were the unknown, and possibly chaos. Then I met that big and growing whiff of freedom and could start to breathe, even before I found a place to unpack.

But it wasn't until Norm and I found an apartment and I could unpack my trunk and hang up *Man with Guitar* that I again had a sense of *home*. It wasn't about a *place* I loved, but a state of mind. For nearly all my life, home would be more a question of with *whom* I was, with whom I felt I belonged. It gets complicated when factoring in the fact that I tended to be a reclusive extrovert, an impassioned rationalist, a practical dreamer, a creative analyst, and a loner who never liked being completely alone.

The small apartment I shared with Norm in the raunchy but extremely convenient Tenderloin for five months was, in fact, home for me. Then the tiny room at the back of Fred's garage in Daly City became my home for nearly two years. Thereafter my home was always with Jeanette, whether on Pueblo Street in San Francisco, on Ross Street in Vancouver, on Ehrensvärdsgatan or on Vårgatan in Malmö. Because *she* was my home. We felt our first real feelings of home in Sweden on returning to Malmö from our long European tour in January 1970, despite being forced to move to a temporary address less than a month later.

Since our first few years in Sweden were based on the premise of being *forced* (in a sense) to make Sweden our home, we'd never had to test what our feelings would be like without that premise. Now that I was suddenly and unexpectedly *allowed* to travel to the US again – and to *live* there again – the rules of the game had changed. We both *believed* that we preferred nearly everything about Sweden, not least due to our disgust with Vietnam, civil rights and Watergate, but we were of the view that any belief worth holding had to be worth testing. So we were looking forward to our trip, not only to see families and friends, but also to see if we missed America after all, to see if any feelings of *home* would come surging back. We were about to test the water. It was thus not merely a trip on a plane, it was a journey in our minds and a voyage in our hearts.

On Thursday, June 20th, Henry picked us up at Vårgatan and drove us to the Malmö Central Station, from where we caught an airport bus that took us via the Limhamn-Dragør ferry to Kastrup, the Copenhagen airport. I gave Henry our spare key; he and Elsa had kindly also volunteered to look after our apartment (the plants, the fish, the mail, etc) for the five weeks we would be away. We were excited, nervous and anxious about this first trip back. Surprisingly to us, waiting in the departure lounge with so many returning American tourists made us uncomfortable; paranoia apparently didn't just switch off when the Selective Service cancelled my induction order. The many Americans waiting at the gate at the airport were all so suspicious-looking, and looked even more so to Jeanette than to me. (Once we arrived in the US, Jeanette began making many of her travelogue entries in Swedish.)

We took a direct flight from Copenhagen to Chicago, arriving in the mid-afternoon. It was *hot* (96°F, 36°C). I was extremely nervous about entering the US, despite the assurances of Aunt Marion's congressman and my brothers' calls to the FBI. Was there an indictment out on me after all – one that the Selective Service forgot to cancel? I didn't find it at all incongruent with America's track record that they might lie, or set a trap. So it was pretty sweaty for that reason too. But everything went well; the only heat was the meteorological kind, which everyone else in the extremely crowded arrival hall also had to endure.

It felt so utterly *strange* to be in the USA again, to *know* we were there, in the place we'd chosen to leave without any certainty that we could *ever* return, for reasons that still felt valid – and more so. The prospect of meeting our families was exciting, of course, but that prospect was also strange. Neither of us had maintained contact with any old friends, so there were none we were expecting (or hoping) to see. I missed (or thought I missed) football (American), baseball and basketball, but July wasn't the right time for those sports, except baseball. And even that would have to wait; Mom didn't have a TV. I'd missed a few consumables, former favorites that weren't available in Sweden: peanut butter, root beer, Twinkies and Mexican food. The peanut butter was still good, but the root beer and Twinkies were far too sweet for my altered taste. And the Mexican would have to wait for the Californian leg of our trip. On the whole, it was a letdown, the unexpected meeting of long-lost favorites.

Since Mom couldn't drive, and didn't know whether our flight would be delayed, we insisted that she should *not* meet us at the airport. (We also suspected that if she came to meet us, Uncle Ralph would be the driver.) We took an old, dirty taxi instead. I had to give the inexperienced driver instructions all the way; he didn't even know where Oak Park was. Almost as soon as we arrived on US soil, Jeanette said it felt to her like we'd never left – a feeling she didn't look pleased about.

Mom hurried out to greet us with open arms when the taxi pulled up at 1231 North Euclid. Uncle Ralph was indeed waiting in the wings, but he stayed only briefly, just long enough to assure himself that Mom could handle our being there (as I later found out). We were hot, sweaty and exhausted, and our nerves were still unnecessarily frazzled about the immigration procedure; it turned out to be completely undramatic. Mom's first and entirely predictable impulse was to pray – out loud and with high drama – to her Invisible Friend. Jeanette and I didn't respond at all, but stood there looking at each other impatiently until Mom finished.

We were, probably fortunately for all concerned, unable to stay up long that first evening. Mom understood this and – to our surprise – encouraged us to get to bed early. That might have had something to do with the fact that we'd stood there silently and passively by while she loudly proclaimed her arrival prayer of thanks to the Lord for our safe journey. I was thinking that Boeing, the pilot and the air traffic controllers had a role there. It was weird and awkward for Jeanette, and a good reminder for me – of how far removed I'd become from that kind of thing.

The sweltering heat oppressed us through the night (no air conditioning), and the morning brought no relief. Mom had several assignments for us during our stay, so after breakfast, we went out and bought everything we'd need to repaint the basement floor with two coats. Mom was eager and able to talk freely about Dad – his illness, his sudden death, her own grief, everything. She told us – again! – that she was still a little upset about Al and Nancy having had a baby "so soon" after Dad's death, but I told her firmly – again! – not to say or think such nonsense, there was no disrespect whatsoever, Dad would have loved it, and she quickly backed down – again!

Mom told us that she understood from what she'd heard at the hospital that the medication Dad received to combat his Hodgkin's was too strong and had caused his adrenal gland to rupture and precipitate his death. I'm sure the doctor and the West Suburban Hospital were greatly relieved to find that my parents had never been the kind of people to file lawsuits. That was one of the good things I'd learned from them.

The temperature continued to rise slowly throughout the day. Mom said there were tornado warnings out. The sky was filled with churning, roiling cumulonimbus clouds that were turning the dark shades of yellow-green-gray I remembered – nothing new for a Midwestern boy like me – but Jeanette found it scary. I knew what it meant: first explosive drama with huge bolts of lightning and torrential rain, possibly hail, then temporary relief from the sweltering heat. I was looking forward to the whole drama, especially the heat relief. I knew that the proximity of Lake Michigan to Oak Park and the entire Chicago area meant that we wouldn't have to worry about tornados. (Although they were a "normal" summer occurrence in Illinois, they were extremely rare in Metropolitan Chicago; I'd never seen one in my 13 years there.) But the huge thunderstorm was dramatic enough. It hit us, replete with heavy hail and blinding bolts of lightning immediately followed by deafening thunder, whiffs of ozone, great sheets of rain, and gusty wind whipping the rain sideways and all other directions (perhaps not upwards...). The temperature plunged from about 38°C to a comfortable 22°C, at least for a while. Even after the rain stopped, the thunder and lightning went on and on, all night. At least, at last, we no longer had to sleep in our own sweat. Jeanette had to admit that the flashes of lightning were spectacular, almost to the point of being entertaining.

Before we could start painting the basement floor the next morning, I had to dismantle some of the train tables, which felt strange and sad. I was glimpsing Dad every other second, looking up for him, hearing his voice, seeing his gentle smile. Some people claim to get closure from funerals, I got mine from taking tables apart. On day three we gave the floor the second coat.

> [Allow me to digress for a moment, in a kind of literary *cadenza*, to relate an incident from a business trip I took in October 2000. I was in Chicago for a couple of days between business meetings in Atlanta and Columbus [Ohio], for the purpose of revisiting Oak Park for the first time since 1974. I wanted to take some photos of my old home, my schools and familiar neighborhoods. While photographing the house at 1231 N. Euclid, I first noticed that the new residents had a *Vote for Gore* sign on the front lawn (the presidential election was the following month), which both surprised and thrilled me. I'd never thought I'd see such a welcome sight in conservative Oak Park!
>
> Then I noticed that behind the screen door, the front door was ajar. I'd been walking back forth in front of the house taking pictures from all angles, and feared I might have caused the residents some unnecessary alarm. So I walked up to the door and rang the bell. A sweet elderly lady came to the door. I told her about my picture-taking, and explained that I'd grown up in the house – and that my parents had had it built in 1951. She was delighted to meet me, then told me that the ones who'd bought it from my mom in 1975 only lived there for half a year, then sold it to her and her husband, whose lunch she was preparing. Then she asked me if I'd like to come in and have a look around!
>
> I was thrilled and accepted her invitation without hesitation. Among many other things, I noticed that the basement floor hadn't been painted since Jeanette and I did it in 1974!]

Our next assignment from Mom was to paint the garage, then to trim the bushes and do some other yard work.

Following our total unresponsiveness to Mom's lengthy prayer on our arrival, she didn't do much preaching – at first – and things started out well. Our assignments were keeping us busy and were a welcome distraction from the rising tide of boredom. Mom didn't go to Meeting once during our visit; it would have been quite all right with us if she had. But we still needed an escape; Jeanette wasn't used to a life based on Meeting values and limited to Meeting-approved activities and topics. (I'd eventually freed myself from it long ago, but it remained distastefully familiar to me.) I hadn't regarded 1231 North Euclid as my home since 1964; it never had been home for Jeanette, and it was even doubtful that it was still home for Mom now that Dad was no longer there.

For Jeanette and me, it wasn't just that we couldn't talk about movies we'd seen. We couldn't watch TV to give our jaws and vocal cords a rest, play a few hands of cards for fun, have a glass of wine for our stomachs' sake, let slip an occasional word that was on Mom's *verboten* list to relax, tell the kinds of jokes we usually told to have a laugh, plunge into our food before Mom talked to her imaginary friend, listen to the music we liked, or see anybody who wasn't from that tight-assed bunch who called themselves the Little Flock or the Chosen Few. It was more than that.

We felt a strong need to meet some "normal" people, to talk about normal things. So on Saturday, after asking Mom whether she had any plans for the evening (she said no), two days after our arrival, I called Jim and John Erickson (the only old high school buddies I could locate (actually, just about the closest thing to high school buddies I'd ever had) and we went out for some beers that evening, in Berwyn (Oak Park was still dry). Jim picked us up. Before going out, I asked Mom for a house key. "*Oh, you won't need that! I stay up late anyway, till 10 at least, sometimes till 10.30!*" – which I immediately recognized as her back-door way of telling her adult son and his adult wife at what time she felt her little children ought to be back. I said I thought it could be good for me to have a key anyway – my back-door way of telling her that Jeanette and I would prefer to decide our time of return ourselves. After that mostly non-verbal conversation, she somewhat reluctantly gave me a key. (We got home just before 1 AM; I'm quite sure she was well aware of that.)

It was strange meeting the Erickson twins, who were friendly, genuinely friendly. Jim even kindly offered us the use of his car while we were in Oak Park. Jeanette and I met Jim in '69, on our way to Sweden. He hadn't changed much (more) since then. But I hadn't met John (who was also my former football teammate) in 11 years. He'd put on quite a lot of weight – which might have served him better in his former role as a football lineman.

But I felt strongly that *I'd* changed so much more than the Erickson twins, not just in appearance but in terms of attitudes, outlooks and values. In just two days, it was already beginning to dawn on Jeanette and me what profoundly different changes had taken place in *us* – even more than the very profound changes in the US, and that most of these changes showed that we'd been moving in opposite directions from the country of our birth.

Jim mentioned that the year before – in 1973 – he'd been to the 10-year reunion of our graduating class from Oak Park High. I spontaneously burst out,

"Oh! I wish I could've been there!" He looked at me with a somewhat sardonic smile and said "I don't think so." I asked him what he meant by that. He said that quite a few of the guys, especially my former football teammates, were looking for me there, and said they were going to *kill* me if they found me. (Jim and John didn't share those sentiments at all.) I laughed, a bit nervously, not understanding why, not making any connections. Jim wasn't laughing at all. Nor was John. Then it dawned on me (a lot of dawning went on after dusk that evening). Everyone at the reunion seemed had probably read the Chicago papers, in which it was erroneously reported that I'd received "political asylum" in Sweden – and this was ultra-right-wing Oak Park. Those former classmates of mine hadn't been joking at all.

Then I also remembered something horrible that Dave Henderson (Norm's cousin and my Oak Park High classmate) told me a few years before, something by which I could calibrate the seriousness of the threat. In 1963, the year I finished high school, most of my classmates probably couldn't even spell "Vietnam". Just a couple of years later, when Dave's younger brother Danny was at Oak Park High, the War was underway, and the protests were revving up. According to Dave, a classmate of Danny's came to school one day wearing an anti-war badge. The guys from the school football team got together and herded the "offender" into an isolated corridor or an empty classroom, threw him onto his back over a table, pinned him down and held one arm extended over the edge of the table at the height of his elbow. Then they broke it backwards over the table edge – and repeated the procedure with the other arm. The pain must have been excruciating.

There was a small-scale inquiry, kept well out of the news. The dean ruled that the mutilated victim, by wearing the anti-war badge to school, had provoked the attack; the culprits were merely issued a verbal reprimand (and possibly a brief suspension). They were not expelled. No charges were brought. So much for the Land of the Free and freedom of speech. So much for feeling "back home"! I felt as far from home in Oak Park as I might have felt swimming halfway across a broad stretch of a piranha-infested river in the Amazon. I felt that I had to watch what I said, not just in front of my mom, but anywhere in public, for the sake of my survival. With the Ericksons' story in mind, I couldn't dismiss the reported threats to kill me as hyperbole or drunken bravado. When Jeanette and I cleared immigration a few days before, we thought we were safe. I no longer felt safe, particularly not in Oak Park. Jeanette wrote: *"We're glad we're just here as tourists. We're not very happy about what we've seen in this country so far."*

The day before, Mom reminded me that the FBI came calling in early 1973, asking all kinds of questions about me. I mentioned that to the Erickson twins. They told us that it wasn't just *my* parents who'd had such visits; their parents also received them – about *me* – at around that same time. Why? I felt certain it must have been a last-ditch effort to nab me before the draft board was obliged to revoke my induction order, but of course the Feds didn't say anything about why. Nor why they'd visited the Ericksons. I'd never met their parents, never been to their home, never even seen it from the outside, even when I was in high school. I'd had almost no contact with Jim or John since 1963, apart from the one meeting with John in '69, when we were on our way to Sweden. Did the FBI know about that meeting somehow? Had they had agents there in the bar? (*Whoa, Stan, easy on the paranoia!*) How many other homes of my former classmates did the FBI visit concerning me? Were the Feds doing that to the 60,000 or so Vietnam War draft-dodgers? Think how many man-hours that must have involved! What a waste! How very Polish of them!

And yet, we felt that the evening out with the Ericksons was our only relaxed evening, with the only relaxed atmosphere on the entire Oak Park leg of our trip. Mom was loveable, loving and kind (except when she got onto the subject of God's wrath from time to time), but there wasn't much relaxed about having to weigh one's every word so as not to hurt or cause offense. Why do people allow vocabulary to cause them grievous mental anguish? Do they have any right to do that? I guess I shouldn't have been surprised about the incident Dave described; I grew up without free speech.

Among the many initial impressions that hit us on coming back to the US were things we'd simply forgotten or become totally unused to: the sight of all the strange monstrosities known as American cars, the harsh neon signs and billboards everywhere, the pace of life that was faster than the traffic, the almost total lack of pedestrians or bikes. One thing we witnessed while walking (almost alone on the sidewalks) to Sears along North Avenue with Mom was an archetypally American sight, in the sense that it seemed inconceivable that it could be found anywhere else: two white-haired, bejeweled White ladies of advancing age came cruising down the street in a huge powder-blue Cadillac, one of them driving, each of them holding a large plastic milkshake cup, and sucking on bendable plastic straws. Jeanette and I stared at them in bemused disbelief, as if we'd found ourselves on the set of a satirical film.

Another strange feeling was our propensity to overreact – to turn around and look – whenever anybody in our vicinity spoke. We kept thinking it might be somebody we knew, because for the past five years, the chances of knowing a person who spoke American English near us were literally millions of times greater than here in the States. This knee-jerk reaction lasted about two weeks.

It was also hard to grasp that so many Americans got only two weeks a year of paid vacation; that they meekly and contentedly – *and* proudly! – accepted the fact that their lack of universal free healthcare could financially destabilize or ruin them (and probably *would* ruin them if they'd had the misfortune to lose their job at the whim of an employer before falling ill); that paid maternity leave could be as little as a few weeks or days – or none at all!; that people could be fired on the spot; that higher education cost a fortune and thus wasn't for everyone; that the once-powerful student activism on political issues was now, suddenly, largely reduced to juvenile pranks or apathy; and that Blacks were *still* facing massive discrimination, racism, prejudice and injustice, despite the Civil Rights legislation of the 1960s. This was "home"?! This was the "land of the free"? The Americans say it best themselves: "*Are you kidding me?!*"

That Sunday, the thing happened that I'd known to generally happen when Meeting people congregate: they strove to outshine each other in demonstrating their willingness and zeal to "witness for Him" when Lost Souls are present. In this case it was Ralph, Maxine and Ed, as well as Nobe and Shirley, who all came over to Mom's for Sunday dinner after Morning Meeting. (Mom stayed home from Meeting to prepare it.)

Mom asked Ralph to do the honors of "giving thanks" – saying the mandatory pre-dinner prayer. He made raw and unsubtle use of his unchallenged pulpit to let Jeanette and me know that the lives we were leading were leading us to Hell. I felt like standing up and punching him in the face. (I'd felt that way for many years about most Meeting people, but in fact I've never punched anyone anywhere, except Howie, once, in the solar plexus, when we were about 14.) *Having* such feelings is natural. *Not acting* on them is what's called civilized. Civilization is thus *un*natural. (That's something to bear in mind when someone tries to sell you something "because it's *100% natural*".) I could tell that Jeanette was also livid and would have loved to chew them out.

Immediately after dinner, while we were still seated (i.e. before Jeanette and I could get up), Mom brought out a horrid little garishly colored metal box of molded aluminum. The box was shaped like a small loaf of bread ("*the bread of life"*, John 6:35) and contained rigid cards (about 1 x 3") with a Scripture verse on one side and a "poem" (poem only in the sense that the lines rhymed, tripe in every other sense) on the other. Maxine had acquired such a box when I was a kid, and I always hated it when we had dinner at their place. Now Mom had one too. In accordance with the after-dinner procedure familiar to all of them, they passed the box around the table; each person was to take a card (no queen of hearts here!), then read (piously) both sides of his or her card *aloud*. Jeanette and I were unappreciative – to put it mildly – of this further gesture, another overt attempt to put us on the spot, to forcibly recruit us into mouthing their nonsense. They were doing their best to make us uncomfortable – and they were succeeding. I managed to exact a kind of revenge (to even out the atmosphere and level the playing field a bit) immediately thereafter by relating a few stories of some extreme examples of revolting Asian food. It may have dampened their enthusiasm for further efforts at religious recruitment, at least for the time being.

How Jeanette and I missed my dad! Jeanette described him as the only one who'd been in that group and who had feelings yet no meanness! In her travelogue she wrote:

> *"I've never in my life encountered such a mentality. I was watching their faces and body language and couldn't believe what I was hearing, with smiles: gossip, condemnations, materialistic values, etc etc, all expressed with the most angelic faces. It's been a tiring day, and I feel disappointed that I need to put up with such contacts for Stan's sake. Maybe I'll learn something here, but it's very difficult."*

In the afternoon we all drove out to the cemetery because *they* felt we should see Dad's grave – a totally bizarre and distasteful experience for me. (Grandma, of course, who existed as a sort of a benign presence during our visit, did not join us; we had almost nothing to say to each other, which was no different from my relationship with her as a child.) Being in that strange, hollow cemetery just felt stupid and weird to Jeanette and me. Dad wasn't *there*. I'd never seen him there. Although he'd picked out the location, I had no memory associations of him there. He was in our basement, leaning over the train tables I'd dismantled. He was everywhere in the house and the yard. He was in our hearts. Jeanette wrote:

> *"It was macabre how Stan's family went over to a 'children's cemetery' to look at the*

> *graves of unknown children, and then all around to look for Carlssons, Anderssons – another identity, another shield – and look for Bible verses, all in the name of a so-called loving god, this ugly masquerade, and there lay Stan's dad. I don't like these thoughts and these sermonizers."*

Towards evening, when Maxine and Ralph were preparing to leave for Gospel Meeting, I suggested that Mom could go with them, and Jeanette and I could stay home and look after Grandma. Then Maxine interjected, saying that *she* could remain with Grandma so that Jeanette and I could go along to Meeting. Both Jeanette and I knew that if we'd disliked being the targets of my family's proselytizing efforts at home, the Meeting would be targeting us with their version of the Marines at a Gospel Meeting. However pathetic those efforts might have been, we didn't want to waste an evening and get our already-explosive ire aroused any further and thus give Mom grief, so I repressed my impulse to belt out "*Fat chance, you oversized rectal orifice!!*" at Maxine. Instead I just looked her in the eye and said with unmistakable, unassailable firmness, "No, thank you!" And that was the end of that round.

On Monday, Jeanette finished painting the garage while I did the heavy gardening work, the last of our assignments. It kept slipping my mind that Jeanette, unlike me, was in an environment in which she had no past experience, and never learned to recognize (much less shrug off) the constant barrage of religious innuendos, from both Mom and Maxine, as well as anybody else who happened to stop by. Mom's entire social calendar consisted of extremely religious people – people who knew that Mom's beloved but wayward son was "unprodigally" in town and needed redeeming, and was accompanied by his – *shudder!* – Catholic wife about whom they presumed to know much, but in fact knew nothing at all.

Their innuendos were by no means innocuous, even though my upbringing had inoculated me. For Jeanette, as it turned out, it was torture, once again borne out by her travelogue, which I didn't know about at the time:

> *"I'm so very tired of all of this and can't understand why I bother about anything. I understand less and less each day. These values that come up from those we meet are for me totally crazy. They're so petty and I'm behaving like I'm small. I don't want my role to be suffering – what condemnations! I find it so hard to understand, let alone accept. Why don't I just leave? Why?"*

Most of the time, I remained blithely unaware of the depths of Jeanette's predicament. Thus when Norm Wood, a Meeting guy I'd sort of known once upon a time, phoned to ask me to join him for touch football that afternoon with some of the others (meaning a Conversion Brigade of eight or so young Meeting men with whom I'd occasionally played when I had no other options during my youth in Oak Park), I accepted enthusiastically. Even though they weren't much good at football (some were hopeless at it), I longed for any kind of football game again, with anybody, so Norm Wood picked me up and I left Jeanette at the mercy of my mom. After a half-assed pretext of a game, the Brigade circled around me and began nagging at me to come to Meeting with them. I politely declined. They continued nagging. I firmly declined. They continued. I told them to shove it. I didn't respond well to textbook group pressure. Meanwhile, Jeanette apparently survived Mom's accelerated zeal in my absence by retreating to the bathroom and then taking a nap when Mom became overbearing.

On Tuesday, June 25th, the three of us took the bus and the Lake Street "L" to the Loop, and went shopping at the huge Marshall Field's department store. When we got home, I phoned Carroll Anderson to ask where we stood on my painting, and he promptly and somewhat tersely invited us to their home in Elmhurst for dinner. (I guessed that the dinner part was at Mrs Anderson's insistence.)

I looked forward to the opportunity to see my very first painting again, to show it to Jeanette, and to photograph it. I found Mr Anderson to be formal and reserved when we got there (I have no memory of whose car we borrowed), although his wife was friendly enough, but a bit on edge. He explained that he'd removed my painting from their walls years ago (*December 1969, perhaps?*), that he no longer liked it, that their son had it until recently but had sent it home to his parents at Mr Anderson's request, that it was now in their closet waiting for me to buy it back. The price was now $40 (he'd apparently done the math – $40 in 1974 was rounded upwards from the inflation-adjusted value of the $25 he paid for it in 1965). During the fairly awkward dinner conversation, I was initially alarmed to discover how reactionary he'd become, but on reflection I realized that when I knew him in high school I was also a real right-winger, and since then had un-become one. He hadn't.

After dinner, when he started talking about how "Black people are creeping into the school system," as though he were talking about the bubonic plague or other kinds of infection and rot, I knew I'd have to get the hell out of there or

Slings and Arrows

end up in a huge argument that I couldn't lose (because I was arguing the case for human decency) but couldn't win (because he was never going to accept any appeals to decency). So I asked him if I could buy back my painting now. I paid him the $40, took the painting, and we left (with all due thanks to his wife for the meal and *her* hospitality). Mr Anderson's whole deportment behind the icy civility fairly shouted at me all evening that he, too, read the Chicago papers in December 1969, and that he decided that I was a traitor with whom he wanted nothing more to do. As if I'd want anything more to do with *him*!

Although we left with a treasured painting, there was also a bad taste in our mouths, especially mine. And suddenly we found ourselves with an extra piece of luggage. Jeanette said she thought her parents would love to have my painting. I wasn't too sure about that, but gladly agreed to give it to them for Jeanette's sake. The painting would be just too hard to transport to all our remaining stopovers anyway. When we got home from the Andersons at around 9 PM, another Meeting couple, the Kuypers (about my brother John's age), were there to meet us, or at least to meet people they thought they could re-make into people they wanted to meet.

At my request, we spent the next day with Mom at Chicago's incredible Museum of Science and Industry, a place I loved almost more than any other museum I'd ever been to. Jeanette was bowled over, and expressed the view that children should be taken there at least twice a week, instead of school, if they were to learn anything in a creative way. Late that afternoon, we were invited to visit the Burtnesses, Mom's Norwegian Christian-in-spite-of-not-being-Meeting neighbors whose grandson had tormented my dog Ollie, resulting in Ollie's execution. The invitation came as a complete surprise to me, considering that I'd only been in their home *once* before, as a child, despite having been close neighbors throughout my childhood and most of my teens.

As usual, Mom and Mrs Burtness started by exchanging biblical clichés, a social interlude like the neck-contortion rituals of mating albatrosses, a totally unfamiliar ritual to Jeanette, and totally bizarre to both of us. But in some way, these "rituals" were the clothes they wore, their costumes. Once they completed the obligatory affirmations and reassurances to each other that they were, as uniquely as possible, on the fast track to heaven, they could subside into something more like humanity and be more pleasant. Jeanette saw through it all with a clarity I wished I'd had as a child; I'd been defenseless then. After we went back to Mom's place, we finished the evening by looking through Dad's old slide collection, including a few of me that Jeanette said she found adorable. She loved seeing old photos of me, when I was a kid, just like I loved seeing photos from her childhood, even though they were few.

On Thursday the 27th, we went to downtown Oak Park – that part of Lake Street between Oak Park Avenue and Harlem, with relatively many memories for me and a few new and interesting sights for Jeanette, like the Frank Lloyd Wright architecture. In the evening we visited two more of my paintings: the two I'd sold to Lloyd (no longer "Butch", his childhood nickname) and Stearly Holt, who were now residing in Wheaton, of all places. Jeanette and I were invited to their home for dinner, and I was glad to see my paintings prominently displayed. Lloyd and Stearly were still Meeting folk but, like my brother John, had gravitated to the more hedonistic wing. (I avoid using the word "liberal" advisedly, since the Holts' politics certainly were not!) They treated us to Champagne, as well as wine with dinner. At least they didn't try to convert us or get us to go to Meeting with them! When it was time for dessert, there was a weird surprise (for Jeanette and me both, but in quite different ways): a visit from Mary Lou and her husband (they also happened to be living in Wheaton). Jeanette had no idea who they were; neither of us knew why they came (was it just curiosity?). I wondered what her husband thought.

On the Friday, Mom pleaded weariness, so Jeanette and I went out on our own, to the Art Institute in downtown Chicago. We both found – as I'd always found – the collection of Impressionist works absolutely rapturous. Jeanette was particularly taken by Dubuffet's *Genuflection of the Bishop*. So was I. I'd never paid much attention to his work before, but could readily identify with it now, at least as far as the use of two dimensional, overlapping objects or random geometric shapes to create three-dimensional space.

The sense of relief from being free from all those Meeting people that day was palpable. Had our host been anyone but my Mom, I would have told every last one of them precisely why they were so full of shit their eyes were brown. Their entire belief system seemed to me to be a badly constructed house of cards with nothing resembling evidence in sight. But I felt I just couldn't hurt Mom's feelings. Jeanette understood me, and although she might have been a lot more willing to blow their house of cards down, *she* couldn't bring herself to hurt *my* feelings.

And so it goes: people endure irrationality to spare the feelings of others who are hell-bent on being offended if they can't have their house of cards in peace, yet they use that very house of cards as a weapon, to set the norms whereby they inflict misery on those around them and the generations that follow.

On the Saturday, Ralph and Maxine took us out to Nobe and Shirley's place. They were no longer living in Des Moines, but in Rockford (where Al's wife Nancy was from), about 85 miles west of Oak Park. By this time, Jeanette was sick of what happened to every conversation when this constellation got together, and she dreaded the prospect. As we toured the Gammell's home, we discovered that Uncle Nobe had a pool table in the basement, and Jeanette and I leaped at the opportunity to play pool with Nobe, at his invitation (neither of us was a pool enthusiast!). Mom and Maxine must have thought *"We got trouble!"* because I knew that the others (except Shirley) felt the same way about pool as the good citizens of River City, Iowa (cf. the musical *The Music Man*), So Jeanette and I (perhaps Nobe too) got some respite from their ceaseless fundamentalist evangelizing, even though Nobe didn't go so far as to invite us to a Scotch or even a glass of wine. Maxine was obviously chagrined by our absence from their preaching venue. Later, Shirley showed me some of Stephen's recent artwork, which impressed the hell out of me.

During our last few days in Oak Park, Mom became increasingly preachy, *obsessively* preachy. It became almost her only topic. Since I still didn't want to hurt her by refuting her – not that she would have been receptive to rational refutations anyway – I just let her babble along, while I looked around the room in boredom, without displaying any response, and thus without overtly concurring or objecting. But couldn't she *see* the connection between her incessant preaching and our eagerness to find other places to be than in her company, in spite of our love for her? She made it as impossible for us to be with her as we would have made it for her if we'd been wearing T-shirts emblazoned with *"I'm an atheist"* or subjected her to non-stop preaching about the foolishness of her faith. We weren't out to "convert" her (or "detox" her). If she wanted to keep her faith, we had no problem with it. But she couldn't leave us alone. So instead of answering in kind, we bowed out.

She kept telling us that so *many* of the Meeting people (whom I knew by name and fanaticism only, who didn't know me at all despite having met me, and who'd never even met Jeanette) *really* wanted to see us. So I said, *"Let them come over, then!"* I wasn't about to go to their turf to satisfy *their* curiosity, nor was I going to hide.

It didn't occur to me that Mom might take me literally. On Sunday, the Sclaters (Meeting friends of my Mom's, almost strangers to me) came by. So did a guy named Robert Thonney, a year or two older than me, whom I met once or twice shortly before I left Oak Park. I'd always thought him a total creep, and we'd *never* had *any*thing in common. He was apparently on his way to becoming a Laboring Brother, so I guessed that his need to see me and Jeanette was to attempt to take his final merit badge or something like that. He was truly pathetic, like a fleshy Uriah Heep. Since Sunday evening was the last possible chance for anyone to get us to Meeting (a Gospel Meeting, no less), he and several others discharged their duties by pleading with us to come. Since Mom was standing right there, we declined politely. (I was prepared to be highly impolite as a last resort if need be.) They understood we weren't coming. Instead, as soon as their Gospel Meeting was over, Mom's phone began ringing incessantly, people wanting to say hello to a couple they didn't know and who were totally uninterested in meeting them. At 10.30 PM, Clem Dear, my old Sunday School teacher, came by to meet me. His real errand was to unload a stack of BTP books on me. I politely took them, again for Mom's sake only.

I truly loved Mom. I believe Jeanette did too. But we just couldn't *breathe* there. The constant strain of minimizing offense to her was wearing us down, because the list of things she took offense at was so damn long. It was a real dilemma for Jeanette *and* me. I didn't want to say goodbye, but I couldn't endure another day (nor could Jeanette, as it turned out) – at least not on Mom's turf, and not by her rules. Fortunately, we had to spend most of Monday morning packing, including finding suitable protective wrapping for the painting, since we were already scheduled to leave Chicago that afternoon.

Our flight out in the late afternoon on Monday, July 1st, from O'Hare to Los Angeles, was our first-ever flight on a Boeing 747 (Jumbo Jet), and we were mightily impressed with the plane. Jeanette was a bit worried that we might be facing more of the same Meeting shit when we got to John and Marj's place, but I told her not to worry. They weren't nearly as extreme; they pretty much took from the Meeting only as much as they wanted (although they'd been duly trained to want a lot!) and took pleasure where they wanted it. I kept forgetting that while the Meeting defined extreme for me, I'd been so inundated with it that anything – even a few cautious steps away from fundamentalism – was no longer extreme to me but would still be to Jeanette. But I also explained to her that I wasn't about to play the deferential-son role towards my brothers; if they gave us a hard time, they'd get a hard time right back.

As it turned out, we had a great time with John and Marj during the four days we were there, completely different from stifling Oak Park. Not only was the dry, desert-like heat of Southern California more bearable than the suffocating, sticky, sultry summer heat of Illinois. We were also among people with whom we felt we had little necessity to watch our every word or weigh our every response, and that we wouldn't be totally bored by Oak Park's severely limited list of approved subjects of conversation or activities. We were spared the gantlet of curious Meeting proselytizers lined up to do their duty to annoy the crap out of us by insisting that their pathetic nonsense was the Only Truth.

Together with John and his family, we did a few touristy things like visiting malls and Knott's Berry Farm. Their kids, Brian (now nearly 13) and Janet (around 10), were extremely sweet, friendly and polite, although a bit shy at first; they were kids. Marj was still the fantastic cook I remembered, and a warm, altogether pleasant person. John liked wine and jokes (although not all of mine in front of his kids). I handed John the stack of books that Clem had panned off on me, and told him he could have them or show me what garbage can to use. He laughed a little nervously. I left them with him. But John countered by giving me one of his latest Francis Schaeffer books, which I looked at and looked at him as if to say *"Seriously? Will you never learn?!"*

Perhaps proselytizing is in the nature of fundamentalist and evangelical belief? After all, if you're *thoroughly* convinced that anyone who doesn't share your beliefs is going to be doomed to eternal suffering, it's understandable that you'd almost be panicking if your loved ones didn't share your "truth". Naturally, such a position wouldn't make for the smoothest relationships ever known if people with a variety of *different* fundamentalist beliefs got together. The thing about *non*-believers is that they lack the weapons to beat each other over the head with. And they would seem to be in the best position to live and let live, which I was fully prepared to do – until and/or unless I was attacked for my non-beliefs.

On one of our two full evenings together, when John and I were alone together in the late evening (fortunately for her, Jeanette was already in bed), John simply couldn't resist setting out to convince me that Christianity was the only way to go. After I listened attentively to and dissected each one of his arguments, John seemed to realize that he had nothing real to offer. He appeared nervous about the instability of his own positions – his house of cards. It was strange seeing him again after five years. He hadn't changed much. His worldview had been gradually settling into comfortable rigidity; he'd deferred for too long challenging questionable ideas once forced on him, until they became part of him. He'd spent so many years not *acting* for himself (he explained that he didn't want to while our parents were still alive!!), that he apparently lost the ability to *think* for himself, at least concerning "spiritual matters". Any thoughts of breaking free he might have had were now morphing and congealing into what he fancied to be his *own* ideas. Perhaps he thought that breaking away from the Meeting was all the breaking free he would ever dare to do? [*My subjective speculations!*]

On the Oak Park leg of our trip, I was largely back in the Meeting atmosphere of my Mom's home and her friends, and everything seemed pretty much the way it always was, apart from the tangible absence of Dad. I deeply missed Dad's gracious equanimity. But on leaving the backwater Oak Park world of my mom, we entered what was more like mainstream America, despite John and family still being in the Meeting. Only then did we begin to become aware of the full extent of change in America since 1969. The Vietnam War was over; Watergate had come and gone; the ensuing apathy (especially of students and young people) seemed to have dragged the activism of the civil rights movement and the entire engaged spirit of the 60s down with it. Nobody was demonstrating, but disgustingly much of the racial discrimination remained. Everything we'd seen was confirming what we'd first suspected. Nobody we met wanted to talk to us about anything but superficialities. *And nobody we met on our entire trip asked us anything at all about Sweden!!* How was that possible? There was to be no controversy, nothing that might provoke thinking, no meaning. Everything had to be "safe" and dull.

After LA, we were off to San Francisco to be with Jeanette's family for a while, another strange experience. To our great surprise, the whole family (including aunts and uncles) turned out to meet us at the airport and I was glad to see that Jeanette felt their welcome and appeared to be buoyant. Now it was my turn to spend some time in the wings. I welcomed the break.

It turned out that Michael (Jeanette's brother, no longer "Mike" now that he was living at home again with Mike, his father), who we thought had returned from Vietnam unscathed (physically at least), had in fact contracted some sort of physical jungle disease in Vietnam, and still wasn't over it completely. (He said nothing about it when he stayed with us for nearly seven months!) He asked us only the most superficial questions about Sweden (or ourselves), despite all the time he spent there with us. And he offered no insights into his own life. We were able to deduce that he was now working at the same haulage company as his father; that he apparently still had no friends; and that he still spent much of his free his time watching escapist TV and reading by himself.

We went around, mostly with Marilyn and Vic (Michael sometimes joined us) to all the tourist sights (or sites) in San Francisco, a city so beautiful it is pretty much a tourist site in its entirety. There were some significant changes: the new subway system (BART), a whole new Japantown, and the sudden appearance of skyscrapers in the financial district. But most of our favorite hangouts were still there: Ocean Beach, Aquatic Park, the cable cars, Market Street (I ventured into The Emporium for a brief visit, but felt uncomfortable and left), Golden Gate Park and Bridge, Coit Tower, Chinatown, and even the ACT, where we saw a play one evening. And of course we enjoyed a few amazing home-cooked Italian meals. We loved San Francisco – so much that we both wished it were located in Europe.

Mike and Rose were not well. Mike had developed angina, which Rose had had for some years now. She'd also had two heart attacks and the doctor told her that only a third of her heart was still working properly. I knew that this news made Jeanette terribly anxious, but she didn't want to talk about it – she *refused* to talk about it – so I could only guess how much it upset her. She didn't let it show, or maybe I didn't dare to see.

Jeanette told me later, after our trip, that in spite of the warm welcome from her family at the airport, it felt like none of them had changed at all, but that *she* had changed, and that nobody in her family was the least bit interested in finding out how or why. (The lack of interest in asking about life in Sweden came across to her as further evidence of a lack of interest in our lives, period.) It was a difficult insight for her to deal with. She hadn't exactly expected anything like rapport from her father, but she hoped for *some*thing from her siblings, especially from Marilyn. On the surface, our dealings with her family seemed friendly enough to me, but any questions that might have led to anything of real substance were "back-door" questions, by which I mean the type of question that allows the subject to be changed instantly if the answer leads in an uncomfortable direction. They were thus always asked in circumstances that would allow a quick escape to another topic or task if the answers caused anything approaching discomfort or risked upsetting the *status quo*. Questions with potential depth were asked by-the-way casually, when others were around to call upon for release, or while undertaking a chore that could suddenly, if needed, demand one's full attention.

Were they interested but didn't know how to show it? Maybe they just didn't know how to deal with talking about feelings, especially about strong feelings? Maybe they had the misfortune of belonging to that huge part of the human race that finds it so much easier to express anger, irritation and platitudes than to express true love? Maybe Jeanette sensed that too, but still wanted more, needed more, to feel that she was there? In her travelogue entry for July 22nd, she remarkably made no mention of any 30th birthday celebration – for her or for Michael. (I have no memory that there was any such celebration.)

But the *surface* was always friendly and casual. I suppose that's better than hostile and vicious, but to Jeanette and me, "superficial friendliness" was pretty much an oxymoron. Surely friendliness is not merely the absence of hostility? Words like "friend" and "love" were becoming increasingly important to us, because their increasing overuse, their careless and frivolous use, was taking away all meaning, leaving no words left with which to describe true friendship and true love. Sure, people can feel without words; animals feel and don't have words. But we need words to be able to *reflect* on feelings, to distinguish nuances of feelings, to refine and reinforce feelings, so it's not just a fuzzy blur. Using words that enable distinctions is a way of finding one's way through the blur. Clichés are clouds, fog. Superficial friendliness is a mask. Maybe there's true friendship behind it, but maybe not. One can't know. What the hell did *I* know?

I could easily understand Jeanette's feeling of being largely invisible to her family, because I felt like the hint of a shadow of the invisible in their presence. They barely acknowledged my gift of the painting; although they did ask me to put it up in a prominent place in their living room, they said nothing about it. Every effort I made to start a conversation, whether it was to discuss anything of substance or make idle chat, invariably fell flat. One Saturday afternoon, Rosanne's steady boyfriend Matt hurried into the Minihane kitchen and announced that he was looking for some guys to join him for an impromptu baseball game. My eyes instantly lit up, and I started to open my mouth, when Vic bounced up and the two of them were off. I would have loved to play, but I was clearly not under consideration. Michael didn't seem to react at all; I guessed that he'd been passed over too many times already.

Michael, Vic and I did have two evenings out, however. We went to a Giants game at Candlestick Park – the first Major League game I'd been to since Wrigley

Field in the early 1960s. We also went to see *The Exorcist*, a well-made science-fiction horror movie that a lot of Americans apparently regarded as having the veracity of a well-researched documentary. Since on both occasions we were watching something, and were guys, there were back doors all over the place and there was no need for depth of any kind.

Jeanette and I played a little tennis with Marilyn and Vic one day, and Jeanette contacted her old friend Carol and went to see her for an afternoon. Carol was in the process of divorce and had two small girls. One of the little girls was playing hairdresser and poked a comb in Jeanette's eye, giving her a bruise on her eyeball that made her eye painfully swollen and watery for several days.

One evening, Jeanette and I decided we needed a break from her family. I'd somehow procured Norm's phone number (through Mom?) and phoned him. He immediately invited us out to their place for dinner in San Ramon, in the East Bay. Not having seen Norm for more than eight years, I was excited to see and hear how he was doing. I'd only met his wife Barbara twice, at their wedding rehearsal and at the wedding itself. I'd never seen their little boy. Jeanette met Norm once or twice 10 years earlier, but didn't feel she knew him at all.

We borrowed Mike's car. The first thing that struck us when we pulled up to Norm's fashionable, fairly classy (by our standards) home was the huge Cadillac parked in the driveway in front of their two-car garage. The thought occurred to both Jeanette and me that Norm might have left it out there to show off. This relatively unexpected meeting of long-lost friends felt awkward, like Norm was posturing and boasting and keeping everything impersonal. It certainly didn't feel like a heartfelt reunion, the kind that could have exploded into tears of joy. It felt like a moderately pleasant evening with total strangers, and that was it. For all we didn't know, his life could have been in shambles, or he might have been sitting on top of the world as a financial wizard. Whatever things might have been going on beneath the surface of Norm's world, we certainly had no way of guessing anything he chose not to reveal.

One comment that Jeanette and I heard from several different people on our trip was that we'd picked up a Swedish accent. We were baffled. Bob had received a similar comment from his brother – in his case about a German accent – which seemed equally unfounded. Then I think I figured it out. After years of speaking mostly to people whose native language is not English, you learn almost automatically to enunciate much more clearly than native speakers need to do to be understood. You also tend to round off the worst of the local twangs you once had. Another factor is that slang words and expressions quickly fall (or get shoved) by the wayside, because anachronistic slang, however groovy it once may have been, is of no use to anyone. And if you frequently have to explain English grammar to others, you tend to speak more grammatically yourself. The result of it all is that you speak much more clearly and correctly than most native speakers, which means there's something "different" about your speech, but you can't put your finger on it; so you call it an accent.

Jeanette and I experienced quite a lot of sadness about leaving San Francisco, but we agreed that it was mostly the sadness of having looked forward, almost urgently, to something with the *potential* to be the high point of our trip, only to find that our wistful little expectations had been far too high. Jeanette said, with the shadow of a smile, that as a child she never found the closeness to her family she sought, so why should she expect to find it now? I knew (or thought I knew) exactly what she was talking about. Although my mom was more capable of expressing feelings than anyone else we met on our trip (and more than most anywhere), and although I knew and felt that I was truly loved by her, there were always the conditions, the criteria, the codicils and caveats, the prerequisites of her world of superstition that got in the way, at least most of the time. She expressed far too many feelings I didn't like and wanted to challenge, but I felt obliged to refrain. I was used to that; Jeanette wasn't.

As we headed for Seattle, neither of us was particularly looking forward to this final four-day leg of our journey. We just wanted to get *home* – to Sweden. Although Al and Nancy were congenial people in most ways, and their boys were fun, there was always tension in the air. Al generally relaxed a bit when he was on his own; he was *almost Al* then. I could tell him off-color jokes that he'd laugh heartily at; he'd have a glass of wine or even a shot of whiskey (my purchase) with Jeanette and me; he'd open up and lose a lot of his uptightness. But never when Nancy was present. The difference in his behavior was striking, and I found it hard to understand how he could be unaware of it, or why it had come to be that way.

Jeanette had a hard time understanding anything of what was going on. It seemed to me that Al's post-Thursday-Night-Massacre persona – the person he became during the two years in which he was focused on molding Nancy into a born-again Meeting person – was in fact a different person than he'd been molding *himself* into: the person he now was. He'd clearly succeeded (all too well) in pulling Nancy into the Fold, making her much more of a religious zealot than he ever was himself prior to the Massacre. Perhaps he'd been pulling too hard?

Their baby, Amy, was just two months old and adorable. She provided all the necessary and unnecessary back doors during our short stay. One of those evenings, after Jeanette (and Nancy) went to bed, Al opened up the topic of religion (surprise, surprise!), in much the same manner John did, sort of picking up where John left off, or gave up. (I wondered whether they spoke to each other about it in the interim, passed the baton, as it were.) I wasn't quite sure how or why they thought that their *efforts* would convince me, since they had nothing of *substance* to offer – no evidence, nothing rational. It just sounded bizarre and silly to me. Didn't they realize I had a brain – and used it? Didn't they realize that their precious faith sounded just as weird and nonsensical to me as bullshit like Scientology sounded to them?

We visited the Space Needle and a couple of good restaurants, but our minds were heading (and longing) for home. I hadn't shaved since we left San Francisco. I'd always hated shaving, but had limited my beard to a Van Dyke. Now I decided to let it all grow, and a full beard was underway by the time we returned to Europe.

The trip home was arduous. For Jeanette there seemed to have been a great deal more tension and disappointment than for me – perhaps my expectations were never high enough to earn disappointment. The flight was late leaving SeaTac, which didn't do anything to improve her mood. It turned dark in the mid-afternoon. *Why was I looking at that stewardess?* To get her attention to ask her to bring us some water. *Who was that girl in the lounge you were staring at?* I have no idea who you mean! *Why are you denying it?* Please, Jeanette, I don't understand where this is coming from!

It went on and on like that for some time, each of us becoming more and more agitated and desperate for disparate reasons. I knew she was disappointed and exhausted, and that there was a post-trip letdown going on, but I couldn't see into her mind to know what was driving her in this way. I wanted to help her, but I didn't know how.

It didn't help matters that we had to change planes in London, and that because our plane was late arriving, we had to hurry to our connecting flight to Copenhagen, but as a result our bags didn't make it, so we had to wait for our bags an extra two hours after arriving in Denmark. By the time we got home, we hadn't slept for 26 hours, and our nerves were frazzled. But Jeanette was beginning to regain control over her feelings, and apologized for her jealous outbursts.

The good thing was that we'd now tested the American water and decided that we'd found something better – for *us* – something far more suited to *our* needs, and we didn't need to become anyone other than ourselves in Sweden. [*I was and am keenly aware of the need to emphasize that in stating what felt right for us, it has never been my intention to claim that our personal choices and preferences would or should be anyone else's.*]

CHAPTER 9

Shifting void

Almost immediately after our return to Malmö, it dawned on me how much effort I'd been making for the past five years to adapt myself to every aspect of Swedish life. This awareness came to me primarily as the tangible absence of feeling any need for such efforts now. It simply disappeared. Not having been able to travel to the States made it necessary (in my mind at least) to do everything possible to "de-Americanize" myself, as if the only way to achieve that would be to "Swedish-ize" myself. Now that I was unexpectedly able to travel to the US again, I could feel more neutral about *both* Sweden and America. I no longer felt compelled to adapt myself to either external identity, but could be guided primarily by whatever internal identity I felt comfortable or compatible with.

I'd never noticed any attempt by Rob and Chris to "de-English-ize" or "Swedish-ize" themselves, although they were very different from each other. Probably due to Chris's close ties to Denmark, she seemed to fit in well in either country, and thus also in Sweden (given the relatively many similarities between the two Scandinavian countries). Rob, on the other hand, seemed to me more like the stereotypical Briton who is never a foreigner in any other country; it's the natives who are foreigners, or at least they behave as strangely as if they were. Most Americans abroad are no different, at least among those I've observed. But Rob was still new to the life of an ex-pat. He was also becoming restless about his lack of sufficient work for Hamadi and was looking for work at other language schools. We still played tennis with them occasionally, and also maintained some other forms of social contact with them.

In examining various aspects of my identity, one of the things I realized was that I would probably never speak Swedish well enough to be taken for a Swede (by Swedes). Before our trip, that bothered me (although far less so after the *semlor* incident!). Now it didn't bother me at all, and I hoped it never would again. I could communicate well in Swedish and could understand Swedes, or at least their language. Swedes had their own broad variety of accents, depending on what part of the country they came from. On my mother's side, I came from the Swedish diaspora. Why not be able to tell that?

I'd observed that a number of Swedes seemed to enjoy mocking foreigners for mispronouncing Swedish words, even when they understood them without difficulty. The style of mocking could be anything from a cruel, jeering, immature kind (bordering on *schadenfreude*) to a more innocent, bemused, playful kind. One thing the mockers seemed to have in common, however, was to avoid speaking English in the presence of native speakers. Perhaps they feared that *they* would be mocked, and they certainly didn't enjoy that threatening prospect! Bullies seldom enjoy being bullied. (Come to think of it, *nobody* enjoys being bullied, so why bully? Isn't there something called the Golden Rule...?)

I could now accept the fact that I was an American – but one who didn't accept many of the things that America was doing or stood for, and one who could and would now live in Sweden *by choice*. I nevertheless acknowledged that I would always *be* American to some extent, without being an "American" American, and that I would not always be *only* an American. It was always a strain to try to adapt myself to something I could never *fully* adapt myself to anyway, no matter how hard I might have wanted to try. I *liked* Sweden a lot – it's in Europe! And it seemed to be the country – more than any other country I knew enough about to tell – that, if all countries were to adopt Sweden's approach to equality, democracy, human rights, compassion for the disadvantaged, non-belligerence – the world would be a far better place.

Although Jeanette and I were critical – we felt that more needed to be done by Sweden in those areas too (even though Sweden had already done far more than America) – we nevertheless considered Sweden to be the "least bad" place on earth for us. But we'd never been flag-waving patriots, for the US or for Sweden. On this we agreed with Samuel Johnson (the author of the first dictionary of the English language): "*Patriotism is the last refuge of the scoundrel.*" And we still felt that the world as a whole was not a particularly good place for children.

I now felt more relaxed in Sweden than ever before, the wonderful relaxation that comes when one grants oneself the freedom not to conform to every bloody thing that comes along, to every silly tradition that many feel compelled to follow blindly, to every whim and fad and fashion that dictates attitudes and behaviors only to those disposed to subordinate themselves. I hadn't been *allowed* to conform as a child; then no I longer wanted to conform once I was on my own, albeit for different reasons.

There are people who dig for buried treasure, then stop digging once they find something, never considering that there might be much more worth finding further down if only they were to keep digging. I'd found the treasure of escaping the influence of the Meeting; now I was continuing to dig for all the conformity-free treasure that I suspected was still down there.

But since the human mind in every culture seems to have a great fondness (perhaps it's congenital?) for creating rituals and ceremonies, and these rituals and ceremonies quickly become habits, and habits become traditions and traditions become laws – written or unwritten – I knew that freedom from conformity would often be freedom at a price. I also knew that just learning more about myself would be a lifelong struggle. Socrates' one commandment – "*Know thyself*" – seems far more difficult for anyone to keep than Moses' ten.

Our plants and flowers and fish survived our absence quite well, thanks to the Carlssons. Jeanette brought a San Francisco sourdough starter home with her, and was eager to try baking her own sourdough bread, which she did with great success. I could hardly wait to get back to painting. But we both had to get back to work first; Jeanette's boss had a big backlog of work waiting for her, and Hamadi phoned me the first day and wanted me to phone some guy called Stig Troell at Perstorp to discuss future pupils for the school from that major potential client. And just like that, we were back into our routines, our home routines.

We'd been living for nearly four and a half years in a cozy (thanks to our efforts), cheap (158 kronor a month to start, incrementally hiked up to around 245 kronor now), comfortable (apart from the winter), centrally located (easy walking distance to the city center, and a short bike ride to work) apartment that was unfortunately located in an increasingly derelict building. And we were running out of wall space for my paintings.

One significant practical side-effect of our trip to America was that it completely removed any residual doubts about where we wanted to spend our future lives. Our cheap rent over the years had enabled us to save a substantial sum (by our standards) that we were now prepared to invest in better living quarters. After searching the newspapers, however, we soon began to realize it could be difficult to find something suitable (mostly meaning affordable). A place with an equally central location with an extra room and central heating was likely to quadruple our rent (at least), and that we couldn't afford. Condos had lower fees than rental apartments, but most of the prices were far beyond our reach. And all such fees felt like money down the drain.

What about a home of our own? A quick run through the ads showed that even the most modest homes were out of our league (or the league of our savings). It was frustrating, to say the least, but it wasn't an emergency situation, there was no sword of Damocles hanging over our heads, we had no timetable to follow, no deadline to meet. We were quite capable of being patient, particularly when we didn't have to wait. I asked Henry for some advice when they came over for some of Jeanette's deliriously delicious veal scaloppine. Maybe his company had a vacant penthouse for rent in one of their buildings along Limhamnsvägen? Henry just smiled nervously; Elsa looked almost shocked.

After struggling with jetlag and teaching during our first week back, I was aching to get on with my canvases. The notion of being geographically locked into position at birth was at the back of my mind when I painted *And We See You*.[49] A lot of heads are locked in place in overlapping protrusions and "peninsulas" of different muted colors (no specific world geography is intended). The characters *could* look at each other but don't.

My next one, *Blue Room*,[50] is quite small and shows a lonely, plain table in an empty room. The small window above the table is too high to see out – and there is only the void outside anyway. The floor is dark, mottled green. The high wall is deep blue. Is it a prison cell? Or a mood as a prison?

I followed up the questioning *Blue Room* with further questioning in *The Game*.[51] Six groups of hooded players (pieces) in the six colors of the rainbow (red, orange, yellow, green, blue, and violet – OK, I left out indigo) stand on a chessboard. Their faces are barely visible. The lone figure is the coldest (blue), the couple is the warmest (red). They are all waiting – to be played, manipulated? Do they have a choice? Or are they all mere pawns in somebody's game?

On August 8th, Richard Nixon became the first American president ever to resign from the presidency, as a result of his involvement in the Watergate scandal. He was succeeded by Gerald Ford, who'd been appointed by Nixon to succeed Spiro Agnew as Vice-President, and thus Ford became the first President never to have been elected, not even as Vice-President. One month later, Ford granted Nixon a "full, free, and absolute pardon", thereby preventing any criminal charges from being brought against him. (Was that deal sealed as a condition of Nixon's appointment of Ford to be vice-president? Was anybody surprised?)

---

49 Painting #64 (see Appendix 2)
50 Painting #65 (- " -)
51 Painting #66 (- " -)

Mom still hadn't decided what to do about a possible move to Knoxville – she still hadn't bought the land yet – and wrote that she'd like to come and see us the following autumn. We enthusiastically encouraged her to do so. We found that the fun-loving part of what we now perceived as her dual personality made her a pleasure to be around, but if her evangelizing side got going, we knew we'd have to run for the trenches. That side didn't appear so readily when Maxine or other Meeting people weren't around, and they certainly wouldn't be around in Malmö. They were *not* invited.

Jeanette's bouts of moodiness and severe jealousy – totally incomprehensible to me – became more frequent in August, and I was almost frantic to know how to handle them. They weren't rational, so things like reason and evidence had no impact, nor did my attempts to lavish her with love and affection; according to her, I was just displaying guilt-based compensation. And then, just as suddenly, the jealous mood would disappear, and she'd feel at a loss to understand what had come over her. Once it left her, she didn't want to talk about it, and I didn't try to force her to, for fear it would bring on a new attack.

I suggested that maybe we needed a break (or a purge) from our American experience by having a good, solid European "antidote", like a week in Rome. We found another incredibly cheap, affordable charter package, August 25th to September 1st, and Jeanette was thrilled beyond measure. She hadn't yet had the opportunity to "show me Rome", which had been high on her list (we'd already spent a week in Paris and much more in London) ever since her trip there in 1965.

In mid-August, we got two tapes from Bob, one that he recorded for us, the other that his brother Charles recorded for him, in which Charles spent most of it lambasting his wayward sons (Danny and Dwight) who were straying from the True Path of the Meeting, making Charles furious. Bob was so baffled by the mental processes that would have led Charles to consult him, of all people, in a matter where Bob would have been the last person on earth to do anything but lambast Charles for lambasting his sons for failing to follow Charles' foolish and suffocating beliefs and restrictions. Bob was in fact so baffled that he wanted us to listen to Charles' tape, and then he wanted each of our comments on it.

Jeanette wrote that she found Charles' tape extremely bizarre and offensive; she couldn't conceive how anyone with Charles' view about children could ever want to have any. She had no answers, only questions, scores of them. At the end of her letter, she mused:

"Bob, I continue to find it difficult to accept life as it is when I am continually being exposed to such grotesque occurrences, even performed by me. A re-evaluation whenever the opportunity arises is the only . . . is the only what? It is as senseless, or I am, as ever; but I go on, life goes on, the weather is to my complete satisfaction, 18°C, a trip to Rome is on our agenda, you are surely feeling better, we have enjoyed a fine visit to the States, last but not (far from) least, dear Stanley is still dear."

[This is another example of insights into Jeanette's mind that I'd never seen until researching this book (punctuation hers).]

We left for Rome early in the morning on Sunday, August 25th, 1974, five years to the day after our first-ever arrival in Sweden. On the plane on the way down, we followed the travel agent's advice and purchased a bottle of Fernet Branca, an herbal liqueur with a taste so bitter that it has the power to make smiling difficult for weeks. We'd been further advised to begin each day with a shot of it to ward off gastrointestinal maladies of every sort.

Rome and Italy far exceeded my expectations in every respect. You could easily find buildings in cities such as London, Amsterdam, Paris and Madrid that were hundreds of years old, impressive enough to me. In Rome many were *thousands* of years old, ancient! Our hotel, the Grand Olympic, was located near the Castel Sant'Angelo, with its secret passage to the Vatican. The beating wings of history were ready to clobber us at every turn. Churches and cathedrals, with all the ornate grandeur of exceptional talent in a foolish cause. There was such artistic ambivalence on nearly every corner. Even the colors of the buildings in the ordinary streets offered a beautiful range of colors, emphasizing tones from sanguine orange through muted peach and a variety of ochres that pleased us immensely. The level differences in the hilly city's topography meant that stairways to new streets on new levels were popping up all the time to arouse our curiosity. And for some strange reason, there were Italian restaurants on almost every corner. This was as much a vacation for us as the US was not. We had no need to posture or accommodate, to disguise or defer. We could just be ourselves.

But it was hot. While exploring the streets and buildings at the base of the Spanish Steps in the sweltering heat on one of our first days, we paused outside a wine merchant's to have a look at the wines in the window, and decided to enter and search the shelves for possible bargains. At the back of the little shop, we noticed a marble tank, about the size of a large, high bathtub, with cold water running into it (and presumably out of it, since it wasn't overflowing) then we saw a number of bottles of white wine chilling in the tank, and a couple of tiny tables and chairs next to it. We managed to understand from the shop owner that we could refresh ourselves there with a large glass of good chilled white wine at a low price, and take a load off our feet for a while. That place became a daily watering hole for us throughout our stay.

We found a lunch restaurant crowded with Italians (i.e. not tourists), and since we were hungry, we joined the short line waiting to be seated. We chose lasagne and split a carafe of red wine. Minutes after we arrived, a small, slender, middle-aged Italian man (apparently on his lunch break from the office) took the table next to ours, said some words to the waitress, and was soon served a sizeable platter of delicious-looking cold cuts and a basket of bread. He began nibbling on them immediately, while reading his newspaper. He also had a carafe of red wine, the same size as the one Jeanette and I were splitting. As he was finishing his platter, the waitress brought us our generous portions of lasagne. We'd scarcely begun digging into ours when she brought him an equally generous portion of the same lasagne. Jeanette and I looked at each other, wondering whether that diminutive man could finish his, especially on top of a big platter of cold cuts and bread. We finished our lasagne first and were stuffed. Minutes later, he finished his, with no apparent discomfort, to our amazement. As we were enjoying the last of our wine, the waitress brought him a steaming plate with two good-size pork chops and a few vegetables. He had obviously instigated this development, and seemed to relish it. Our eyes grew wider. When he'd finished everything, the waitress took his plate, and he went back to his paper. A few minutes later, she brought him a large platter of assorted cheeses to accompany the last of his wine. We stayed on because we had to see if he would finish that too. He did.

One balmy evening we saw a staggering performance of *Aïda*, set in the ruins of an ancient Roman amphitheater, with live horses on stage and Verdi's music welling forth over the audience. It felt like magic to us, and Jeanette seemed so happy.

We finished the last of our half-bottle of Fernet Branca in the morning, two days before our flight home, and decided that for the remaining two mornings we didn't need to invest in a new bottle of that anti-delicious concoction. After all, our stomachs were fine. The next day (with no Fernet Branca to line them) they weren't, and our exploring range had to be limited to a brisk 15-minute walk back to our hotel bathroom.

We bought half a dozen bottles of wine (*no* Fernet Branca!), in addition to our two-bottles-per-person quota back to Sweden with us on Sunday, September 1st, hoping we wouldn't have to pay duty on it. We were lucky, and walked right through customs without being stopped. Smuggling a few extra bottles was kind of a sport for most Swedes back in the 70s. Wine was so much cheaper outside Sweden then, and just about everybody brought back a little extra. The customs officers seldom bothered about mere wine; they were more concerned about drugs nowadays.

Rome gave us a refreshing break – including a near cessation of Jeanette's bouts of jealousy – as well as a purge from the disappointments of America, and the realization that we and our former homeland were moving in opposite directions more swiftly than ever.

Just five days after we got back to Sweden from Rome, Al and his whole family visited us for a few uneventful days, in connection with some speaking engagements Al had in Copenhagen on the Friday and in Lund on the Monday – a whirlwind tour.

We also heard from Jeanette's mom that Mike (her father) was in the hospital following a heart attack. I could see that the news shook Jeanette considerably, although she tried not to let on, and she didn't want to talk about it. It was just wordlessly perplexing – her father had hardly spoken to her when we were there. Jeanette seemed a bit numbed by it.

She helped me stretch a new round of canvases so I could get back to painting as quickly as possible. After discussing our housing situation with Henry a little, he thought we might want to look into the possibility of buying a so-called "*renoveringsobjekt*" (renovation object, i.e. a "fixer-upper") – an old, run-down house that sorely needed a major overhaul. He said that sometimes they appeared on the market at extremely low prices, relatively speaking, and he correctly guessed that we weren't afraid to roll up our sleeves. So we began scouring the Sunday papers for anything of that type that might come along.

Bob was planning to come to see us on September 28th, and stay for a bit more than two weeks. We were delighted about that. And Mom mentioned that when she came to see us – tentatively the following fall – maybe the three of us could make a trip to Jerusalem. It sounded interesting to us (every new experience sounded interesting), but for entirely different reasons from hers; we said we'd try to out find what the options were. Mom told us that she was leaning towards accommodations at the expensive (from our perspective) King David Hotel; the sound of that particular establishment made Jeanette and me suspicious that it might be religiously conservative and not allow alcohol.

Jeanette's German classes resumed on September 12th. I wished she'd taken a little French as well. For my birthday the next day, she made an exquisite French dish, following a pretty advanced recipe in *Larousse Gastronimique*, a huge French cookbook I gave her courtesy of The Emporium once upon a time. I was wild about the result, and enormously impressed by her cooking skills. So I said, in French, "*Tu es formidable!*" (You're terrific, outstanding!) Her good mood disappeared in a flash. She *presumed* that what I said meant "You are formidable" (terrifying, challenging), and would not listen to the attempts I made to convince her that despite the same spelling and origin, the word had nearly opposite meanings in English and French. Instead she instantly became furious, hostile, suspicious, and (sigh) jealous.

Mom once again sent me pajamas for my birthday (and a nightie for Jeanette). Ever since Jeanette and I got married, Mom almost always sent me pajamas for my birthday, despite my telling her that I didn't sleep, had never slept (since childhood), never intended to sleep, in pajamas. I think she thought it was somehow indecent.

We received word from San Francisco that Mike was "home again and feeling fine," to Jeanette's considerable relief. And I started a new painting, *Wanderers*,[52] inspired by our visit to Rome: cool strangers amid its warm-colored buildings and stairways. We'd been wanderers there – faceless, anonymous, wafting through the streets. I'd painted stairways before, but in this painting the stairway is the focal point.

On Sunday morning, September 22nd, we were reading the newspaper in bed, as was our habit. Since it was Sunday, the day when most of the classified property ads would appear, we were extra eager to see if there might be something of interest among the listings. There was. It was a tiny ad, as might be expected for an unassuming property, but it had the headline we'd learned to watch for: *Renoveringsobjekt*. It had plenty of room (and rooms) on a small lot, it was livable as-is, but a lot of work would be needed to realize the full potential of the property. And then the bottom line: 70,000 Swedish kronor. It was *almost* affordable (meaning it would consume about 10,000 more than the sum of all our savings)!

---

52 Painting #67 (see Appendix 2)

There was a phone number to the agent. We phoned immediately, still in our non-pajamas, said we were interested, and could the agent please meet us at the property that day? He said he could meet us there that afternoon, so we asked for the address – Sandgatan 5 – in a part of town called Kirseberg, less than a kilometer farther out Lundavägen from Vårgatan, up a small hill.

We were terribly excited, threw our clothes on, wolfed down some breakfast, and cycled out there to have a look from the outside before our guided afternoon viewing. Despite its proximity to Vårgatan, we'd never been to Kirseberg before, and despite Sandgatan being one of Malmö's shortest streets, only about 50 meters long, we had no trouble finding the place, the second house from the corner of Källargatan. The neighborhood was old, dominated by small terraced houses built right along the quiet little streets, with no or minimal sidewalks. Most of the houses were single-storey A-frames in brick (or stucco) from the 1860s. A number of them had been modified over the years; this was the only full-two-storey place on its side of the street, and in the three parallel rows of houses from the 1860s. There were also a few turn-of-the-century (19th to 20th) two-storey red brick places in the neighborhood. Most of them were pretty run-down, but one or two had recently been restored beautifully.

Sandgatan was an exceptionally narrow street, one of Malmö's narrowest. Sandgatan 5 was directly opposite a much higher two-storey red brick apartment building from around 1900, which also had a full basement and high ceilings on both floors, plus an attic with a high enough ceiling for apartment conversion, to make a third floor. (There was another red brick building of similar height at the far end of the same block.) But the house at Sandgatan 5 looked plenty big enough to us as we peered through the windows from the street. There was sure to be plenty of studio space. We'd seen enough for our enthusiasm to soar exponentially, and we could hardly wait for our meeting with the realtor. In fact, we phoned him back right after our outdoor viewing to say that although we still wanted to see inside the house that afternoon, we'd already made up our minds: *we would take it!* He chuckled and said he'd meet us there as planned, that afternoon.

We were so focused on our potential new home that we scarcely noticed the realtor when he arrived, except to note that he seemed to be friendly and not a blackguard. That settled, we turned our eyes and attention to the house. We weren't disappointed by the interior, or rather by the *potential* we saw in the interior. There was already a small but functional kitchen and a bathroom, as well as a small, light living room facing a tiny courtyard, and a dark bedroom facing the narrow street and the taller dark building opposite. Then there was an entire upstairs, unfinished – unbegun – with ample space for a studio and a couple more bedrooms (guestrooms, dens, whatever-rooms). There was even a functional bathroom with a shower. Moreover, there was ample attic storage space above the second storey (we could stand up straight there!) – or the second-story ceilings could be opened up to the rafters.

On the far side of the courtyard was another windowless building, parallel with the main building, like a large garage or workshop. That could even be a second studio if I opened up some large windows in the north-facing wall towards the courtyard. *Sculpture*?! The space was there if I ever chose to go in that direction. The roof of this extra building was flat and directly connected to a small porch outside the upstairs of the main building, allowing the possibility of a large L-shaped roof terrace. That building also opened up to the alley behind it.

My heart was pounding. Jeanette's eyes were wide and she could scarcely contain her excitement. If we put all our savings together, we'd *almost* have enough to buy it outright (the amount of work that needed to be done made it doubtful that we would be able to get a mortgage, particularly since our incomes from our part-time jobs were so low). Our parents told us that a small loan might be possible if we found a place, even if we'd have preferred to manage it all on our own. But it *would* work, we'd *make* it work!

We reminded the realtor that we'd already made up our minds to buy it, and would like to make a cash down-payment the next day, after we'd been to the bank. He told us that 10%, or 7000 kronor, would be the right amount for a down-payment. He agreed to meet us at the house again on Monday, September 23rd, at the same time. We walked around the neighborhood a little before making the 3-minute bike ride home to Vårgatan. We couldn't think of anything else; we were so excited we could barely eat or sleep.

The next morning, I was waiting at the bank at Värnhemstorget (a block away from our apartment when they opened at 10. I withdrew the 7000 in seven huge 1000-kronor bills. We arrived at the house at about 12.30 – we didn't want to keep the realtor waiting if he happened to be the early type. As the appointed hour was approaching (we were compulsively checking our watches every three seconds or so), our anticipation was becoming unbearable. One o'clock arrived. No realtor. Half past one. Nothing. No realtor. At two o'clock I anxiously went up to the phone booth at Kirsebergstorget and phoned him, to see if there'd been some delay that he'd been unable to inform us about. (This was, after all, long before the age of mobile phones.) Jeanette waited by the house in case he showed up from the other direction. When he finally answered, I told him who I was, that we were waiting at the house to meet him and make our down-payment, as agreed. He cleared his throat roughly and said, "*Oh, that house? I sold it yesterday afternoon to somebody else!*"

It felt like I would collapse right there in the phone booth. (If I'd been armed and facing him in person, would I have shot him in the face? I honestly don't know.) I struggled to protest, "But we had a *deal*! You promised to sell it to us!!" He seemed totally unperturbed. "*I got a better offer, so I had to take it, and the money's already been transferred.*" I asked him how much better the offer was, and he said 80,000 kronor. I asked for the name of the buyer – I was maybe going to make *him* an offer – so he gave me the man's name and phone number.

Jeanette saw instantly by the look on my face that something had gone horribly wrong. When I related what happened, I thought she was going to explode. After we'd calmed each other down a bit, we decided to try phoning the man who outbid us on a sale that the realtor lied about promising us. The purchaser – a Swede living in Germany – was indeed willing to re-sell the house to us – for 150,000 kronor, more than double the price we'd agreed upon with the realtor, and nearly double what he'd paid for it the day before! After a deep breath, we just hung up.

For a long time, "Sandgatan" would remain as bitter a memory as "Freiburg" had once been. It was more than the shattering of dreams; it was also a glimpse into the rapaciousness of human nature, at least the nature of two humans: the realtor and the buyer (especially the realtor!). We would later learn that the buyer never even moved in; after a few months, he sold the house to others who knew nothing of the wheelings and dealings that went on before. It was back to the drawing board for us (or for a somewhat more disillusioned version of us), but we both felt that if we were to find something to meet our future needs, it would pretty much have to be another *renoveringsobjekt*.

Every once in a while I'd have a pupil from some sector of the building and construction industry, and while teaching them how to talk about their work in English, I picked up lots of information and pointers about how houses are built: foundations, insulation, concrete work, roof construction, tile laying, working with plasterboard,[53] building codes, dealing with the authorities, government

---

53 Plasterboard is also known as drywall, sheetrock and gypsum-board.

grants to weatherproof or winterize houses, etc. It was always interesting and valuable to learn new things, and I felt sure the knowledge about all the house stuff might also prove useful to us someday.

Before Bob's arrival on September 28th, I began a new painting, *Inconclusive Anticipation*.[54] It builds to some degree on the previous painting, with the stairway to an unknown destination and people adrift among buildings, but these buildings have no warmth. The people have faces, but they don't see each other. They all appear to be waiting for something, someone, to descend the stairs. (Waiting for a real estate agent to arrive? Waiting for one to be honest?) But they don't know for certain what, if anything, will ever come – like waiting for Godot. In the meantime, they have no contact with each other. (Jeanette modeled for the figure in the lower left, in her post-Sandgatan mood.) I finished it a few days after Bob's arrival.

Bob was planning to stay with us for two weeks, and we had loads of things to discuss: his health, details of our impressions of our US trip and family relations, Nixon's resignation, the aftermath and continuing saga of Watergate, our continuing house hunt, my latest round of paintings, my ongoing painting, new heights and depths of classical music, the collapse of the Iranian trip, the collapse of any reasonable, residual foundation for religion. It kept us busy.

A letter from Mom requested more Bible translations, which she said that this Mr Gullens suggested to her to ask us for. Of course all three of us could see through why she was doing that. She didn't speak Swedish. If Gullens did, he could look up the corresponding chapters and verses himself! I suggested to her that she let him handle them himself in the future. Changing the subject in a flash (she was outstanding at that!), Mom then informed us that John nearly lost a leg while out white-water rafting. Apparently *His* eye was on the sparrow instead. (If John had lost a testicle – which he didn't – could one say that He kept His eye on the ball?) And a brief letter from Marilyn informed us that Mike was "continuing to improve".

Into the second week of Bob's visit, I was already well into my next painting, *Tables for One*,[55] a different take of the theme of *The Unexpected Meeting* – this time showing two people, at a restaurant, who might like to meet, but cannot let

---

54 Painting #68 (see Appendix 2)

55 Painting #69 (- " -)

their barriers down. They are, in their longing loneliness, completely separated by the void.

On Tuesday evening, October 8th, after a superb anniversary dinner creation from Jeanette, the three of us were just relaxing with some wine and popcorn, talking and listening to music. In the late evening I began experiencing stomach pains that continued and increased throughout the night. It was pretty bad the next morning, even worse in the afternoon. I thought it might be a cramp due to tensing up too much while painting, so I took a hot bath, which only made it worse. The doctor in Bob was aroused, and he asked me to apply pressure to various parts of my abdomen. When he suggested pressing my fingers into the lower-right corner, I nearly shot through the ceiling, the pain was so piercing. "*You've got to get to a hospital now,*" he exclaimed urgently. "*It's appendicitis!*"

Jeanette frantically called a taxi, which was already at our door by the time we got down the stairs to meet it. I was writhing in pain by this time, around 5 PM. It took the hospital staff about one minute to confirm Bob's diagnosis and to give me a sedative to calm down my writhing. Then they held a mask up to my nose and mouth, and asked me to count backwards from 100. I only made it to 98 before the swirling haze whisked me away into the unconscious. It was the first time I'd ever been etherized upon a table. I'd guess that it took less than two more minutes to whisk me off to the operating room.

The next thing I knew was that I was lying in a hospital bed in a dimly lit post-op ward, possibly at around 10 PM, together with about a dozen other sleeping men (I think I was the youngest), with a nurse I'd never seen before standing by my side asking me whether I wanted a sleeping pill for the night. I'd never taken a sleeping pill in my life and automatically declined the offer. I was still groggy from the general anesthetic, which was just beginning to wear off, so I was only feeling a little pain from the incision.

About an hour later I began to wish I'd accepted the offer. Several of the men in my ward were snoring, but there was one whose snoring was like an exaggerated cartoon version, the kind that sounds like an intermittently operated and seriously defective cement mixer. The noise was so loud, the sound was so ridiculous, the circumstances were so novel and bizarre, that I burst into laughter – only to experience excruciating pain as a result. I tried not to listen to the snoring and above all I tried not to laugh, but it took me a long time to get to sleep, probably well past midnight.

Early the next morning, a short, I think it was about 6.30, a muscular bulldog of a nurse burst through the swinging doors of the ward to rouse the sleepy dozen with a penetrating roar, "*Hi there, boys, are you bright-eyed and bushy-tailed?!*" (a rough translation of her Swedish, "*Hej killar! Är ni pigg-pigg-pigg-pigg-pigga?!*"). My first, spontaneous movement was to try to sit up in bed, but the resulting sharp stab of pain made me change my mind. Nurses were scurrying everywhere. One of them handed me a small kidney-shaped stainless steel bowl with a thermometer lying in it. Still groggy, I asked what it was for. She'd already begun to move on, so she just said over her shoulder at me that it was for taking my temperature, of course. I shrugged, picked up the thermometer and stuck it under my tongue, as I'd *always* done in the past – albeit never at a hospital, of which I'd had no experience at all. I immediately let out a loud "*Yeechhh!*" The nurse came running back to see what the problem was. I'd already taken the thermometer out of my mouth, had a thoroughly disgusted look on my face, and was inspecting the remains of a glob of Vaseline on the end of the thermometer while trying to remove the rest of the goo from my mouth. The nurse began laughing, "*It's not for your mouth, silly! It's goes in the other end!*"

They wanted me to get out of bed that very first morning; it felt like my wound would rip open and my guts would spill out on the floor in front of me. I thought of *Catch-22*. I thought the staff had sadistic impulses. *They couldn't be serious?!* Every tiny step convinced me that my next one would be my last. Jeanette and Bob came to see me an hour or two later, while I was still weak and groggy and in great pain from the incision. It turned out that my appendix was very close to rupturing by the time they got in there and removed it. Jeanette tried to look calm, but I could see that she was terrified. I did everything in my power to put on a brave face – not to impress her with my fortitude, but to calm her by downplaying my condition. There was an earnestness, a desperation in her touch that made me think that *she* was the one doing her best to keep the brave face. I was determined to recover as quickly as possible, and did my walking exercises long after the other post-op patients in the ward had returned to their beds.

Bob had already made arrangements with his boss and the airline to stay on with us for an extra week; I think he also saw how alarmed Jeanette was. I was soon walking long stretches up and down the corridors, pushing my wheeled drip stand, in order to get my body up and running as fast as possible so they would let me come home to Jeanette. Two evenings later, I told Jeanette that I would be allowed to come home the following morning. I got up early, and had just painfully dressed when Jeanette burst into the ward. I'd never seen her looking so happy. She fairly radiated happiness and joy to see me. But there was just a faint hint of something else; I couldn't understand what it was.

After another three days, I was back to painting. And eleven days after my operation, I played tennis with Henry, while holding my wound together with my right hand. (How nice to be left-handed!) It only *felt* like I needed to hold my wound, but the fact that I *could* play seemed to help roll back Jeanette's anxiety, and that was the only important thing to me.

In the two weeks after coming home from the hospital, I completed two more paintings. The first, *Departure*,[56] depicts a departing man in the foreground. He seems to be heading for the void, and fleeing the responses of others to his departure. The painting symbolizes our reactions to the US, to realizing that we no longer felt we belonged there (or that *they* felt that we didn't belong there!); to my Mom's anguishing over our departure – and not necessarily from the US. We (I especially) had departed *her* way, which she conveniently called the Lord's Way, and was unwilling to consider any other possibility. We felt everything from mild alienation to outright rejection, when nobody (except Bob) seemed to want to understand our lives, but maintained silence on every topic of depth.

The next painting is sarcastically titled *Dialogue*,[57] in which two people are *not* having a dialogue, but two simultaneous monologues. Both are speaking, neither is listening, they are not even addressing each other. They are separated by the void for the entire height of the painting. Outside, others are crowding and fighting to eavesdrop. Listening is apparently all right when one is not supposed to. Again, this reflected the frustration of finding meaningful conversation anywhere, particularly while in the US.

In a tape Bob made for his brother Charles on October 26th, Bob expressed his profound concern regarding Charles' mistreatment of his sons, Danny and Dwight. The tape was a heartfelt *plea* by Bob for Charles to save his relationship with his sons, especially Danny. Bob was also livid. "*Human beings, at every level and at every age, must be treated as though they were not born slaves!*" (In the tape, Bob informed Charles that he shared tapes with me and Jeanette, that he had no secrets from us.)

Bob also mentioned some things about himself and his parents that I hadn't heard him express with such clarity before. Particularly surprising to me was

---

[56] Painting #70 (see Appendix 2)

[57] Painting #71 (- " -); compare with #15 (*Discussion*) and #38 (*Public Image*).

that Bob clearly felt that his mother had dictated his father's role – I'd always understood that Bob regarded Harold as the Chief Tyrant. Perhaps Bob had emotional ties to his mother that made him tend to withhold criticism of her? Where his father was concerned, however, Bob didn't pull his punches: "*Is it worthwhile being a Christian if you ain't no goddamn human being?!*" (Bob asked this rhetorical question in his tape to Charles – ostensibly about Harold, but clearly directed at Charles as well – in an agitated voice.)

Presenting his plea from another angle, Bob laid bare another dimension of himself: "*I wanted children – especially sons, to be able to show them kindness, which I hadn't known – but it was denied to me. In retrospect, with Sigrid's severe mental illness and my physical problems, that turned out to be fortunate.*" Retaining my composure, on hearing Bob's voice saying this on the tape many years later, turned out to be an impossibility.

On Tuesday, November 5th, I came home from teaching and entered our apartment full of energy and cheery greetings, but was immediately uncertain as to whether Jeanette was at home. Then she emerged slowly from the darkened bedroom, holding onto the doorpost. Her eyes were red and swollen and she was looking down at the floor like she was sinking through it. Two hours earlier, she'd received a phone call from San Francisco. Her father was dead. Heart attack. As usual, I didn't know how to react at first. She was sad, angry, frantic, confused, irritated and overwhelmed, all at once.

We (I) immediately booked a trip leaving for San Francisco two days later, since Jeanette was determined to attend the funeral on the 8th. We originally planned to be away for three weeks, since flights were significantly cheaper than if we stayed only two weeks. But Jeanette's boss felt he couldn't manage without her for that long, so he paid the difference in our fare for a two-week stay. Shortening our stay pleased us both.

On the flight, Jeanette was quiet and withdrawn the whole way. I held her hand and tried to say comforting things to her, but she hardly heard what I said. From time to time she would look long and hard at me strangely and squeeze my hand till it hurt.

The funeral was held at the Epiphany Church, the same church where Jeanette and I got married eight years earlier, with all the funeral trimmings in the best American and Catholic traditions. Since Mike was not a practicing Catholic, the officiating priest didn't know him at all. But that didn't stop him from informing the assembled mourners that because Mike had failed to perform his religious duties, *he was at that very moment suffering the most grotesque tortures of hellfire!* The priest *knew* this. And he ladled it out in gruesome detail (along the lines of the priest at the retreat in James Joyce's *Portrait of the Artist as a Young Man*). I'd been led to believe that such things were part of the past, among the Catholics at least. But they were right there, in the present, in 1974. Jeanette was furious, disgusted and appalled. I was afraid she'd run up to the altar and bite the sonofabitch. So much for funerals offering comfort and closure to the bereaved!

After it was over, Jeanette went on and on about it to me (and to a much lesser extent to her immediate family). She told me, in no uncertain terms, that when she died, there was to be *no* funeral whatsoever, *no* ceremonies, *no* goddamn religion, *no* gravesite. People who wanted to mourn could mourn, people who wanted to remember could remember – they didn't need a fucking church to do it in! After the experience of visiting Dad's grave a few months earlier, that strange location with nothing relating to his life, I had absolutely no reason to disagree with her. Jeanette declared that she wanted to be cremated. I felt the same, and we made a pact that our ashes should be strewn on the sea, without ceremony.

I visited John and Marj for the weekend that came in the middle of our two-week stay in San Francisco. Just a couple of days earlier, John was given two weeks' notice by his employer, after 10 years of service. I'd heard that many American employers frowned on employees taking vacation time or not working on weekends (by "frowned" I mean grounds for dismissal), after the employers had made unrealistic delivery promises to their customers. How shameful that an employee might prioritize a life or family time instead of devotion to making junk products! I was reminded of the medieval nature of American working conditions, the serf-like dependency on the lord of the manor for healthcare, job security and retirement pensions, and how things like four weeks of paid vacation and paid long maternity leave – all universal and legally mandated in Sweden and similarly throughout much of Europe – were extremely rare in the US. But I wasn't terribly surprised about what I discovered on this second trip. As I put it to Bob, "The second jump off the high diving board isn't the same as the first."

I phoned Mom several times during our stay in California. She was making some progress with her plans to move to Knoxville. In connection with Mike's death, Jeanette initiated a lengthy hiatus in her normally frequent notes to Mom (and to nearly everyone else), brought on by Jeanette's renewed disgust with everything relating to religion, and thus also with Mom's incessant and insidious references (at best) and outright nagging (at worst).

Mom directed her next round of nagging at Bob, in a preachy letter of November 14th. "*His Love shines through even greater when the tests are overwhelming – in prison Paul gave the text – 'Rejoice in the Lord always'....*" However strange it may seem, Bob, Jeanette and I had come to feel that it's not necessary to prove one's love for someone by killing their family members and making them sick and miserable.

As the year was drawing to a close, we saw several new house prospects in the form of late-19th- and early-20th-century houses bearing some architectural similarities to the house on Sandgatan. These were in a part of town called Sofielund, and were being sold by the municipality, with a long-term lease on the lot. We were skeptical about such an arrangement, since having to pay a monthly fee on the lease[58] would mean an additional fixed monthly cost, and the feeling of being at the whim of the decisions of municipal governments. Even more uncertain was the fact that these houses weren't being offered for sale at a fixed price – one had to submit a bid to the municipality. Perhaps it could be a good approach, but we didn't feel it was the right fit for us. We didn't like to gamble.

Just before Christmas, I had a talk with Hamadi about my working hours. Rob had more or less disappeared from Hamadi's school following some dispute about Rob's insufficient hours, and filling the gap had fallen back on me. But I feared that my workload was becoming too heavy because of the time I felt I needed for painting, yet I didn't want to leave Hamadi in the lurch. He assured me that he had several other English teachers lined up to relieve me.

He also told Jeanette and me that he was going home to Tunisia for about a month, leaving in mid-December. The purpose of the trip? To get married! He'd never mentioned a girlfriend there, so we were full of questions. He told us she was someone whose family knew his family, and he'd known her for many years. She was a pharmacist, and was planning to take up that profession in Sweden as soon as she learned Swedish and took a few courses to align her knowledge of pharmacology with Swedish practice.

---

58 Swedish: *tomträttsavgäld*

I completed three more paintings in December. The first – *But Maybe I Don't Want to See*[59] – reflects my growing awareness of the lengths to which people – not excluding myself – will go to avoid uncomfortable truths or to challenge their own well-established ideas and beliefs, even in the face of overwhelming evidence to the contrary. The sharp, cold blue points behind the man force him towards the void, from which he shields his eyes with both hands.

Next came *Stranded*,[60] with figures standing in beach huts on a blue beach (strand), each couple isolated from the others. The two in the foreground seem to be isolated from each other as well. The taller one may be looking for contact, but the shorter one has her eyes and face turned completely averted. Individually or collectively, they are all stranded.

My final painting of my most productive painting year ever (a total of 29 paintings in 1974), was significant as a summary of several themes. In this painting, the void itself plays the central role, and the three people around it, isolated from each other, react to it differently, depending on how (or whether) they see it. The first has open yet unseeing eyes, and has a bottle between him and the void; he is grinning madly. The second has his eyes closed and looks melancholy; he has a flower between him and the void. The position of the third is in direct contact with the void; his eyes are averted and he's screaming in terror. The title is *It Depends on Your Point of View*.[61]

Our extra trip to the US eliminated our chances of visiting Bob at Christmas, which we'd been hoping to do. Jeanette had used up all her extra time off work, and the air fare had dealt our house-purchase funds a heavy (but not mortal) blow. So we spent Christmas on our own, just the two of us, licking our wounds and making new ones, in the form of Jeanette's increasingly ferocious bouts of incomprehensible jealousy.

In retrospect, in hindsight, even I can see that the year must have been particularly hard on Jeanette: she was still greatly disturbed about the loss of my father; the excitement and dashed hopes concerning a possible extended stay in Iran; the disillusionment of the US trip on so many levels; the cruel disap-

---

59 Painting #72 (see Appendix 2)
60 Painting #73 (- " -)
61 Painting #74 (- " -)

pointment over Sandgatan; the harsh reminder of my mortality in connection with my appendectomy; and the death of her father, with so many unresolved issues, as well as his horrendous funeral. I'm sure we were both hoping that the new year would be less convulsive.

CHAPTER 10

Moving

From the very beginning of 1975, we had little else on our minds than moving. If only we could find a place! We seemed to be getting nowhere. As of the end of 1974, we had no neighbors at all left in our stairway, and most of the doors to the vacant apartments were broken open. We could hear people moving about in the stairway at night, and more frequently now in the attic above us, not surprisingly feeding our paranoia. Our apartment was unheatable during the chilly winter nights, exacerbated by no longer having any heated units around us. We mourned these developments; we'd made such a lovely home within our own walls.

But so far, house-hunting proved extremely frustrating. The one place we'd wanted – and briefly thought was ours – was ripped from our grasp, and we'd not yet been able to find anything else remotely like it. As a result, we were constantly reassessing our demands and were prepared to lower them considerably if that was what it took.

I painted two paintings in the early part of January, both related to housing and neighbors. The first, *Nobody Home*,[62] shows a man who has turned away from a darkened house, but is looking back intently, the way people do when nobody has answered their knock on a door, as if there might still be an answer at any moment. He looks back one more time, but even if somebody were at home, nobody would receive him. A careful look, however, reveals that there was somebody lurking in the window after all, just not someone who would allow contact.

The second of these two paintings, *Neighbors*,[63] has many similarities to the first. In this case, both houses are blue. In the doorway of the house farthest away, the man seems to be looking for visitors, but he is looking in the opposite direction, yet some light is coming from his doorway. In the foreground, the man is re-entering his house. Both are looking away from each other.

Although Jeanette's interest in my painting was still on the same high level, as was her active encouragement, her bouts of jealousy were increasing in frequency and intensity. I was beginning to feel a sense of despair overwhelming me – of

---

62 Painting #75 (see Appendix 2)

63 Painting #76 (- " -)

a different kind than the one I didn't realize was overwhelming her, and I was faced with that hopelessly futile task of proving this kind of negative. No wonder free societies zealously guard the principle of innocent until proven guilty! But she always sharply rebuffed my suggestions of seeking counselling – for herself and/or for us.

On Sunday morning, January 19th, we saw an ad for a house – another *renoveringsobjekt!* – that made us sit up and take notice. It was also in Kirseberg, and the price was 80,000 kronor. We thought it might be the house on Sandgatan, which the owner for some reason needed to unload again, for the price he'd paid for it. There was a phone number (not the same agent). We called and were told the address, so we could go have a look from the outside that Sunday, but the realtor said he wouldn't be able to meet us there that day. The address was Korngatan 12, on the north side of the street, just one short block over from Sandgatan and parallel to it.

Like Sandgatan, Korngatan was just one block long. Originally, each block was four abutting houses long, but some had been divided into two smaller houses. Each property consisted of a main house and a parallel smaller building (originally outhouses and/or stables). The houses on Korngatan and Sandgatan were separated by a common alley called Källargränd. Korngatan 12 was located on the corner of Källargatan, diagonally behind (or almost back-to-back with) the house we'd looked at on Sandgatan. At their nearest corners, the two properties were a mere seven meters apart.

The fronts of the houses along Korngatan were recessed only about 40 centimeters from the street itself. Korngatan 12 was about 11½ meters long, with brick walls that were painted white but were badly flaked. Some of the bricks were cracked, and chunks were missing. The door and the single-glazed windows seemed to be rotting and would need replacement. The roof was covered in worn-out roofing felt. The façade along Källargatan was nearly 16 meters long, all the way to Källargränd. The profile indicated that there were two parallel buildings, one about eight meters wide, the other only about three and a half meters wide, probably with a garage or small open courtyard space between them; there was a massive rusting solid iron gate facing Källargatan. It appeared that nobody had lived in that house for decades. We cycled back home, disappointed, feeling that the amount of repair needed was likely to be far too overwhelming and costly for a house with a price tag that was already over our budget, especially now that our budget was lower than before, due to the extra trip to San Francisco for the funeral.

After some further thought, we decided to contact the realtor for an appointment anyway; I was more optimistic than Jeanette about the possibility of discovering exciting potential once we'd had a chance to look around inside the house. We agreed to meet him at the house at two o'clock on Tuesday afternoon.

That whole week (except Tuesday afternoon) I again had Stig Svensson as my pupil. By this time, he'd already transformed several of my pencil drawings into laminates, with mostly excellent results. He was curious to hear about our search for a new home, and pointed out to me that if we were ever going to be needing a new kitchen, that I should seriously consider doing something completely different and special for the countertops and cupboard doors: laminated original drawings. He offered to supply me a whole roll of impregnated décor paper in just about any background color I wanted, and I could make my drawings directly on it. He seemed almost more excited about the prospect than I was.

At about 1:30 PM on the Tuesday, as Jeanette and I were heading down the stairs to meet the realtor at the house on Korngatan, we encountered three girls, perhaps 10-15 years old, brightly and flamboyantly dressed in the manner of gypsies, merrily heading up the stairs. We thought it was strange, since we didn't know them, and they didn't live in the building, and there was nobody else living there either. But we were in a hurry and quickly forgot about it.

[*As I write this, in 2016, the jury still seems to be out on whether "gypsy" is to be deemed a derogatory term to be added to the growing list of words condemned (by whatever "authorities" appoint themselves to rule over language) as "politically incorrect", even though the word is still often used by many members of that ethnic group. The word "Romani" was unknown to me in 1975 and for many years thereafter; it hadn't yet had time to be added to that blacklist. Let me emphasize that I neither meant nor mean anything derogatory about that ethnic group which, like all other ethnic groups to walk the face of the earth, includes individuals from across the entire moral spectrum.*]

When the realtor showed up punctually (that in itself was a relief) and took us inside, we were pretty stunned.[64] The room immediately to the right had a concrete floor that was somewhat elevated, thus making the ceiling low. One of the three windows facing the street was mostly boarded up to accommodate extra

---

64 See Appendix 1

electrical cabinets; the premises had been used as small mechanical workshops for decades, and hadn't served as a residence for some 30-40 years!

The room to the left on entering from the street had a wooden floor that appeared to have absorbed years of grease and machine oil spillage. There was some water damage in the part of the floor nearest the street, beneath a section of the ceiling that also showed the telltale stains of water damage. The rest of the downstairs was rather dark and gloomy. There were three very rusty kerosene burners, and a grime-encrusted toilet in a completely dark and dusty little room, with no running water. A door at the back led out into a small courtyard, and beyond it was a low two-storey building in equally forlorn shape.

To the left, occupying half the space between the two buildings, was a wooden garage where a man was welding something. The realtor explained that the garage and the "little house" were being rented out to a branch of a Finnish-based company called Kone. I knew them as an elevator company; this particular branch did mechanical repairs to small parts used in harbor cranes. The courtyard half of that space was full of empty or broken pallets, pieces of scrap metal, and broken bits of the cracked, disintegrating concrete surface of the courtyard itself, with that big iron gate out to Källargatan.

Inside the little house, to the left upon entering, was a low-ceilinged (1.8 m) enclosed space that the realtor called a room, with a crumbling concrete floor, a long workbench and a doorway connecting it directly to the garage – an extension of the workshop. To the right of the entrance was a tiny cubbyhole (another "room" where I couldn't stand upright) full of torn-up boxes, and an even tinier "closet" (in the sense of WC) at the far end of it, containing an aging toilet (apparently functional) and a cold water supply in a tiny filthy sink. Cold, disintegrating concrete floors covered the downstairs. The upstairs of the little house was divided into two rooms, the larger of which was being used as a primitive office, and the other as a makeshift kitchen – with cold running water and a sink.

The only entrance to the upstairs part of the big house was through a door outside, in the corner of the courtyard and up a steep stairway, which led to a relatively large north-facing room (*my future studio?!*) with a low flat ceiling. The southern half, under the steeply sloping roof, was divided into three small rooms that felt tiny because the slope of the ceiling flattened out halfway up and became very low, barely high enough for me to stand up straight. The wooden floors were badly mutilated, as though someone had been dragging huge anvils back and forth across them.

Jeanette and I were growing paler and paler, not only from the raw January chill, but from the daunting scope of the project this property represented. We didn't know what to say to the realtor, or to each other, and we told him we'd need to think about it. He suggested that the owner might be willing to negotiate the price a little, but it seemed to us that it would be too expensive even if we got it the property for free. On our way home, we decided that we'd just have to keep looking.

When we'd almost reached the top of the stairs at Vårgatan and saw the door to our apartment, our blood froze. The window in the door was smashed, and there was glass all over the place. Our hearts were pounding – the unknown burglars could still be in there – but the door was still locked. (We didn't immediately make the connection to the girls we'd seen when we left an hour or so before.) We made noise and listened for scurrying before I unlocked the door, but there were no sounds coming from our place. As much of our hair as had the strength to do so was standing on end.

A year or so earlier, we took the precaution of installing a security lock in the front door, so it couldn't be opened (even from the inside) without a key – it wasn't enough to smash the window and reach through to open the door. Without a key, it remained locked. We surmised that whoever had entered was thus obliged to do so through the fairly narrow window. No grown-up could fit through that narrow window opening; it must have been one of more of those girls. We unlocked the door and entered, still *very* cautiously. The door from the kitchen to the narrow back spiral stairway, which we never used, was open: *that* was their escape route.

Once we'd ascertained that nobody was still in our apartment, we tried to calm ourselves and each other enough to try to figure out what was missing: whatever cash they could find, not a great deal; the remaining traveler's checks from our trip to Rome, which we presumed would be fairly easy to get reimbursed for; a couple of good watches, one of which I'd inherited from Dad; and a few other small items.

One other thing was more significant. Jeanette had lost a fair amount of weight in recent months (she'd never been overweight), and her diamond engagement and wedding rings were now too loose for her to wear without the risk of them falling off, so she'd put them in a drawer until she could get around to having them refitted. They were gone, and were probably worth quite a lot; the prices of gold and diamonds had roughly tripled since I bought them in December 1965.

But we were greatly relieved that they hadn't touched my paintings, and that they'd left our stereo, our record collection, as well as cameras and various other items that might have been easy to fence; they were probably in a great hurry. I boarded up the door *securely*, but for rather many nights we awoke at the slightest noise and lay there listening, pulses racing, for quite a long time. Now we *really* had to get out of there!

The experience didn't exactly make the house at Korngatan 12 more attractive, but it certainly made it a helluva lot less *un*attractive! There was never any question about its potential: it was almost as centrally located as our apartment and offered about three times the living space. A lot to do? So what?!

But the purchase price was still prohibitive, and we didn't yet know where we stood regarding reimbursement for the rings. The insurance company wanted proof, and we managed to find the receipts among our old papers, as well as a photo. When we got married, we (or rather Jeanette's parents) hired a professional wedding photographer. One of the photos she'd arranged showed our hands clasped together, rings clearly visible. We hoped that the photo, together with the receipt for the ring itself, would be sufficient proof.

In the meantime, we felt we had to make a move on that house on Korngatan. We figured we had nothing to lose by making a bold offer, so we called the realtor and offered half the original asking price: 40,000 kronor. Even if the insurance company didn't come through, we could afford that; we had 56,000 kronor saved up, so we still had some negotiating room as well. The realtor sounded skeptical that the owner would accept our offer, but said he'd forward it to the owner and get back to us.

On Monday, January 27th, the realtor February phoned back to say that although the owner wouldn't agree to 40,000, he (the realtor) felt there was a good chance that the owner might meet us halfway, at 60,000 kronor. We gulped and said OK. The realtor phoned the owner, and soon phoned us back to say that our offer had been accepted – we'd bought ourselves a house! When the mail arrived that very same day, it included an answer from the insurance company: we'd be reimbursed 8,000 kronor for our stolen property – we'd be able to pay the full amount for the house, all on our own, and have 4,000 kronor left over!

There was some comic relief during all this high drama. The previous Saturday evening we were among eight or ten people invited to Hamadi's apartment (which also served as his school, my place of work) on Limhamnsvägen for a small party to meet his bride, Saloua. Jeanette and I arrived punctually and were thus among the first to arrive (in breach of another Swedish tradition of arriving a little later than the appointed time – how contrary to my upbringing!). Saloua was tall, statuesque, young and stunning, a real fashion-model beauty. I knew by this time that those qualities were sufficient to have Jeanette watching me like a hawk. I wanted to be polite and friendly without waking Jeanette's green monster. Saloua spoke very little English, and my French was rusty, so most of the conversation had to go through Hamadi.

As soon as we were seated on the sofa, I asked her, in carefully enunciated English, whether she was hoping to become a pharmacist in Sweden. Hamadi didn't translate; instead he almost jumped out of his seat, flashed an extremely agitated look at me, and motioned for me to follow him into the next room. "*No!!*" he hissed urgently. "*She's not that one! The pharmacist was already taken, so I married this one instead!*" There have been few occasions in my life when it has been more difficult to contain the urge to roar and howl with laughter – and few occasions where laughter would have been less appropriate.

The house transaction was not entirely free of red tape. Since we weren't Swedish citizens, we needed to apply for a property acquisition permit (*förvärvstillstånd*). The sale was contingent on our getting this permit. The good news was that in order to encourage and stimulate property owners to reduce energy consumption following the 1973 Oil Crisis, the Swedish government had recently instituted a program of heavily subsidized homeowner loans for that purpose, something we would desperately need if we were going to afford renovation, so our purchase agreement was also contingent on our being granted such a loan. Moreover, Kone, the current tenants of the house (the workshop) had to be given notice that their tenancy would end by March 31st, another codicil in the contract. But these were minor things.

When I told Henry about the house we'd found, he blanched. *Kirseberg!?* This same gut reaction would recur when we told Elsa and virtually every other acquaintance we had who came from Malmö. They all seemed to know something we had no idea about: that Kirseberg was a lawless neighborhood that outsiders entered at their peril. (*Worse than the Tenderloin!*, I thought. *Why does this keep happening?!*) We would later discover that Kirseberg's frightening reputation was formed in the early 1900s, when it was separated from Malmö by farmland, when poverty there was rampant, and outsiders indeed risked being beaten up if they were caught "trespassing". It's just that Malmö in the early 1900s and Malmö in the 1970s had little in common. As a result, most of those who'd bought and revamped houses in Kirseberg in the 1970s and 80s came from other parts of Sweden (as well as Denmark), not from other parts of Malmö. By the mid-1980s, Kirseberg had morphed into an attractive part of town – except in the eyes of old-time Malmö residents. Bad reputations die hard.

When Henry came with me to look at the house on February 9th, he was wearing his construction engineer's glasses and saw only the house itself, its few strengths and its multiplicity of weaknesses. In his slow, measured way, he systematically pointed out every visible area of concern and suggested what other lurking problems we might expect to encounter once hidden faults were exposed. While he was telling me all this, he looked at me frequently, perhaps to see whether his gloomy assessments had penetrated my optimism, perhaps to see at what point I'd break. But I couldn't wait to get started. How else was I ever going to finish?

Two days later, we met with the realtor to sign some papers and make a down-payment of 5,000 kronor, in cash (we'd redeposited the 7,000 in cash for what was to have been the down-payment on Sandgatan). The official handover date was set for April 1st, by which time the tenants (Kone) would have cleared out, we would have received the money from the insurance settlement, and we could pay the balance of 55,000 kronor. We were also thrilled that we'd be able to manage it without borrowing a cent from our mothers or anyone else. Bob told us we could count on some financial support, but I quickly told him we'd covered it. (Banks were totally uninterested in lending money for such a presumably foolhardy project, especially to people with our paltry incomes and frightening lack of assets or construction experience.)

We heard from Mom that my brother John had found a new job in the Bay Area, so he and his family would shortly be pulling up roots from LA and moving to a house in Novato, a town in Marin County, just across the Golden Gate from San Francisco. Al would also be moving to a new and larger house about a mile from their previous one in Bellevue, Washington (just east of Seattle), later that year; and Mom would be moving to Knoxville. Even Marilyn would be moving from San Francisco to San Bruno, a bit to the south.

It should have been, might have been, a time of almost unmitigated joy for us: finding a house with great potential, launching a big and exciting project together, having managed to scrape together enough to do it on our own, loving each other. And indeed there was a lot of joy and love and lots of wonderful peaks. But then there were those troughs, when Jeanette's behavior became so inexplicably hostile and destructive – especially *self*-destructive.

At some point during this period, I painted the last painting I would ever paint at Vårgatan 4A. In the lower-right foreground is an anguished person, reaching out as if to grab the void in a kind of dance of death. An inaccessible stairway emerges from the void or extends into it. I call it *Despair*.[65] [*Reflecting on it while writing* Hindsights, *it becomes clear to me, or at least theoretically plausible, that I was often subconsciously painting Jeanette's innermost feelings, while remaining unconscious of their depth myself – a very chilling thought.*]

Although we had *just* enough money to pay for the house, we had hardly anything left for the massive restoration job that awaited us – the magnitude of which was completely unknown to us. If we *had* known, we'd undoubtedly have backed away from the project, walked away, run away head over heels. But now we were committed and had to press on.

The house as it stood had no insulation anywhere, and that fact alone entitled us to apply for that advantageous government loan. We wanted to borrow as little as possible in order to keep our fixed costs down, so we asked for 70,000 kronor. We also had to apply to the municipality for a building permit, and in both cases we needed drawings of what the house looked like externally (façade drawings from all sides) and how it was laid out (floor plans, upstairs and downstairs), both in its existing state, and how we intended it to look when finished.[66]

First I made crude sketches of everything, then Jeanette and I took all the measurements and added them to the sketches. Next I sat down and converted the sketches into fairly accurate scale drawings, and Jeanette joined me in planning what rooms we wanted to have where. Once we were done, I made a new set of scale drawings, and took them all to Henry, who got his company's team of draftsmen to turn my small-scale drawings into official, professional, architectural drawings, the kind that would impress the pants off the people who issue permits.

---

65 Painting #77 (see Appendix 2)
66 See Appendix 1

Henry told us that one of the terms of the government loan (he said he'd been expecting us to borrow *at least* triple the amount we were asking for) was that the work should be completed within two years from the date of the permit, whereas the municipal building permit had an indefinite completion date. We were concerned about managing all of it within that timeframe, and I wondered if it were possible to get a permit for the government loan based only on the big house, but to get the city permit for both buildings, right from the start. Henry said he'd talk to them about it. Henry also helped us apply for the property acquisition permit. Thanks to his kind help, everything about the house was running smoothly.

On Thursday, February 20th, the realtor phoned to see how the paperwork and permits were coming along, and we told him everything was on track. He said he'd spoken to the owner, who in turn spoke to the current tenants, who said they had no objections if we wanted to get going on ripping stuff out of the big house (the tenants' rental contract didn't extend to the big house anyway). If we wished, we could pick up a spare key from the current tenants at any time. We were thrilled. He also said that the tenants promised to take all their junk and scrap and tools and equipment with them by end of March.

On Sunday, February 23rd, we invited Henry and his wife Elsa to Vårgatan for a lasagne dinner in the early afternoon. They accepted enthusiastically (they knew Jeanette's cooking, and were very curious to know the latest on our massive project). Henry asked if we'd gotten our own key yet and sounded pleased that we had. When they arrived, I presented them with one of my favorite paintings – *Sun, Plant and Lamp* (#31) – as a gesture of gratitude for Henry's many kindnesses and practical help with the house, drawings, paperwork etc. I discussed the gift with Jeanette first, and reluctant as she was to part with any of my paintings, she agreed that in this special case it would be "appropriate". Although neither Henry nor Elsa had ever expressed much interest in my paintings, they seemed genuinely delighted.

Jeanette used a lasagne recipe she'd "inherited" from her mother, allegedly going back to her mother's Italian ancestors (which ones – from Naples or Sicily or Wappingers Falls – I don't know). The meat sauce was made with ground beef (browned in olive oil), lots of finely chopped onions, numerous cloves of crushed garlic, lots of red wine, crushed tomatoes, tomato purée and copious quantities of herbs: basil, oregano, marjoram, thyme, tarragon, rosemary, bay leaves and any other herbs she felt like throwing in; and a dash of sugar. There was no *béchamel*.

It was just alternate layers of meat sauce, lasagne pasta, and thinly sliced hard cheese, layer after layer, with a little grated parmesan on top (or added to the individual portions when served).

They loved it, of course, but Henry seemed to be in a bit of a hurry. As soon as we finished, he said he'd like to show our new home to Elsa, and could we please cycle over there while they drove? It sounded like a strange request, but we took our bikes and hurried on over. A minute later, they pulled up – not in Henry's usual big Mercedes, but in a pick-up truck! In the back, Henry had a truckload of gifts for us, including a used but sturdy wheelbarrow, a big iron pike (I didn't even know what it was for) and a heavy-duty sledgehammer! After a quick tour of the place (Elsa's eyes were wide in disbelief and semi-shock), we returned to Vårgatan for dessert and to pick up their painting.

On Thursday, February 27th, we gave three months' notice on our apartment. Our plan was to move out as soon as we could, but to keep the apartment until the end of May, so we would have a place to go back to and cook hot meals, have a bath after a dirty, sweaty day. (We were *certain* we'd have made enough progress to be able to cook and take showers by the time we left our old apartment. *Ha!*) During these three months, we'd take a new load of our possessions each day, in bags hanging on our handlebars and in a box on the rack on the back of each of our bikes, thus gradually transferring everything before we had to vacate our apartment for good.

Jeanette and I (or sometimes just me) were now going to the house whenever we found a few extra hours, ripping out everything that was cracked and broken in the main building (which we soon began calling "the big house"). That turned out to mean nearly *everything*. We started upstairs. The low, patchwork ceilings consisted of plasterboard in some places and old tongue-and-groove paneling in others (I rescued what paneling I could for later use). One section of the ceiling was of pure plaster applied on chicken wire and straw that was nailed onto rough-hewn boards, which in turn were nailed to the undersides of the tie beams. The space above that section and above the tie beams was empty – except for copious quantities of ashes, dirt and dust. Removing the ceilings was incredibly filthy, but made a huge difference: it opened up to the peak of the roof and suddenly made the rooms feel bigger and airier (once the dust had cleared).

The roof of the big house was originally an A-frame, but some previous owner (probably in the early 1900s) decided to build up the entire wall between the houses to a height of two meters, in order to increase the living space upstairs, and to put an upstairs door into the wall along the courtyard, accessed by a second staircase outdoors. The courtyard staircase and door had been removed by a subsequent owner, but it was possible to see where the door had been.

The big problem resulting from raising that wall was that the house was no longer an A-frame, which meant that all those tie beams no longer tied to anything. A load-bearing brick wall divided the downstairs lengthwise into two halves. When they took away the A-frame upstairs, they simply added a second story to that brick wall, up to the height of where the tie beams had been, and rested those beams on the new wall. Then they hid the rest with the low ceilings. But since the tie beams were no longer tied and the roof beams were insufficiently supported higher up, they'd made pillars of *loose* bricks (no mortar whatsoever!) on the brick wall directly beneath each roof beam, to provide additional "support". And that wall had several major full-height cracks....

The roof above one of the two dormer windows upstairs, facing the street, had clearly been leaking for a long time. The floor beneath the leak was rotting, which explained the water damage in the ceiling downstairs, as well as the rot in many of the downstairs floorboards. I would have to start by rebuilding both dormer windows, which I probably would have had to do at some point anyway, since they were too narrow to allow any insulation. Then I would have to remove the rotten or water-damaged upstairs floorboards to be able to check the beams that supported them (and repair or replace those that might be rotten).

Downstairs, it was obvious that the oil-drenched, rotting floorboards on the one side would have to go. It was equally obvious that on the other side, the horrible concrete floor would have to go. That would take a jack-hammer. And what kind of floor did we want to have instead? For one thing, it had to be a lot lower (since we couldn't make the ceiling any higher). Conversations I'd been having with some of my pupils and with Henry indicated that once we'd cleared out all that was there, and maybe dug out a little more, we could put down a special kind of compressed mineral wool insulation, then place some steel reinforcement mesh on top of it, and finally pour a concrete slab to get a level, insulated, structurally sound floor. On top of that we could lay floor tiles, preferably not too dark, but more or less brick-like in format. We didn't want very low, head-banging ceilings downstairs, and since we did want under-floor insulation, but didn't want the risks entailed by going below the ground level, the kind of floor construction Henry suggested seemed to be our only choice.

One block from the language school, at Tessins väg 2, I'd seen a fairly big store specializing in floor tiles, where on March 8th we found just what we were looking for. The quality was Höganäs (a Swedish brand with a sterling reputation), the color was variable shades of ochre, and the format was perfect. Because they were not part of the standard Höganäs range – the color was an experimental run – they were on offer for about a third of the normal price. We told the proprietor we wanted 70 square meters of them, but would prefer not to take delivery for about six months. He laughed and said they could hold them for one month at most, and that I would need to make a down-payment the following week, which I did on the Tuesday.

At the far end of Korngatan, meaning four doors down from us, lived a single woman in her 30s whose father apparently owned several properties in the area, and manufactured display-window mannequins (*skyltdockor* in Swedish). One of those properties had at one time been the house on Sandgatan that we almost purchased. Jeanette was quick to spot the daughter, our neighbor, and dubbed her *Skyltdockan*. This woman, whose name I don't remember, was blonde and normally dressed in painted-on jeans. She was, in my view, exceptionally *unattractive* and tacky, who walked with her nose in the air as though the world were falling at her feet, or at least should have been. For some reason I could never understand, she instantly became a trigger for Jeanette's extreme jealousy; her suspicions began brewing and rumbling, and I thought *Oh no, not again*.

I didn't know how to handle it. I tried the rational approach; I was totally *un*attracted, even repulsed. That brought an accusation: *You're lying!* Anything I said to try to make Jeanette see how totally unfounded her feelings were only inflamed her anger. I couldn't understand her, couldn't deal with her rage, and we'd both end up upset as hell. And then it would end, abruptly. It was "just" in her mind, she said. This gut-wrenching drama exploded over and over, and we were none the wiser for it. I had no clue about how to prevent it from recurring, and Jeanette repeatedly refused my every suggestion of counselling.

There were so many times when I (and sometimes we) just had to sit down and wonder what the hell we'd been thinking. I sometimes wondered how those Swedes – my mom's grandparents – who'd emigrated from Sweden to America in the 1860s – must have felt when they arrived in the "rough and ready" American frontier, not speaking the language, barely a penny to their names, knowing nobody, every last thing strange and threatening, many out to trick and deceive them. I think we understood *something* of those feelings, and certainly a whole lot more than we'd understood before we took upon ourselves the roles of immigrants and settlers.

Starting March 10th, I had a full week of teaching; in fact, it was my fifth straight week of full-time work. We needed the money to buy building materials, after all. My pupil that fifth week was Annika, a pretty girl about my age, from Kramfors in Norrland. She was an eager learner. I left our apartment every morning at half past eight, cycled across town, through Slottsparken, to Hamadi's school (now also home to Saloua). Annika and I had our lessons in the classroom, went to Per's Krog for lunch, and usually took a long walk afterwards before going back to the classroom, and before I cycled home at half past five.

On the Thursday I became aware that she was flirting with me, or that her flirting of previous days was now too obvious even for me not to notice.

After lunch on Friday, while on a walk in Slottsparken after lunch, she suddenly pulled me around, leaned in and kissed me. My brain, except for my libido (if that counts as brain – it felt like it was somewhere else) shut down, slammed shut, right then and there, and I kissed her back. We ended up walking quickly to her hotel, where we spent the afternoon doing everything we shouldn't. It was very erotic. She kept telling me I was wonderful. I kept thinking that it felt wonderful – purely (or impurely) physically – but was otherwise just terribly confusing. I was trying to find ways of rationalizing to myself something that I absolutely should not have done. *Jeanette's so jealous anyway, I might as well do something to deserve it!* That lame excuse worked for me, for a few minutes. Then I felt awful again. I'd cheated on the one woman I'd ever truly loved. What an incredible, pathetic jerk I was!!

I'd heard many times about couples who practiced "tell each other everything", but I'd never heard of any good ever coming from that. The truth isn't always liberating; it sometime enslaves people to painful memories that can never be obliterated, to words that can never be unspoken, to mental images that can never be eradicated, to remorse, recriminations, longstanding distrust and heartache, and outright downright anguish. I'd had enough experience in concealing my ill deeds at The Emporium from others (except Jeanette), so I resolved not to cause her even more pain by forcing her to deal with something in reality that she didn't even know was there for her to deal with in her fantasy. And perhaps the efforts I made to repress the memory of my foolish philandering helped me to control my wandering eye and to deal with Jeanette's unabated bouts of jealousy; after all, I could no longer think of them as unreasonable, could I?

[*Looking back at myself, my deeds and misdeeds more than four decades ago, I often shake my head in disbelief and disapproval. I could easily have simply skipped writing about things I'm not proud of having done. But I did them. Do I dare to write about them only because I found it unlikely – at the time I first wrote them – that my writings would ever be published? I hope that is not the reason; writing honestly about the person I was is now much more important to me than writing only about the person I should have been. But it's quite possible that I felt greater freedom to write with uncompromising honesty than I would have if I felt or knew it would be published, in much the same way as I felt greater freedom to paint what I needed to paint thanks to not feeling obliged to sell.*]

The next day, Saturday, brought good news and bad news. The bad news was that *both* of our bikes had been stolen during the night, and we had to find replacements immediately, since they were our only means of independent transportation, apart from walking. The good news was that American Express reimbursed us for the stolen traveler's checks, *and* the insurance company paid our claim, meaning that we now had the money to cover the balance on our house that was due two weeks later. Moreover, we received our *förvärvstillstånd* – we now had the government permit to buy the property.

I had my sixth and final consecutive week of full-time work the following week. Then, armed with photos and drawings, we were off to see Bob for a week. We had a pleasantly uneventful time in Binningen, with a lot of music and Jeanette's good cooking, some intensive cleaning and sorting, and plenty of good conversation. Bob's interest in Watergate had more or less faded out, like that epic scandal itself. Much of the talk was about our new house, and Bob seemed to be nearly as thrilled as we were – and he was a lot more curious than he'd been at first. For us, it was more like the calm before the storm, the lightning in the distance that crashes all around you minutes later.

We got back home on Sunday, March 30th, and started making lists of everything we would bring with us to the house once the deal was sealed. The next day I went to the bank to withdraw nearly all our money in cash, in order to make the final payment the next day. To avoid being burdened with too thick a wad of cash, I asked to have the 55,000 kronor in the form of five 1,000 kronor bills and five 10,000 kronor bills – the first and only time I would ever handle that larger denomination. The 10,000-kronor bills were gigantic: 210x121 millimeters. Before heading out for our rendezvous with the realtor and the seller at a café on Södergatan, close to Stortorget, at one o'clock, I carefully folded up the big bills. I put an empty envelope in the pocket of my sport jacket, but instead of putting the money there as well, I put it in my shoe. (I'd never heard of anyone getting "pickshoed".) We arrived early at the café so I could air the money before putting it into the plain envelope.

The seller, whom we met for the first and only time, was an elderly man named Knut Englesson (he was representing the actual owner, his sister). He told us that our house was at some point in its history locally known as "Järnbagareborg" – "Iron-Baker Fortress" – because it was once owned by a scrap-iron dealer who became a baker (or vice-versa), and that the house had something of the look of a fortress, due to its large, windowless end-wall façade and big iron gate. To any outsider, the meeting at the café would have looked completely unspectacular. The only unusual thing was that we all signed a document or two, and I handed the seller an envelope, which he inspected (without smelling). But to us, Tuesday, April 1st was high drama, a milestone in our lives. There was no turning back.

Henry then helped us to obtain special permission from the municipal authorities to be allowed to start working on the house before the building permit was finalized. Now that the tenants were gone, we were doubly eager to begin. They'd duly taken all their stuff with them except for a sturdy vice that was bolted to a worn-out workbench in the room they'd been using downstairs in the little house. The bench looked like thick (about 8 cm), hard wood with severe acne (and gangrene in places).

After signing the papers and making the payment, Jeanette and I cycled over to the house – *our* house! – to get a better look at the parts the tenants vacated, and to see how we most quickly and easily could transform those close quarters into a temporary place where we could stay while working on the rest. The upstairs – the former small office and even smaller coffee-break room, was the only possibility for that. Although the roof sloped, the ceiling below it was flat and low (I could bump my head on it if I stood on tiptoe) and sagging somewhat, despite there being no insulation at all. The whole roof would have to be raised some day, but the full restoration of the *little* house was going to be a totally separate project from the *big* house, so that aspect of it had to be put on ice.

But as a temporary solution to give ourselves temporary living quarters at the site, we bought a couple of large cans of cheap, white, interior paint for all the walls and ceilings upstairs (except for the rough-cut panel-clad end wall in the office). The office, about 5½ x 3½ meters, would have to become our living room *and* bedroom *and* closet. If we sacrificed one meter of the length of that room by putting up a curtain (an arras?), and a sturdy rod on which to hang our clothes, we could put our black leather sofa along the curtain, and still have room for our small desk, our stereo, a small table, and our black leather easy chair, plus just enough free floor space to pull the sofa cushions down onto the floor to serve as our temporary bed (as we'd been doing in Binningen). We also used one of our four trunks (the black one I'd bought for moving from Oak Park to San Francisco) as a coffee table. And we ripped out the forest-green wall-to-wall carpeting we'd installed ourselves at Vårgatan, in order to hide the grimy, broken linoleum that was currently covering the floor in our new quarters.

The former coffee-break room would become our interim kitchen. There was already a filthy stainless-steel sink with cold running water. (A once-over with steel wool helped a lot.) The sink was mounted onto a cabinet in the far corner, beneath a small window overlooking Källargatan. That was, in fact, the only window along that entire Källargatan façade. We'd bring as many of our kitchen cabinets from Vårgatan as we could fit in (including two drawer cabinets), as well as our relatively big fridge, and our small table with two pull-out leaf extensions (which would have to remain unextended), our four chairs, and the terracotta-colored carpeting from our apartment living room. Then, all we'd need was a small countertop stove with two burners and a tiny oven, and we'd have a fairly functional kitchen, around 3 x 3½ meters.

Making use of the cozy fluorescent lighting fixtures in both rooms, we started painting that same evening. We didn't need to be too careful – everything was going to be white anyway, and the ugly floor was soon going to be covered. We finished rolling on the first coat late that evening; we were both glowing.

A second coat was a must, and it went even more quickly the next day; we'd both taken the week off. I measured the cabinets we had in our kitchen on Vårgatan, and we worked out how many we could fit in without making the floor space too small for the table and chairs. We also decided that we'd have to use the former workshop downstairs as a storage room for everything we couldn't fit into the two small rooms upstairs: most of the paintings, the three remaining big trunks (filled with dishes, rugs, utensils, extra bedding, and extra clothing), as well as nearly all the books (meaning close to 70 new cartons from Systembolaget). Once the second coat of painting was done, we went back to Vårgatan and began cutting the carpets to get pieces of sufficient size to cover the floors in the two rooms.

On the Thursday, we put up the curtain rods and the clothing rod in our new living quarters. Henry told us that as of late Friday afternoon, after working hours, we would have the use of the pick-up he and Elsa used some weeks before to deliver our wheelbarrow. He would even have the building workers deliver the pick-up to Vårgatan – what an incredible help! And he told us we'd be able to borrow it again once in a while. What an amazingly kind man he was!

We immediately began loading up the pick-up with the carpets and kitchen cabinets, the sofa, the biggest paintings (*A Cry, Man Reading a Book, the Midian Children* and *Funeral*), and one of the trunks, down five flights of stairs. When it was time to load the paintings, Jeanette waited by the van while I scurried up and down the stairs; we were still a little paranoid. Then we took off for Korngatan. It was possible to open both halves of the big iron gate and drive the pick-up right into the courtyard, which facilitated unloading considerably.

When I came back downstairs from the little house after having left off a couple of cabinets, I suddenly heard a deep, rough, strange, clearly drunken male voice booming, "*Välkomna till Backarna!*" ("Welcome to 'The Hills,'" the name the locals used for Kirseberg.) It got my adrenalin pumping, but fortunately my response was neither flight nor fight this time. I spun around to face a huge bear of a man, scruffily clad, severely unshaven, coarse, thick features – with a huge outstretched hand and an impishly inebriated, silly smile.

His voice was severely slurred, as if he'd woken up from having been in hibernation with a drip bag of vodka. His eyes were blurry and baggy, and he seemed to stagger even while standing still. But he was as gentle as a lamb and was just trying to be neighborly, seemingly unaware of his startling, frightening aspect. His name was Ivan (all associations with Ivan the Terrible are purely coincidental). He explained that he and his wife lived in the house diagonally opposite ours, on Källargatan, and that their daughter and her family lived next door. He was at least sufficiently sober to realize how frantically busy we were, so he waved goodbye and shuffled out of the courtyard. I then took the precaution of closing the gate.

When we'd finished unloading everything and had it all pretty much in place, we were pleased to see that our things fit the way we'd hoped they would. We were exhausted, and it was now dark. We drove back to Vårgatan, took a bath, and Jeanette made dinner. After dinner, we loaded a few more things into the back of the pick-up, drove back to Korngatan, and spent our first overwhelmingly exciting night ever in our new home, lying on the sofa cushions on the floor, in each other's arms, listening to (and for) all the new sounds, on Friday, April 4th, 1975.

CHAPTER 11

Tearing

It took quite a long time to learn to tell where sounds were coming from at our new home. There were stone or brick walls everywhere, not only the walls of our own two houses, but those in unbroken rows along the narrow streets of the neighborhood. The sounds didn't echo, they bounced, they caromed – and they kept us guessing.

First thing on Saturday morning, April 5th, we drove back to Vårgatan to have breakfast, fill up the pick-up, and take off again. While unloading each new round, we began meeting several more new neighbors, who strolled into the courtyard, mostly one at a time, to see who these new people on the block were. Some of them in turn informed us about other neighbors who *didn't* stop by. We weren't used to having neighbors, or at least any *contact* with neighbors, at any of the places we'd ever lived (apart from the Falcones in Vancouver, of course, but they were also our landlords), so it was something of a novel experience for us.

Our first visitor that Saturday morning was a Danish neighbor who lived in one of the few houses in the neighborhood that was already beautifully restored. He'd done nearly all the work himself. His name was Tage Thagaard, a photographer by trade, now semi-retired. (His name is pronounced something like TA-geh TA-gored; *aa* in Danish corresponds to the Swedish å and is pronounced something like a long *o*. In Danish, the single *a* is pronounced something like the *a* in *apple*.) Tage closely resembled the head of Sweden's small Communist party, C H Hermansson (whose views Tage shared). He was mild-mannered and pleasant, and said he guessed we'd soon be needing a large dumpster to get rid of all the debris we'd already begun accumulating in the big house. He gave me the name and phone number of a guy who provided dumpster service for just 50 kronor for a large 10-cubic-meter bin, to be parked on the sidewalk outside our gate until we phoned to say it was full, whereupon it would magically be picked up, emptied, and returned for the next round of rubble and the next 50 kronor.

Tage told me he'd been through all the steps of restoring old houses and wondered if we had any thoughts about modernizing. I told him we wanted modern appliances and heating, as well as plenty of thermal insulation, but otherwise we were hoping to do everything in the old style, with emphasis on restoration, not modernization. I thought he would start jumping up and down, he seemed so pleased. He also said he had lots of connections and tips about where to find bargains on building materials, or reliable craftsmen for jobs I couldn't do myself. (I was certain we'd need an electrician, a plumber, and a tinsmith.) How wonderful to have met such a neighborly neighbor! If only it wasn't so difficult for me to understand his Danish-Swedish!

The neighbor directly behind us, and directly across Källargatan from Tage, was a grumpy-looking (and -acting) geezer by the name of Ivarsson. He was a real busybody who sneered at everybody (Tage in particular) and everything. The sound of a car door closing in the street brought him out to the sidewalk in a flash to stare and glare with undisguised hostility at the new arrival, as though his personal domain had been rudely invaded. (He seemed to regard the whole of Backarna as his personal and private domain.) He neither smiled nor waved, nor did he make any attempt to control his snarling stare. He just stood there, glaring daggers. At least he didn't say much.

His house was of brick, but the color must have displeased him, because he painted it all a glossy crimson, then painted all the mortar gray. It was always flaking, and he was extremely pedantic about maintaining his chosen level of ugliness. He was out there most days (except in the winter) with his little can of paint and paintbrush, touching up the crimson and gray, glaring at all passers-by.

Ivarsson's grumpiness was similar in intensity to that of a somewhat elderly lady who lived a couple of doors down on Sandgatan (next door to the house we almost bought), but her grumpiness was the outspoken kind. She had highly vocal views about everything and everybody (especially Tage), and none of them were good. When she stuck her nose into our yard while passing by sometime that weekend, she had two proclamations to issue: one was that we *had* to use Mexitegel on the entire façade. (Mexitegel was a rough-hewn white flint-lime brick imitation that had about the same aesthetic appeal as a seagull turd on a pizza, in addition to which this 1960s material was as suitable for the restoration of an 1860s house as it would have been to paint an Edsel into a Rembrandt painting.) Her second message was that we should avoid any contact with "*that horrible Thagaard*", whose name she had no intention of pronouncing correctly, and who was, she alleged, trying to destroy the neighborhood with his careful selection of materials, tasteful designs and historically appropriate methods. For perhaps the first year, I was given to believe that her name was Kärringen Wijk (Wijk is pronounced "veek"; I surmised that she had a Dutch ancestor somewhere back there), because most of the other neighbors I spoke with referred to her that way (it roughly translates as "Wijk the Bitch"; "kärring" means "old hag"). She was just as vehemently *certain* about her twisted edicts and judgments as a significant number of Christian Evangelicals I'd met.

Directly across the street from our gate lived a couple in their 60s. He was a lineman for the phone company, back in the day when the phone company – Televerket – was the Swedish *national* phone company. (This was shortly before the waves of "deregulation" – privatization – swept over Sweden, "deregulation" being a euphemism for "removal of protection", allowing profit-driven business to replace public services that everyone in the society is dependent on: water, sewage, electrical power, phone service, education and health care, etc. All of these would eventually be swept away or weakened, one by one, in the name of "freedom of choice", another euphemism for "you get what you can pay for" or "if you can't afford it, you'll be stuck with a second-rate alternative." So why deregulate/privatize? Sweden had very high taxes – but very high national standards of education, healthcare etc. After all, such public services cost money, and that money comes from taxes. But the wealthier people become, the more they seem to begrudge paying taxes to provide a high standard of public service to *everyone*. If you lower taxes – which the Conservatives were always clamoring for, then the standards of public services will be lower – for everyone. Unless you deregulate. Then you can have alternative services that not everyone can afford, but the wealthy will retain their high level, and their taxes will be lower. OK, the less wealthy will sometimes have to settle for a lower level of service, but why would any wealthy person have a problem with *that*?)

But I digress: those neighbors' names were Gustaf and Magna Jeppsson. He had a grumpy exterior but a heart of gold; she was solid gold. They kept pretty much to themselves, mostly out of respect for others' privacy (or perhaps they were just shy), but they gradually opened up to us.

Next to the Jeppssons lived an old man, alone except for his collection of pigeons – not only in a shed-sized coop in the yard, but apparently with him inside his run-down house as well, judging by the splotches of pigeon shit all over him at all times. We referred to him as the pigeon man; I never heard him say a word (nor a coo).

The three-storey apartment building (from around 1900) opposite Ivarsson on Sandgatan was mostly empty, abandoned. The only tenant I knew of when we moved to Kirseberg was a wizened old man named Axel, who had more pigeon shit on him than the pigeon man. He appeared to be constantly drunk or hung over, and had a visage of unbearable long-term grief and remorse. He managed always to be beyond unshaven yet never quite had a beard, and he always wore the same black overcoat (with whitish pigeon shit like semi-liquid epaulettes pouring over his shoulders) year-round. His approach manifested itself well in advance of his arrival if he was upwind. Perhaps he hadn't bathed for quite a few years. I tried several times to engage him in conversation, to find out if there was some way we could help him with anything, but I never could understand a word of the discombobulated syllables he struggled to emit. Few consonants emerged intact.

Like the properties along Korngatan and Sandgatan, some of the properties along Källargatan consisted of two parallel buildings. Thagaard and his family lived in both of theirs, the Jeppssons and the pigeon man had only one house each, facing the next street over, Kirsebergsgatan (the Jeppssons also had a small garage facing Källargatan). The next property along Källargatan, next to the pigeon man's, also comprised two houses, both owned by the Rundströms, a family of five. The wife was an unusually large woman who seemed to be pleasant, although she kept pretty much to herself. Our initial surprise at her imposing size disappeared once we found out that she was the daughter of Ivan, the mountain-of-a-man, who lived next door to her. But her size became all the more astonishing when we met her husband Klas, who could easily have hidden behind her.

Klas Rundström was the kind of unintentionally comical person you almost had to see to believe. He was probably about five or ten years older than me, incredibly impulsive, and seemed to be doing everything in his power to look like Elvis: the long sideburns, the dark, slicked-back, huge-waved hair, the swagger and the sneer. The fact that he was so short, however, was only one of the differences; he was also so cross-eyed that it was impossible to tell whether he was looking at you or at something quite far in either direction beside you. But I never heard him sing or play a guitar.

He spoke with the broadest Malmö dialect I'd ever heard, causing me to blurt out the Swedish equivalent of *Huh?* after everything he said. A few weeks after a fleeting first meeting, while I was ripping out stuff to throw into our dumpster, Klas knocked on our door. As soon as I answered, and before I had a chance to say hello, he blurted out at high speed, *"Deu, jah hao lide skid, kan jah hodda i bingen?"* I didn't understand a syllable. I just stood there looking like he'd hit me with a fish. *Uhhh...?* I said. He tried again, slowly, for my Yankee benefit. *"Jah* *hao lide skräp, kan jah feå slänga det i din contain*å?" and I was able to guess that he had a little scrap that he wanted to throw into our dumpster.

We'd apparently been dubbed "the Yankees" by our neighbors more or less on arrival, which I suppose was their way of excusing us for failing to understand the local version of the Malmö dialect. We soon realized that most of the Swedish we'd been listening to and learning from came from TV and radio, with a bit more from speaking with people in shops and with a few articulate Swedes like Elsa Braun, Henry and others. But we'd hardly ever spoken Swedish with any neighbors – not at Ehrensvärdsgatan, nor at Vårgatan – and we had some catching up to do on the vernacular, particularly in Kirseberg.

Klas and family lived in the house facing Kirsebergsgatan; the other house on their property – next to Ivan's and facing our corner – was being rented out to a family we never met, never saw, and whom Klas didn't like at all, but whose rental contract he didn't know how to terminate (he frequently anguished about that to me). Then came the house belonging to Ivan; and on the corner up at Vattenverksvägen was a two-storey red brick building (also from the early 1900s) that was a tobacconist's downstairs and one or two small apartments upstairs. Vattenverksvägen was the arterial, with a bus stop in either direction. On the far side of it, bordered by Källargatan and Vattenverksvägen, was the square, Kirsebergstorget. There were commercial buildings along the eastern and southern perimeters, including a Co-op grocery store, a bank, a post office, and a pre- and post-natal clinic. Along the north side of Vattenverksvägen we also had a pharmacy and a bakery. Just about the only amenity we didn't have within 50 meters of our front door was *Systembolaget* (the liquor store), perhaps just as well.

Nobody lived in the house directly opposite ours on Korngatan; it was a one-man perfume manufacturing operation, at least initially. But beyond nodding hello at each other, we never had any contact with the German guy who ran it. The house next to it on Korngatan was abandoned and in worse shape than ours.

Next door to us lived a Danish family working with auto repair. The father, Mogens Saabye, spoke a mixture of English, Danish and Swedish with us. He'd spent a number of years working at America's Thule Air Force Base in northwesternmost Greenland, where he learned most of his English. Although the family had been living in Malmö for a number of years, his wife Ellen spoke only Danish, and we found it all but impossible to understand her. They had two sons: Allan, the eldest, spoke Danish, Swedish and English (the latter two with a strong Danish accent); and Per, who was fluent and accent-free in all three languages. The Saabyes were friendly, as well as funny to talk to, and they were always ready to tell a joke or lend a hand, almost before I'd had a chance to ask. And yet they and Tage seemed to avoid each other like the plague, for reasons I never figured out.

At some point in April, the board of the Perstorp chemical company, Hamadi's biggest client, and thus indirectly mine, decided to make a change at the very top, and replaced their creative CEO Gunnar Wessman with the more stolid Karl-Erik Sahlberg, who immediately plotted a new course for the company, reducing the emphasis on internationalization – and the accompanying emphasis on having key employees take intensive language courses. There would still be a few such courses, but nothing like the volume of business the school had once enjoyed.

Instead, Perstorp was opting for an hour or two of lessons per week per pupil, to be held during office hours at the company headquarters in the eponymous village, 85 kilometers to the north and slightly east of Malmö. Stig Troell, the education manager, offered me a job there (and a fixed salary!), teaching (and perhaps some translating), but Jeanette and I had just bought our house. Taking a job *in* Perstorp would have required us to move to that painfully boring village, where I would have to teach in a format I knew to be far less effective (and therefore far less professionally gratifying), and Jeanette would have to give up her job and try to find something else. All the arguments we'd found against a move to Gränna nearly three years earlier were still valid (and Perstorp was far more boring than Gränna). I turned him down.

On April 16th, we got the official, registered deed to our property. At the same time, we were informed that the tax assessment value was a mere 32,000 kronor. No wonder no bank would even look at a mortgage for that worthless a property! But it didn't stop us.

On April 30th, the US pulled the last of its personnel out of Vietnam, bringing that fiasco to an end at last, after pointlessly devastating the lives of untold millions – particularly among the Vietnamese. The US was starting to feel distant, even foreign to us.

Once we'd painted the walls upstairs in the little house, refitted the carpets from our apartment, installed the cabinets and fridge, and bought a small countertop stove with two burners and a tiny oven, we'd achieved a functional kitchen and living room-bedroom, compact-living style. We now began a race against the clock to turn the tiny downstairs room in the little house into a bedroom – a minimalist bedroom (just over two by three meters) with an extremely compact (less than one by three meters) *en suite* bathroom (toilet, sink and shower) – in the overly ambitious hope of achieving this before we would no longer have access to our apartment on Vårgatan at the end of May.

The ceiling in that room was low – even Jeanette couldn't stand up straight – because of a very thick layer of low-grade concrete on the floor. It was full of cracks, so I felt I could break it up using the sledge hammer and the iron pike (Henry's gifts), and not need a jack hammer until it was time to rip out the downstairs floor in the big house. I had no idea what I might find beneath the concrete....

I began by tearing down the wall that separated the future tiny bedroom from its future tiny bathroom, to get better access to the floor. Then I began whacking away at the concrete floor with the sledge hammer, until I achieved big enough cracks to insert the pike and pry loose huge concrete chunks from the rest, like calving glaciers. If they were too big for me to lift, I had to break them up further. Then I'd load as much as I could into the wheelbarrow, wheel it out to the sidewalk, and finally wrestle the concrete chunks up and into the dumpster. It didn't take many weeks of this kind of strenuous work before I began putting on a lot of muscle.

The concrete layer was nearly 25 centimeters thick, but it was of poor quality (they'd clearly skimped on the Portland cement) and not reinforced. As a result, it wasn't that difficult – just awfully heavy and dusty. Beneath it there seemed to be only sand – the sand of the old hills of *Backarna*. When I'd cleared nearly half of the future bedroom floor, however, I came upon some bricks in the ground beneath the concrete – what looked like the remnants of an old wall. I couldn't figure it out. I took the iron pike and laid into the bricks, some of which went crashing and falling *inwards*, into a black void, making a gaping hole. I ran to get a big flashlight, and saw a tiny cellar room down there, with just the faintest cracks of daylight coming in along one part of the wall to the left. The mysterious underground room was filled with rubble – and roughly 6,287,914 monstrous spiders, as counted by a person who'd always had a clear case of arachnophobia.

Where were the cracks of daylight coming from? They appeared to be from along the wall towards the yard. Then I remembered having seen a thick, heavy iron plate, a little bigger than one-by-one meter, lying apathetically on the surface of the courtyard, in the corner closest to the entrance to the little house, near the garage. I went out with the iron pike to see if I could move the plate. It slid off fairly easily, revealing a hole about 80 x 80 centimeters, straight down nearly two meters, filled with more rubble and more spiders. After pulling out a few things, I could clearly see that there was an opening through the foundation of the little house into that cellar room – a room that neither the previous owner nor the tenants ever mentioned, probably because they hadn't known about it. And now, curséd spite, I was born to put it right.

First I emptied a couple of cans of insect spray into the cellar, not realizing that insect spray wouldn't kill spiders, at least not directly (possibly if they ate insects that the spray killed). But it did seem to make them lethargic. I pulled out as much stuff as I could from above, some via our future bedroom, more through the hole in the ground in the courtyard, but eventually I had to climb down there, taking a construction lamp with me. I was wearing overalls buttoned up to my neck, boots, gloves, a cap, and a pained and slightly panic-stricken frown. I threw stuff out to the yard for Jeanette to sort, and to squash any spiders I'd missed. *Maybe there'd be some hidden treasure that would finance our entire renovation?!*

I did find a small rusty metal box containing a few pea-size pieces of amber (easily worth a couple of kronor), and a few old beer bottles and small ink bottles (all empty, most of them chipped), as well as one five-liter deep-blue bottle still half full of peppermint oil (purity and purpose unknown). But the rest of the cellar rubble consisted of pieces of crushed stone, rotting wood, soggy cardboard, glass shards, bent nails, rusty fittings and broken fixtures, with a total market value of zero kronor.

As the contours of the cellar walls were becoming visible, I could see that there was a second, even smaller cellar room extending in under part of the former workshop room (now our storage room). The floors in both cellar rooms were of hard-packed, muddy, sandy soil. In the first and biggest there were cast-iron drain pipes and municipal water connections entering the cellar from the alley side and exiting it for points unknown on our property. My first thought on discovering the cellar was simply to fill it up and close it off forever, but the drain and water connections made that impossible; I would have to keep the one cellar room and fix it up enough to enable future access somehow.

The whole thing was like an interlocking Chinese puzzle, nightmarish in the sense of keeping me awake at nights trying to figure out how to solve it. I couldn't simply fill up either cellar room from below. That would have to be done from above, once the floor above both rooms had been removed. But I couldn't remove that floor now, because the stairway to our upstairs living quarters rested on it, and we had no other place to live for all the months it would take to rebuild all that.

The sheer complexity of working through layer upon layer of rotten, half-disintegrated shit that had once been somebody's building materials, not knowing what new horror the removal of each crumbling layer would reveal, was not unlike the other major undertaking of my life: stripping away layer upon layer of religious indoctrination, removing what didn't stand up to scrutiny, ferreting out and examining what had once been drummed in, rooting out the faulty and fallacious first premises. I never did any of that lightly; it took me more than 10 years in all. I hoped that rebuilding this house would take less time.

I could see from the part I'd laid bare that the floor above the cellar was a pretty scary construction. I felt fairly certain that there hadn't been a cellar when the house was first built in 1864, but that at some point, one of the previous owners must have dug it out to bring in those connections to the municipal water supply and sewage system. (The little house was originally used as stables and outhouses.) To support the floor above the cellar, it appeared that one or more of the mysterious previous owners had put down a few 10 x 10" wooden beams as joists. On top of those they'd nailed a thin piece of sheet metal. And on top of that they poured a thick layer of low-grade concrete. By the time I discovered it, the wooden beams were so rotten and water-logged that I could break off crumbly chunks of them with my hands; the sheet metal was completely rusted through, making it look more like a large, thin, rusty, moldy gray slice of Emmentaler cheese; and the concrete was full of cracks, presumably remaining in place only by the power of the inertia of rest, or because it had simply forgotten how to fall down.

Since the cellar extended more than halfway (over one meter) in under the future bedroom, I decided that for the time being I would try to remove only that part of the concrete floor, so we could achieve a bedroom, and retain the rest so as not to have to remove the existing stairway up to our main living quarters. We realized that all this unexpected work would prevent us from meeting our deadline to achieve a functional bathroom and separate bedroom before we had to abandon Vårgatan by the end of May. We were working full-time at our jobs *and* on the house. We were, in short, burning the candle at both ends. But it gave a lovely light. During the periods of greatest struggle, my Jenny's jealousy was nowhere in sight and we were happy to be working side by side.

On May 21st, the electrical company came to take the final reading of the meter at Vårgatan. Then they shut off the electricity. This meant that we could no longer return there to take baths at the end of our dirty working days. We had, however, discovered a place called Rörsjöbadet, a small and charming public bathhouse on Drottninggatan, along the way we used to walk to our Swedish lessons. We would have to rely on that facility, as long as we got there well before closing time, at around 6 PM most days. Otherwise, until our new bathroom was ready, we were consigned to heating water in a pot and then taking sponge baths, like back in the "good old days" on Ehrensvärdsgatan.

Rörsjöbadet was divided into two parts, one each for men and women, respectively. Five days a week, the men had access to a 25-meter pool with chilly water (about 16°C), which all but necessitated a hot, dry sauna before jumping in. One day a week, the men and women switched sides. The women's part consisted of a small mosaic-tiled and sculpted pool surrounded by tropical plants and filled with warm water. The women's sauna was smaller and not so hot. No matter what day it was (except Sundays, when it was closed), Rörsjöbadet was a great place to get clean and to utilize the sauna to sweat out cement dust and insulation fibers from our pores.

On Saturday, May 24th, we once again had the use of Henry's pick-up and made the last few trips with the remainder of our stuff, including the water heater and bathtub (which we initially stored in the big house), and the kitchen sink (better than the one at Korngatan, so why not?), as well as the last of the cartons of books and trunks. Since we knew that the entire building was going to be modernized, we asked the caretaker if we could take some of the old paneled inner doors with us. He said we could take as many as we wanted (we assumed he was authorized to give us permission). We took most of the ones from our apartment, and we also harvested several from a couple of the other vacant apartments. Most of the old doors had dozens of layers of paint on them, and Jeanette took it upon herself to start stripping the paint off with caustic soda, one side of a door at a time, wearing goggles, overalls and rubber gloves. But soon another neighbor of ours, Gert Isgren, who lived next door to Tage on the far side from us, took over tenancy of the house opposite ours and installed a paint-stripping bath for doors and old furniture on the premises of the former perfume factory, so Jeanette could return to safer tasks.

We had little time – far too little – to reflect on the profound changes that were taking place in our lives. When did these latest changes start? With the deaths of our fathers? Did we have any idea at the time of the scope of the impact they'd had on us? Did our first return visit to the US make the huge gaps between us and our respective families greater or only make them more painfully apparent? Could I assume that Jeanette's reactions were identical to mine? We recognized very clearly that the country of our birth was no longer a place that felt like home to us. But were we fully aware of the implications this might have on our emotional make-up?

What could account for Jeanette's increasingly deep and erratic mood swings? She seemed to be aware of them only after they'd passed, and then she – not I – would dismiss them as pre-menstrual hormonal imbalance. But then why wouldn't she seek help, medication, therapy? Why didn't I insist and persist? How would she have reacted if I had? Was I unconsciously behaving in a way that exacerbated her jealousy? Did my foolish attempt to make her previously false accusations real have any real but unconscious effect on either or both of us?

We knew we couldn't remain in our apartment on Vårgatan, despite five years of a simple, mostly comfortable and idyllic life there. But the building was falling apart around us; it was no longer a safe environment. It was as if someone who wanted to live in the woods chose a house in a wooded community, only to have all the neighbors start felling all their trees. Free will? There are *all kinds of limitations*!

Our lives had been increasingly centered on music, Jeanette's good cooking and further education, and my painting. In our efforts to pursue that life with greater space and safety, however, we suddenly found ourselves in an environment with a primitive kitchen, where nearly all the paintings had to be stacked on an old workbench against a wall in a storage room, with no place for me to paint, with nobody for my muse to weave her magic for, with a project of a magnitude and complexity that we could not foresee, with an overwhelming amount of work that consumed all our resources and energy, and gave us constant anxiety about making ends meet. What did that do to our sense of freedom and well-being?

Was Jeanette's relationship with Bob the same as mine, or did I just assume that? Were we both comfortable with our Swedish-language environment, or did I just assume that as well? What about children? Jeanette had long and repeatedly been emphatically opposed to having any. But might I have persuaded her? Should I have? Would pregnancy have put her hormones right? *Can one use children as hormone therapy?*

What if none of these factors had any relevance to anything problematic in our lives? What if it were a combination of them? What if it involved factors we knew nothing about and those possible actors were beyond our control? What if it were all about some imbalance in brain chemistry? What if insight came with same-day delivery instead of with the laggardly mirror of hindsight?

I managed to remove all the concrete floor from the future bedroom without further endangering the support for the stairway and the wall that separated the stairwell from the future bedroom, thanks to some careful chiseling as I approached that wall. I also removed the two newly exposed soggy, rotten wooden joists, making a large gap with easy access to the cellar via a ladder from indoors – from the future bedroom.

Next I had to learn how to lay bricks, in order to repair the top of the brick cellar wall beneath the future bedroom and to wall up the former entrance to the cellar from the yard. I'd never before in my life even *touched* a brick, at least not for the purpose of laying it. I found some old loose bricks in the big house and knew that I needed to stick some "mortar" in between them. I also knew that mortar was made of cement. Tage gave me an extra sack of the stuff and a couple of his extra, well-worn trowels. I learned that *lime* cement is used for making mortar and for plastering, while *Portland* cement is for making concrete. I learned those and many other building terms first in Swedish, then in English. I phoned the cement company to ask what kind of consistency I should aim for when mixing lime cement with sand and water. They seemed aghast and somewhat amused by such an elementary question from an adult member of the general public, but they told me what I needed to know. I didn't care whether my questions sounded foolish or not, so long as I got the answers.

Having emerged victorious from my battle with the spiders, I walled up the entrance to the cellar from the yard. Before doing so, I dug out the floor in the main cellar room a little so that when I would later pour a concrete floor, the original floor level would be maintained. I threw the excess dirt into the extra cellar room and then walled up that entrance too. (I would fill that room completely in connection with breaking up the concrete floor of the storage room at some point in a future that was far less foreseeable than I could ever have imagined.)

Now it was time to call in a plumber to take care of whatever connections might be needed from the water and drain lines from the cellar to wherever they would go next. Tage told me of a young plumber named Kjell who did good work at reasonable prices, so I phoned him. He said he'd be happy to take care of it for us, but that he was tied up with other jobs until late June – another unforeseen delay we could do nothing about. It meant that we wouldn't have our bedroom and shower by the time we had to vacate Vårgatan. [*Looking back, if we'd known, it's clear that we should have kept Vårgatan until late August instead of late May.*]

So we turned our attention to other things, like filling one dumpster after another with rubble from the big house. By the time the restoration work on the whole property (both houses) was completed in the early 80s, I'd filled 33 dumpsters with rubble. (At 10m^3 each, that represents a volume close to the entire volume of the big house, from the downstairs floor to the peak of the roof upstairs.)

While I was bricking up the cellar wall, I began thinking about the garage. Three of its four walls were the walls of other buildings: the little house, the big house, and the high brick wall we shared with the Saabyes (behind which they had their car repair workshop). The fourth side was a simple wooden wall that divided our yard into two equal halves. One of those halves was the garage space, covered by a simple wooden roof that was also in need of repair. The other half was for our yard, which was in effect useful for nothing more than a driveway for a car we didn't have. What if we were simply to tear down that wall and roof, put up a new garage where the yard was, and leave the space originally occupied by the garage as an atrium – an inner courtyard? We could then put some windows in the future kitchen and make it brighter, and could turn the new garage roof into a terrace or deck, with a door out from the studio upstairs and eventually another door out from the upstairs of the little house? Jeanette was very enthusiastic about the idea. We wasted no time dismantling the old garage in a few days (and started filling another dumpster). We saved every piece of wood that had potential for reuse, and we left the concrete garage floor as it was for the time being, to make it easier to store building materials on it during the construction phase. We also saved the garage doors; the width of them was a near-perfect match for the width of the big, noisy, insecure (the lock was loose)) iron gate from the yard to the street. We'd planned to replace that industrial gate some day anyway.

I phoned Henry to check whether switching the positions of the yard and garage would require submitting new drawings for our building permit, but he said no; all the modifications made during the restoration could be included in another set of drawings which could be submitted in connection with obtaining final approval after the work was done. (He also conjectured that the planning people might not even notice the exchanged locations of the words "garage" and "yard" on the final drawings – the only indicators of this significant change!) This news gave us all kinds of freedom.

The greatest limitation on our building freedom was our almost total lack of money. Having spent nearly every penny we owned just to buy the place, there was precious little left over for building materials, which forced us to be creative about sourcing. If a neighbor had just completed a building project and had some materials left over, Tage was sure to know about it and tell me so I could swoop down to buy the leftovers at a big discount. Sometimes that discount would be 100%; the neighbor in question would let me retrieve them from their dumpsters for free (they were usually glad to be rid of them).

We also scoured the classified ads in the Sunday paper for cut-rate leftovers. And much of our stuff came from demolition companies (*all* our bricks, beams and floorboards). In fact, for the first six months, we regarded ordinary lumber yards or other purveyors of *new* building materials as a court of last resort.

Henry asked how we intended to make the new garage roof, and I said I thought I'd try to find some iron girders somewhere to support the whole thing. He said that his contacts had a lot of them lying around at various sites and depots, so if I could just give him the dimensions we needed, he'd have them sent over! It was unbelievable that he was *so kind*! Mogens and Allan said they'd be happy to cut the girders to size, then bolt or weld them and help put them in place as required. *They* were also so kind!

We often had to revise our plans and priorities quickly, on the fly, to keep up the pace so that the unforeseen – gigantic! – scope of the project wouldn't overwhelm us. Getting that new garage roof in place suddenly had top priority, despite not even having been part of our plan a week or two earlier. But we had to do something while waiting for the plumber.

We had to get rid of all the old disintegrating concrete from the original yard (another dumpster), then dig it out a little (another dumpster) to make room for a layer of coarse gravel before casting the concrete for the new garage floor. But first we had to build some molds to cast concrete plinths to support the vertical girders. When the girders were delivered (thanks to Henry), Mogens and Allan cut them to the exact lengths of my specifications, then welded them together. We wanted the roof to slope diagonally down from one corner on the street side to the opposite corner on the yard side, to assure the run-off of rainwater, while compensating for the level difference between the big and little houses. The roof terrace floor could still be made flat by cutting its supporting joists to compensate for the diagonal slope of the underlying roof, with a lower section at the door to the terrace from the little house, to allow it to be opened (allegedly an important criterion for doors).

Switching places with the yard and garage had an added benefit: the doors from the yard to both houses would now be sheltered by the new garage roof, meaning we would be able to go between houses without getting wet, whatever the weather. After the Saabyes' and my combined and concerted efforts to get the girders in place, I bought a lot of *new* two-by-fours from a lumber company to use as closely spaced joists. Then I bought about 35 square meters of old, thick floorboards from a demolition company (which meant removing well over a thousand nails and cleaning the tongues and grooves) to make a sturdy floor, and then protect it with three layers of roofing felt. We would have to add a few rows of bricks to the wall towards Källargatan before using the new garage roof as a terrace, but that would also be a future project.

We needed a source of water in the garage. The immediate need was for mixing mortar and concrete, but some day there might be a need to water plants in the little atrium. This required a frost-proof faucet to which a hose could be attached. And if we had water, we'd also need a drain, which would have to be an extension of the drainpipe for the shower on the other side of the garage wall, in the corner of the little house.

On June 17th we finally got our official municipal building permit, which meant that the government loan could now be issued. It also meant that the clock was now ticking to complete the renovation of the big house within two years, by June 16th, 1977. Instead of granting us the 70,000 kronor we'd asked for, they gave us a line of building credit for up to 100,000 kronor. Apparently they didn't find our more modest request feasible. (But we remained determined to stick to our 70,000 budget.)

Kjell finally came and connected the water pipes, as well as the drains to the existing drainpipe in the cellar, for our future *en suite* bathroom, our temporary upstairs kitchen, and our new garage. He added blind connections for those that one day would enter the big house from the yard. The new main water pipe now came from a connection in the sidewalk along Källargatan, with a shut-off valve for all water to the entire property.

At last I could install two pressure-treated two-by-eights above the open gap to the cellar from our future bedroom and lay the floorboards, and tile in the bathroom. The cellar was now sealed off until it was time to rebuild the rest of the little house. Finally, I insulated the walls.

In the corner of the tiny bedroom I built a kind of closet or cupboard that shared a wall with the shower corner in the tinier bathroom. This closet was for the main water pipe, shut-off valve, water meter, and the wall-mounted water heater we'd brought with us from our apartment. The shared wall obviated the need for having exposed water pipes in the shower cubicle – they could come straight into the faucets through the shared wall.

The electrician came before I'd finished the walls, put up the connection boxes for outlets, switches, heater, and the conduits for the wires to connect it all. I built the door openings in the walls to the bedroom and bathroom to fit two of the smaller doors we'd brought with us from Vårgatan. While waiting for the plumber and electrician to complete their installations, I built a bed to fit the available space. After the electrician was done, I put up the plasterboard and Jeanette put up the weave on the walls and painted them.

Then we ordered a mattress to fit the bed, from the place that had cut to measure the cushions we had on the sofa-bed at Vårgatan. We took our first shower in the first week of August, and slept in our new bedroom for the first time that night. It felt so luxurious, and our living room felt much bigger now that we no longer had to leave strategic floor space for the sofa cushions every night.

However pleased we'd been by the atmosphere and relative convenience of Rörsjöbadet, it was a tremendous relief not to *have* to go there anymore. It also meant that we could continue working through the long summer evenings, without having to keep an eye on the clock so we could be at the bathhouse before it closed for the day.

Slings and Arrows

Every day during June and July, if weather permitted and when I couldn't do more on our new bedroom, I worked on rebuilding the dormer windows along Korngatan. I was particularly eager to stop the leakage in the one nearest the Saabyes. While I was sitting up there one day, about four or five meters above the street level, two young men, all dressed up in white shirts and ties despite the warm summer day, came strolling along and stopped down below me. They were looking straight up at me. I had my suspicions. "*Hi!*" one of them said, in English. "*We were wondering whether you've ever read the Bible?*" I answered *yes*, emphatically, and they looked very surprised. But they quickly recovered, and started telling me, in effect, how important it was for me to believe what they believed. I could hear that they were Americans, probably more than five years younger than me, perhaps 10. I'd heard that the neighbors beyond Saabyes were a family of Jehovah's Witnesses whom I'd never met. I guessed that our JW neighbor had heard that I was an American, so he probably got his local assembly to round up a couple of Americans to preach at me. I asked if they were Jehovah's Witnesses, which they confirmed.

"So what is it about your Jehovah that a civilized person would want to worship?" I challenged. They were taken aback by my blunt question and started cherry-picking a few choice Bible verses. I gave them whole chapters in return – chapter after chapter of the horrendous deeds of their wonderful God. I admitted that while the Bible may have misrepresented God's true nature, the Bible itself certainly didn't support any claim that the biblical god could be a good one, and that if there were a good one, it seemed odd to me that he would allow himself to be so monstrously misrepresented by the Bible and yet demand worship. My would-be proselytizers were turning paler and paler. They kept looking at each other, as if they were hoping the other had a solution for extricating themselves from the dilemma they created by trying to peddle their beliefs to me. Suddenly they concluded that we had nothing more to talk about, and they scurried away, never to return.

One warm and sunny summer morning Jeanette and I awoke to the loud and destructive noise of a big machine nearby, maybe a tractor. We threw on some clothes and hurried outside to see a bulldozer attacking the house where Klas Rundström's tenants lived. Klas himself was pacing nervously up and down, watching the heavy saw-toothed steel scoop ripping away at the roof. I went over to ask him what was going on. Either he was speaking extra carefully for my sake that day or I had already picked up more of the local lingo than I realized, but

I understood directly the gist of his words, if not his actions. His hated tenants had embarked upon a dangerous combination: not paying the rent and going away on vacation. So Klas seized the opportunity to tear down their home (it was his house) in their absence. I wondered why he didn't just expand his own family's living space into the second house on their property, but he was afraid that the tenants could find some legal way of getting it back, which they couldn't do if the house didn't exist. Besides, Klas wanted a garage and a bigger yard. The adrenalin rush he seemed to be experiencing made me wonder whether he'd soon start shaking his pelvis.

By late afternoon, all traces of the (former) tenants' house were gone, and Klas looked mighty pleased with himself. The large windowless side wall of his parents-in-law's house next door was now exposed towards Klas's yard, making an unusual sight in the neighborhood. A few hours later in the long, balmy Scandinavian summer evening, at around 11 (by which time it was dark), Jeanette and I again heard some commotion from across the street and looked out the window of our temporary kitchen. Klas was frantically mixing cement in a large bucket, then flicking one trowel of it after another into large cracks that had begun to appear in his in-laws' newly exposed end-wall – a wall that Klas had undermined in his zeal to rid his property of every last vestige of that hateful house.

His wife and kids were holding flashlights to augment the streetlight in the dimly lit late evening. A couple of other neighbors were scurrying over to assist him or to inspect the problem and provide all kinds of advice or predictions, or just to gawk. Suddenly Klas ran out into the street, yelling for everyone to get back. We heard a deep rattling, groaning, rumbling sound, and then, like the Jericho of Backarna, the whole wall came tumbling outward from the in-law's house, and fell flat on Klas's new yard with a thunderous *WHOOMP!!*, breaking apart as it crashed, and raising a gigantic cloud of dust that obliged us to close our window and go outdoors instead. The in-laws' living room, kitchen, and two upstairs bedrooms were immediately exposed to the elements and the dust. Everyone (including us) stood there staring in wide-eyed, drop-jawed disbelief.

When the in-laws, who had also been away at the time, returned a couple of days later to an unlivable home, the exposed façade had been covered by a plastic sheet. They were obliged to move to a small apartment a few blocks away; it took nearly half a year before the insurance issues were sorted out and repair work could even begin. The house was eventually sold, then totally revamped (by Tage). A new owner moved in a year later. I never heard anything about the reactions of his former tenants. Klas built his garage and remained forever defiant about his actions.

We were now completely focused on finishing the dormer windows, and putting a new layer of roofing felt on the entire roof. But we were skeptical about the longevity of roofing felt as a final outermost surface material, and began looking for roof tiles. Hopefully, we'd be able to find some old ones.

But first we had to shop around for new yet affordable windows. (Mom sent us $1000 at this point, which was highly appreciated and needed.) The new window we bought for the bedroom was excellent, but was also far too expensive, considering our need for some 20 more new windows, all larger than the one we'd bought, as well as four outer doors (all to face the courtyard) with windows in them. Although the government energy-saving loan didn't stipulate triple glazing, we went for that anyway to minimize energy consumption and long-term fixed costs. Nothing we had to buy new would be cheap.

Abema, a newcomer to the market, seemed to be the local building materials supplier with the best prices. We explained our total renovation project to one of their reps, and told him we were looking for a supplier for our whole project. He promised us even better prices. We urgently needed two windows (and 18 more to follow), as well as some lumber (I'd made a list), roofing felt and various kinds and lengths of nails.

Once the dormer windows were finished, and the new roofing felt was in place, we no longer had to worry about further leakage from rain. The next step was to strip away everything else that was broken and rotten from the big house, which basically meant stripping away *everything*. Hercules (as in *labors of*) came to mind. When I ripped up some of the rotten floorboards upstairs by the dormer windows, several rotten joists were revealed beneath them. My heart sank. It was impossible to remove and replace an entire joist, since each one ran the entire width of the house, and at the halfway mark there was that upstairs brick wall (with big cracks in it) resting on the joists, and supporting the roof. It felt like another goddamn Chinese puzzle: you have to do B before you can do A, but C before you do B, and A before you do C. I had six consecutive weeks off work that summer, and Jeanette had four, so we were determined somehow to get A, B and C taken care of, in whatever arduous order they arose.

When we partially exposed the joists from above, we saw (with a huge sigh) that the spaces between the joists (i.e. between upstairs and downstairs) were filled with ashes, cinders, gravel, broken bottles, a couple of mummified rats, fragments of broken bricks, remnants of old magazines and newspapers – but no gold ducats. (The space had probably been filled with whatever shit they wanted to get rid of, to provide some sort of thermal or noise insulation between the floors.) We also realized, however, that by removing the exceptionally ugly ceilings downstairs, we could achieve exposed-beam ceilings there, something we hadn't known how badly we wanted until we saw that we could get it.

When the work inside was too heavy for Jeanette – she refused to be excluded from anything but the very heaviest work – she took it upon herself to move outside with a mason's hammer and start knocking off the old white-plastic-painted cement wash that was cracking and disintegrating all over the façade. The plastic paint that didn't "breathe", causing whatever moisture there was in the wall to burst though it each spring, disintegrating a few of the bricks in the process. The plastic paint had to go. It was a tedious job that required a lot more patience than I had, but Jeanette said she thought it was fun. And it saved us the considerable cost of having someone sand-blast it.

The next step for me was to remove all the ceilings downstairs. The construction was the same as the one section had been upstairs: thick rough-hewn boards nailed into the beams, chicken wire, straw and plaster attached to the boards, but then more recent plasterboard on top of (actually below) that. The big difficulty downstairs was the cascade of ashes and dust that filled the room each time I managed to pry a board loose with the crowbar, my tool of choice for a while. I tried to wear a dust-filter mask and goggles, but they were affordably cheap ones that didn't seal tightly. The combination caused my goggles to steam up, capturing the dust in the condensation on the goggles, and making it impossible for me to see. So I opted to keep the goggles on and leave the mask off, then run like hell each time I unleashed a new cascade, and wait impatiently for the dust to settle before returning for the next board. (Patience was never my thing; it would turn out that I only waited until I could *see* safely, not necessarily until I could *breathe* safely.)

The removal of the downstairs ceilings, with the seemingly endless amount of dust and rubble that accompanied it, was probably the most daunting and overwhelming task I would undertake in the whole restoration project. I looked like a coal miner. When I blew my nose, which clogged up twice a minute, out came a dark charcoal-gray paste. The dust even had the audacity to follow me outdoors, as if seeking to deny me that little refuge. And there was *so* much of it!

Each time I re-entered the house to pull down the next board, the air seemed to have become more saturated than ever with fine dust particles. Even when I was able to wear the goggles, my eyes were stinging. But I could see no other way to get the job done, and it had to be done. There was no turning back. [*I strongly suspect that all my work in this thick dust, in combination with my heavy smoking a couple of years later, led to my future respiratory problems.*]

Perhaps the analogy between removing the frustratingly numerous layers of rot and ruin on one hand, and the 10 years of stripping away 18 years of evangelical Christian indoctrination (another type of rot) on the other, actually encouraged me not to lose heart, knowing that the end results – freedom from religion and a beautiful home, respectively – would be worth the effort, pain and tears (in addition to the blood and sweat). Maybe Jeanette, not having had quite as many layers of indoctrination to divest, didn't feel the analogy as strongly as I did.

Once all the ceilings in the big house were down, all the beams exposed, and the rubble cleared away, I could start breaking up the downstairs floor. The floors in our future kitchen were made of worn-out wood, which made it easy. The joists that supported them were lying directly on the sandy ground and were rotten too. The floors in the main part of the downstairs were concrete, so after a few pointless and futile attempts to break them up with the sledgehammer, I had to concede that I would need to rent a jackhammer.

Before that, however, I discovered that the two brick walls that formed the entry just inside the front door were not affixed to anything – they just rose up from the floor to the joists and stopped there, as if they'd done what was expected of them and would do no more. With a hard push, the walls would sway slightly. I took them down carefully, because I wanted to salvage as many as possible of the bricks for re-use.

Then there were the two chimneys, both in such awful shape that they would have to come down. I would only rebuild one. I started at the top, out on the roof. I could literally pry loose almost any brick anywhere in either of them with my bare hands, row by row, layer by layer, onwards and downwards. When I came to the roof peak, I continued by reaching down through the opening in the roof as far as I could. Then I secured a small covering over the hole through the roof, moved inside, and stood on a stepladder to continue the demolition. I occasionally came to a row of bricks that had some adhesion left, but a fairly gentle tap with my mason's hammer was enough to loosen them. When I'd come down to the upstairs floor level, I again reached through the floor and picked them off by hand. Finally, I went downstairs and removed the rest.

We would need to rebuild one of the chimneys again soon, but did we really need *two*? They took up a lot of space, especially the one in what was going to be in the living room. Then Jeanette got a brilliant idea: we could put a fireplace in the corner of the kitchen where the one chimney stood. I could take some of the bricks that had formed the entry walls and build up the one wall again, so that the new chimney and fireplace wouldn't be abutting a wood-framed wall. Unfortunately, most of the bricks that had formed the original chimneys were too badly damaged by soot and cracking to be of any use, so into the dumpster they went. We'd have to acquire some new bricks (or at least other, better bricks) to build up the new chimney, once we'd decided on what kind of fireplace to have.

Finally, it was time to attack the concrete floor, using a rented jackhammer to defeat it. It quickly became apparent that there wasn't just one layer of concrete, but four or five, of varying thicknesses and grades. The cutaway profile reminded me of the Grand Canyon, with its multiple geological layers. It suggested that whenever a new workshop had moved in during the past few decades, they'd simply added a new layer of concrete, gradually raising the height of the floor. That had required resizing the doors, so they simply sawed off the lower part of the old panel doors separating the rooms, rendering those doors worthless. Fortunately, we had a good supply of old panel doors of various sizes from Vårgatan. I was glad I could build the door openings to fit the doors we already had, rather than having to find doors of the right size or having them custom-built.

In the far end of the living room I discovered an old disconnected sewage pipe and an already-filled-up cellar of about four square meters. The pipe contained some greenish-black sludge that had the most putrid stench I'd ever smelled. [*Years later, I would experience the exact same smell when a neighbor served* surströmming, *a specialty of northern Sweden consisting of fermented herring. I could only compare the smell, since I hadn't tasted the sludge....*]

Each big chunk of concrete felt like it weighed a ton. I had to learn the hard way how big a chunk would still be possible to lift up into the wheelbarrow, then lift again and thrust up into the dumpster. I also had to learn about density and volume the hard way. After filling a dumpster with big chunks of concrete rubble from the floor, I phoned the dumpster guy to come and empty it. He soon appeared on the scene and began attaching the chains for lifting the full dumpster up onto the flatbed part of his special truck. But it wouldn't budge. Instead of lifting the dumpster off the ground, the entire front of his truck began to rear into the air like a frightened horse. He had to let it back down while I climbed into the dumpster and started throwing big chunks of concrete back out, onto the side of the street, until I had removed enough weight to allow his truck to lift it. Once he'd returned with the empty dumpster, I had the dubious pleasure of throwing all those excess chunks back into the dumpster – thus lifting them for the *fourth* time!

After having undertaken the kind of strenuous exercise and weight-lifting that some people spend a lot of money to get at gyms, the last of the concrete floor downstairs was gone. We then dug it out a bit more (without going beneath the street level) in order to have as high ceilings as possible. (And there had to be room for the insulation matting, a new concrete slab, and the floor tiles, about 25 cm in total.) The house was now stripped bare, a hollow shell with four walls and little else. We'd already filled something like 20 dumpsters – 200 cubic meters of rubble.

Once we'd leveled out the ground, we needed Kjell the plumber again, since the drain pipes had to be dug down in the ground under the big house before the insulation matting could be laid out. Kjell said he'd come the following week to install it, but he didn't show up. I phoned again. He would come the following week. He didn't. It went on and on and on like that, for a couple of months. The frustration was exasperating, excruciating, infuriating.

In the meantime, I had to do something about that upstairs wall, the rotten joists and the floor. This was particularly crucial because in the kitchen half of the downstairs, a three-meter stretch of the load-bearing wall that ran the length of the downstairs in the middle had long ago been removed to create a more open workshop. In its stead they'd placed a steel girder – a horizontal I-beam – supported at each end by vertical I-beams. The problem was that the I-profile should have been positioned vertically for maximum strength, but instead it too was horizontal (like a squashed H), which minimized its load-bearing strength. In fact, it was sagging noticeably – and this was the girder that supported the joists, which in turn supported the upstairs load-bearing brick wall, which was cracked, and that wall was in turn supporting the roof! I had to find a solution, urgently. I'd lived in a Bruce-built house in Oak Park; this one must have been built by his renegade brother Jerry.

I thought out a way to stand an old, solid eight-by-eight wooden beam vertically beneath the midpoint of the incorrectly positioned I-beam, to be supported by the new concrete floor. The only trouble was that it would take quite some time before there *was* a new concrete floor. We'd have to take a chance that the sag of the I-beam would not decide to increase any time soon, so I could start repairing the upstairs brick wall first.

That was also a challenging task – no surprise there! I couldn't take down the existing, cracked wall all at once, because there'd be nothing left to support the roof. I had to do it in sections, roughly two meters at a time, while trussing up the roof beams directly above the part of the wall that I was rebuilding; then remove the old, damaged floorboards above what was to be the living room; then saw off the rotten halves of the joists, so that the remaining half would be supported by the load-bearing wall downstairs; then put in a new joist to replace the rotten part, also resting on the downstairs load-bearing wall; then lay new floorboards on the joists; then build up that section of the upstairs brick wall, all the way up to support the roof beams directly, for the first time ever.

Tage had tipped me off about a demolition company based in Kyrkheddinge (near Lund), from whom we could buy old, thick floorboards and old beams. We were pleased to buy old stuff, not only because it was a fraction of the price (seven kronor per square meter for the floorboards versus 200 kronor for new ones), but because we felt that old materials were better suited to restoring an old house. We discovered that the demolition company also had some old, black-glazed roof tiles that we fell for, so we bought those too, and stored them on the new garage roof until we were ready to use them. When I told the owner of the demolition company that I needed bricks, he told me where they were tearing down a building that week, and said I could go there any time after working hours and help myself. A neighbor with a pick-up offered to help out, so we began going to different demolition sites on Saturday and/or Sunday mornings. I brought my mason's hammer along to whack off as much of the old mortar as possible, and my neighbor helped me load the bricks into the pick-up. A couple hundred bricks at a time was all the pick-up could manage, but 200 bricks was enough to keep me busy for quite some time. And there were always new demolition sites.

Starting at the place where the new spliced joists were resting on the load-bearing downstairs wall, I used four-inch nails to secure a few rows of the thick floorboards and to prevent any lateral movement of the joists. Then, using five-inch nails, I added an extra row of the thick floorboards as a base on which to build the new brick wall, two meters at a time. Then I built a proper brick wall all the way up to the roof peak (no loose bricks this time!), securing the loose ends of the former tie beams in it as well. I repeated the procedure for the next two meters, leaving appropriate spaces for doors to match the ones we'd brought from Vårgatan, until I'd completed about two-thirds of the upstairs load-bearing wall, reaching almost as far as where the new chimney would come from the kitchen area downstairs and out through the roof.

We were now into October. Jeanette was continuing with her German course, making great progress, and was enthusiastic about everything – apart from speaking German when anybody could hear her. She was also writing lots of notes and reminders to herself in German. And she said she was considering studying Italian as well.

One evening after a long day's work, she suddenly (and for no particular reason that I could discern) reiterated her strong desire *not* to have children. I said that *her* happiness was all that mattered to me, and that *she* was enough for me. I also said that if she was certain about it, perhaps I should consider getting a vasectomy, like my brother John (who had laughingly told me "*It's the only way to fly!*" – the slogan of Western Airlines – after he'd had one a couple of years before), so we would no longer have to use condoms. She said it sounded like a great idea. But amid so much else going on with the house, the issue was largely forgotten for a while.

In mid-October, we ordered all our 20-some remaining windows and four Dutch doors from Abema. Delivery was scheduled for early January 1976, but we were beginning to worry about the timing. Without being able to pour the concrete slab, we might end up having to move the windows back and forth several times, and they were *heavy*. We finally decided we'd have to give up on Kjell after months of unreturned and increasingly anxious phone calls (I'd already added "Kjell" to the anxiety-inducing list with "Freiburg" and "Sandgatan"!), and we began asking around for another plumber. By November we finally heard from one of our neighbors about a good plumber, a young man named Bengt Norén, who was just setting up his own business. He came by the day after we phoned him and took a look at what we needed. I told him if he could give us a good price for the whole job, I was pretty sure I could help him get a lot of other jobs by actively advocating his services to neighbors who were starting to think of installing flush toilets and undertaking major restoration jobs.

I should mention that when Jeanette and I moved into our house, the great majority of our neighbors' homes had only latrines – no flushing toilets. The waste from their outhouses was deposited in thick-walled metal cans, which were collected once or twice a week by a guy who arrived in a special flat-bed truck. He wore overalls, and went into each outhouse to retrieve a sealed can, which he carried on his shoulder. That shoulder of his overalls was stained to an extent that didn't look like it could ever be washed clean.

Norén gave us an extremely good price for the whole project, I gave him the go-ahead, and he stopped by a couple of days later and had all the drain pipes measured, cut and connected within a day or two. The electrician also came by to install a new power cable from the mains box in the street. The cable entered the house via a small trench he dug beneath the front door frame to a new fuse box he mounted on the back wall of what was and would again be the entry. But it was turning cold now, the days were short, and our bodies were aching. We felt it best to wait for warmer weather to pour the concrete.

I had a couple of new colleagues at work to relieve me when my obsession with work on the house became too great. Rob had left Hamadi's school in disgust about getting too little work (he had, after all, been promised a full-time job), although Jeanette and I continued to meet him and Chris occasionally. Isobel (née McCafferty) was one of the new ones. She was Irish, a Catholic from Londonderry, and was married to a tall and skinny Swede named Björn. Isobel talked incessantly, and sometimes produced an excess of frothy saliva when she got ahead of herself and forgot to swallow. She had a fair complexion, a receding chin and a round face. Her raven hair was cropped short. Her head sometimes reminded me of a bowling ball. She was outgoing, but too hasty to spew out her immutable opinions (with which I often found it impossible to concur); the concepts of *truth* and *wishful thinking* tended to merge in her world. The other new colleague was Lynn, an American from Minnesota, who was married to a Swedish hockey player from Ängelholm, a town in northwestern Skåne. She was short and effervescent; he was huge and taciturn, the strong silent type. Jeanette and I met both couples socially, but infrequently, and never simultaneously.

During our break from work on the house, we were both working hard at our jobs to try to pay for it all, but as Christmas was approaching, things at the school were slowing down noticeably. Bob could no longer contain his curiosity about our house, and despite the primitive conditions we had to offer, he joined us for more than two weeks over the Christmas holidays. [*About two decades later I would learn that during 1975, Bob made me the sole beneficiary of his will.*] He was overwhelmed and inspired by the tremendous potential of the house – and daunted by the enormity of the tasks already undertaken and still before us.

Recognizing that the intensity of our work left little time for correspondence, Bob proposed that weekly updates by phone might frequently be used to replace our correspondence. The cassette tapes had proved too awkward. Remembering the multiple drafts of letters he tended to make in all his correspondence, and the fact that few of his letters ever contained any corrections, I realized that correspondence was no easy task for him either.

On December 18th Jeanette wrote to thank Mom (who was now living in Knoxville) for her gifts to us and to Rose, as well as to Rosanne for her wedding. Jeanette suspected that they wouldn't manage to thank my mom, and Jeanette knew how sensitive Mom was to perceived ingratitude; failure to express thanks would immediately remove a person from Mom's gift recipients' list. [*In connection with research for this book, I noticed that Jeanette's handwriting was considerably altered as from this letter – broader and more careless. Was that significant in any way, I wonder now? And if so, I wonder how?*]

Although we endured cramped quarters during Christmas, I still managed to break out my easel and do one last painting for the year: *Tell Us Another One.*[67] People are sitting at a table, drinking. A central figure is telling jokes. He, at least, is amused. Another man could be laughing into his hand, but could just as well be yawning. The other two are turned away; one is covering his ear. This might have been an attempt to create a counterweight to the anxiety and stress we were feeling that our lives had become. It was the first painting I'd done in nearly nine months, and only the fourth I managed to paint in 1975. It would also turn out to be my last painting for quite a long time. I finished it on New Year's Eve, 1975. But I had to face the fact that it was now just too difficult to go on painting in the confinement of the little house, and besides, I was getting more than enough creative fulfillment out of working on the house.

---

67 Painting #78 (see Appendix 2)

CHAPTER 12

Intensity

1976 was approaching. I wondered, Shouldn't it be time for the pendulum to start swinging *our* way? Except there's absolutely no reason for thinking that the "should" part was any less a product of my culturally conditioned imagination than the pendulum metaphor itself. On the contrary (almost), there's abundant evidence that the individual life is not about back-and-forth, but a process with a beginning and an end. Or perhaps more like a line, a timeline, but in the form of a chain with links that both bind and separate events and developments to and from each other. In either case, despite our best efforts and intentions, the future doesn't always do what we want it to do, no matter how carefully we plan or how fervent our desire or how vain our faith. And the past doesn't – *can*not – undo that which is done, no matter how great our pain, nor how many regrets we might have, nor how much we pretend what happened never did. It's only the future that can repair or regenerate, if that can ever be done at all.

We had, at least, pretty much come to the end of the stripping-away process where the big house was concerned. We'd reduced it to an empty shell, and exoskeleton of itself, down to the sandy dirt of the hill it stood on, naked walls, ceilings with exposed beams, as blank a slate as it was ever going to be. And for the first time we could now see that all our work to make it that way, to rid ourselves of all that was broken and rotten, had paved the way for the great new building-up process to begin.

The month of January was largely a much-needed break for us. It was far too cold and raw to be working hour after hour in an unheated, drafty house. (I had some experience in avoiding the draft....) But we were still under pressure to complete work on the big house within two years of the issue date of the building permit, and more than half a year had passed since then. We'd seen, all too many times by now, how a carefully planned task normally ended up taking roughly four times what we'd calculated, so we felt the pressure keenly – and had we had little or no experience in most of the tasks that still lay before us, many of which I'd never understood existed, let alone that we'd be facing them.

In the early weeks of January we spent a lot of our spare time planning. The windows and doors would soon be arriving. I would have to start replacing the old rotten ones, and I had no idea how. I had to build up a fireplace in conjunction with rebuilding the brick entry wall, which meant finding some kind of fireplace unit, then building the chimney (preferably after first learning how). I knew I'd need a lot more bricks. Then there was the façade; Jeanette, in her unflagging persistence, had somehow managed to knock down nearly all the old plastic-painted cement wash from the exterior walls. She would soon be going after the rest, and then I would do a new cement wash. Finally we'd, whitewash the whole house outside, but not until the new windows were in place. And we needed a new front door – from where? The new concrete slab was going to be a huge task, and had to precede putting up all the studs, electrical connections, insulation, and plasterboard. It was essential to do it all, and to do it in the right order. But the more we planned, the more daunting and staggering, it seemed, kind of like having swallowed something that starts to swell once it's inside your guts (or still in your throat). And yet it was all moving in the right direction, towards completion, towards a new and lovely home, the desired swing of that illusory pendulum.

Shortly before Christmas 1975, Stig Svensson delivered a large roll of yellowish (instead of unpigmented white) impregnated paper (Jeanette and I had chosen the color to emphasize warm light) on which I was would make drawings to turn into laminates for our kitchen worktops, splashbacks and cabinet doors. We no longer faced a windowless kitchen; by moving the garage and giving ourselves an atrium, we could now have a couple of windows facing the yard, but probably it still wouldn't be a bright place. Jeanette agreed that the laminate design I was going to make should give us something to compensate for all the houseplants we wouldn't be able to have in those north-facing windows. I suggested cheerful drawings of greenery using various shades of marker pens. Jeanette was thrilled with the idea. And the greenery should have a light yellow background, hence the color choice for the impregnated paper.

Before I could start, we had to plan the kitchen layout in great detail, with millimeter tolerance, at a time when the future kitchen still looked more like a demolition site. Accurate scale drawings of cupboards, sinks, and appliances were coming out our ears and turning our eyes red as we tweaked the drawings over and over until we had made our kitchen layout exactly the way we wanted it. (I should perhaps remind age-challenged readers that in the mid-1970s we had no computers, no design or architectural programs or apps, nothing but paper, pencils and rulers.)

It was tricky making the drawings for the laminate, bearing in mind that the drawings were not going to be *transferred* to a laminate; the original drawings were going to *be* the laminate, a scale of 1:1. My idea – drawings rather than a pattern, meaning no repetitions – didn't make the task any easier. Our cabinet arrangement would entail two tall cabinet doors (nearly floor to ceiling, or baseboard to beam), and it was only here where the complete concept would be found in a single piece of laminate: at the bottom, root-like structures in various shades of green, with little cartoon-like pink men hiding playfully among them (also the motif for all the lower cabinet doors); from the roots emerge green stems (also the motif for the countertops); the stems then develop into bright pink flowers and buds (also on the splashbacks); and finally, some of the stems continue on up and develop into the little pink men again, except this time somewhat larger and emerging jubilantly and triumphantly from the "buds" (also on the wall-mounted upper cabinets). Everything had to fit together, perfectly; there could be no trimming or altering afterwards.

All our windows and Dutch doors arrived on schedule (albeit not *our* desired schedule) on January 8th, and we hardly knew where to put them. I think we may have put them in the garage. They were far too heavy for Jeanette to lift, but she kept me company whenever she could. She sometimes set up a pot of tea and warm rolls on little table with a couple of chairs, where she would read a book and put it down each time I could or had to take a break. My Jenny was so sweet that I felt I would melt.

Several more people in the neighborhood were now beginning to renovate (we remained the first and only on Korngatan for a year or two). And Tage was the spider in the web, coordinating a kind of jungle telegraph about where to find bargains, make joint purchases, where demolition work was going on, etc. A neighbor who was also looking for stuff tipped me off about an old apartment building being torn down in the Södervärn part of town, and he drove us out there. It was a four- or five-storey building, and up in the attic part, overlooking the yard, I spotted a kind of dormer with a pair of doors clad with herringbone paneling. They looked exactly like what I wanted for our front door. (The damaged front door of our house was probably from the 1950s, and didn't have the look of anything but the 1950s.) A beam stuck out from above the attic doors, with a pulley mounted on the end of it for hauling heavy or bulky things up to the attic. The guys from the demolition company said they had no use for the doors, so I got them free of charge.

We brought them home, together with some things for my neighbor. The combined width of the doors was a perfect match for our existing door frame, but they were nearly 15 centimeters too short. However, since we wanted an outside kick-plate anyway, I added some boards to the bottom of the doors, then covered the outside of the extension with the black metal kick-plate. The next step was to screw a thin framework of 25x50 mm laths onto the inside of the doors, fill it with sheets of polystyrene insulation, then affix paneling to the framework. Each door had a small square single-glazed window (with broken glass) that had to be replaced anyway. I'd noticed that the old rotten window at the top of the stairs in the big house had some old, slightly bubbly glass in the nine panes, so I took six of those panes to a local glazier who made them into two triple-glazed windows of the right size for our new front doors. And, if we could find some new hinges, a pair of wrought-iron door handles, an appropriate mailbox and a new lock, we'd be set.

One day in January, when I was taking some measurements downstairs in our empty shell of a big house, there was a knock on the door. A middle-aged man with a kind face introduced himself as Lennart (he spoke a very formal kind of Swedish). He said he was considering buying the empty ruin of a house diagonally opposite ours, and noticed that we'd undertaken a project of similar scope. He wanted to know whether it could be regarded as a worthwhile endeavor. He seemed very encouraged by what he saw in our place – an assessment that was somewhat at odds with the frequent bouts of *dis*couragement we'd been feeling. Notwithstanding, he decided to go ahead and buy the property, making him and his family our new neighbors, or at least future neighbors; it would take several years before they had enough of their house ready to move in.

Jeanette was getting fed up with her job by now, due to the erratic and often bad-tempered and sometimes mean-spirited behavior of her boss. In her growing restlessness, she was also becoming more and more emotionally involved in the world's vast array of political hotspots: the Troubles in Northern Ireland, the rivalries in German politics, the fractious and ferocious guerrilla warfare in Angola, to mention a few. [*She kept a diary covering about half the days in January, from which I've sourced a great deal of information in writing* Hindsights. *In doing so, I was reading most of it for the first time ever.*] She had long talks with my colleague Isobel about the situation in Northern Ireland; Isobel was a Catholic from Londonderry, which was in itself a significant risk factor for

Isobel's well-being there.

On January 10th, Jeanette commented in her diary on having recently read *Fear of Flying* by Erica Jong: "*I enjoyed it on the whole; somewhat bitchy in places, but isn't that how 'we women' are?*" The next day she wrote that she thought she would soon be getting her period. "*I'm extraordinarily aggressive, short-tempered, sensitive, and suspicious. [...] I feel rejected and hateful towards others. I've been able to recognize this attitude and with Stan's help and affection, it is fairly easily and quickly controlled.*"

January was, as usual, the coldest month of the year, and we urgently needed a change of scene, more from our restoration obsession than from the chill. I thought that Jeanette might want to travel to someplace warmer, but in fact she wanted to go back to London for a week. We found a package deal from Spies (the Danish charter company) for 380 kronor each including the flights and a very good hotel, so we decided to splurge on a hectically relaxing holiday in one of our favorite cities. We arrived at Stanstead Airport just after noon on Friday, January 23rd. It took an hour and a half to get to our hotel, the Cunard International, in Hammersmith, a part of London we'd never seen before. We were not expecting such a modern, luxurious hotel at the very low price we'd paid for the whole package, and it felt particularly good after some eight months of primitive living in aged dust.

We spent our whole first afternoon and evening walking, discovering new places, finding connections and shortcuts to old ones, making frequent pub stops in an effort to stay warm in the raw chill of January in London. The next day we headed for the Portobello Road flea market, which was great fun. We soon noticed how much our search for quirky bargains was drifting towards things for our home: brass and wrought-iron door handles, interesting wall-mounted hooks, and a wrought-iron letter-box perfect for mounting into our new front door.

Even the architecture of the buildings seemed to have changed – because it was suddenly there! Details on buildings that on previous visits had completely escaped our notice were now popping into focus everywhere. There were all kinds of flashings that we'd never seen before, even though they'd obviously been there all along. Window frames, eaves, dormer windows, sills, jambs, downpipes, the number of hinges per door, the profiles of moldings – endless details now jostled and jousted with the tourist sites for our attention.

After walking the whole day, we headed back to our hotel in the late afternoon to rest our aching feet and unburden ourselves of our purchases. In her trip diary,

Jeanette wrote, "*I can't get over how well we feel touring in London. We seem to harmonize so beautifully here, which probably is why I love our London trips.*"

In the early evening, we took a bus into town to go to the Queen's Theatre to see a witty performance of *Otherwise Engaged*, starring Alan Bates. Since it finished early, we had a quick Chinese meal, then took in a movie, followed by another pub visit, before heading back to our hotel.

After breakfast on Sunday morning, we got on a bus, intending to visit Hyde Park Corner to hear people holding forth on their literal or figurative soapboxes, proclaiming their literal or figurative truths, but we somehow missed our stop and ended up at St. Paul's Cathedral. We entered Christopher Wren's majestic building, but found it too hard to take the ongoing service seriously (too many hilariously disturbing similarities to Hyde Park Corner), and, not wanting to disturb those who did take it seriously, we left quietly and started walking in the general direction of Covent Garden, to see whether we would be able to get tickets to see Mozart's fabulous opera *Le nozze di Figaro*, only to find the theater closed (or perhaps not open *yet* – it wasn't even noon). We walked on towards Piccadilly, and along the way we spotted some posters about concerts at the Royal Festival Hall on the other side of the Thames, so we hurried along, arriving before the box office opened at two o'clock. We were first in line. We had so many Classical favorites already, very few of which we'd ever heard in concert before, so we were thrilled at the amazing selection and bought tickets for four concerts during our remaining five days. It felt like we were indulging ourselves, even though the price of a ticket was the equivalent of about 20 minutes' work at my low-paying job.

The first of these concerts was to start an hour later, so we hurried back across the Thames to find a pub, only to find that they'd closed minutes earlier – this was Sunday in Britain. Instead we bought some rolls and fruit and sat on a bench near the river to feed ourselves and the pigeons. We found the performance at that first concert disappointing, despite it being Mozart's 24th piano concerto. The conductor and pianist seemed bored, and managed to convey that.

Afterwards we took in a meal at a restaurant we'd spotted earlier, near the Colosseum Theatre, but we had to hurry once more; we had another concert to attend, now at the Queen Elizabeth Hall. Mozart was again on the program, and this time it was sublimely beautiful: sonatas for violin and piano in G, E, F, A, and B-flat, played exquisitely by Radu Lupu, a young Romanian pianist; and by Szymon Goldberg, an older Polish violinist. After enjoying the encores elicited by the enthusiastic audience (ourselves included), we took a drink at a pub before returning to our hotel, still glowing.

Immediately after breakfast on Monday, January 26th, we took an early bus to the Strand and walked up to Covent Garden to try to get our longed-for opera tickets for Wednesday evening's performance. We were almost shocked to be able to get great orchestra stall seats for a mere seven pounds each. Invigorated, we walked along Rosebery Avenue to the Sadler's Wells Theatre, where we got cheap (£1.25) tickets to the Wednesday matinée performance of Gilbert and Sullivan's *Patience*.

Bob had introduced us to the Gilbert and Sullivan operettas as well, and we found them delightful. He revealed that he'd sung in a couple of them that were staged at Rochester University when he was attending medical school there. He seemed to have committed most of them to memory, and would often recite whole arias from *Pinafore* or *The Mikado*, or just throw in an appropriate line here and there (*"And happy to meet you all once more!"*). It would be our first live Gilbert and Sullivan performance ever. Jeanette wrote, *"We've been having a contrasting, hectic and relaxing holiday, but totally enjoyable."*

Tickets in hand, we spent most of the day shopping, as well as walking in Kensington Gardens. We then hurried back to the hotel to drop off our shopping bags, have a quick cognac, and take off for the Purcell Room at Queen Elizabeth Hall for a recital with Rosalind Plowright. Due to a surprise onslaught of sleet, the traffic through town was horrendous, and came to a complete stop at Piccadilly, so we got off the bus and ran the rest of the way, unfortunately just missing the closing of the doors for the first part of the recital. But we enjoyed the remainder of the program once they let us in after the intermission.

On Tuesday, we started by taking the bus to Charing Cross Road, where we bought books and records at Foyle's, adding to our collection of the superb recordings of Bach's Cantatas on original instruments, a huge project undertaken by a group called *Concentus Musicus* in Vienna, under Nicolaus Harnoncourt. I hoped to add these to the reel-to-reel tapes I'd been making to paint by. We also bought new and better tennis rackets, since we'd been playing more often with Rob and Chris, and I was still playing regularly with Henry. We indulged ourselves even further by paying a visit to the Dunhill shop on Old Bond Street, where I bought a diminutive cedar box of 30 small cigars (cheroots) for three pounds. Jeanette occasionally joined me for one.

We had another concert in the evening, and although it was still afternoon, we didn't want to end up late like the day before, so we arrived in the area of the concert hall very early – so early that we were forced to find a pub to wait in, although the nearest one was about 15 minutes' walk from the concert hall. At about quarter past seven, Jeanette asked me the time and I told her, while casually glancing at our tickets to confirm the eight o'clock starting time – except that the concert was going to start at half past seven, and we had to run through the streets of London once again. This time we made it at the last minute, and heard a very pleasant piano recital of sonatas by Mozart and Beethoven, as well as Schubert's Impromptus.

Wednesday was the big music day, starting with the matinée performance of *Patience*, performed by the venerable D'Oyly Carte Opera Company. It was easy to understand why Bob was so ecstatic, both about Gilbert and Sullivan and about that particular opera company. Jeanette wrote: *"It was most assuredly a wonderful experience being entertained on so many levels so humorously and delightfully. We ate delicious cheesecake and drank tea during the intermission. Can life have such pleasure?"*

On our way to the evening's opera performance, we stopped for a very tasty Chinese meal, then reached Covent Garden in plenty of time for the musical experience of a lifetime: the music (conducted by Colin Davis) was divine, the scenography and costumes were impressive, and the singers were enthralling – and we experienced it all from seats W3 and W4. We'd listened to our recording of *The Marriage of Figaro* numerous times before, but this live performance was a new experience altogether. With movingly beautiful arias like *Voi Che Sapete* and *Dove Somo* still coursing through our veins, we returned to our hotel room, had a sherry and a small cigar, and lay in each other's arms, urgently wishing to keep this feeling, this glory in the flower, forever and ever.

On Thursday morning, practical matters came first. We had to try to pack all our things to see whether we would need to buy an extra suitcase to carry home all our purchases. Fortunately, we didn't, although our bags were bulging. That taken care of, we headed directly for the Tate Gallery, where we spent a lot of time with Turner and Francis Bacon. From there we went to the National Gallery at Trafalgar Square and enjoyed the Impressionists, especially Van Gogh.

Since it was our last day in London, and we hadn't yet done all things London, we stopped for fish and chips after the gallery visits. And since it was our last evening, we decided go to the West End one last time and take in an early evening performance of *Rosencrantz and Guildenstern Are Dead*, by Tom Stoppard. We got very poor seats, but moved much closer to the stage during the first interval (it was far from a full house). Afterwards, as a sort of antidote to the somewhat unsatisfactory fish and chips, we stopped at a kiosk to try a Turkish lamb kebab in pita bread – a new and delicious experience for us both.

We got home to Malmö on Friday evening at around six o'clock, and had to break into our own gate because somebody had apparently jammed the lock in our absence, turning our homecoming into a bit of a crash landing after an incredibly exciting, gratifying and jealousy-free week. Would we ever experience another one like it?

Back from London meant back to intense drudgery for both of us. Jeanette had a dissatisfying job for a capricious boss she no longer respected, while helping out all she could to support me with the arduous work on the house. I had all those bothersome pupils, when all I wanted to do was reach the elusive end of the goddamn house project, an end that never seemed to be within our grasp. But at least we'd started to build.

In February and March, the focus was on bricklaying. Except for the wooden construction of the two upstairs dormer windows, every one of the 20-odd windows that needed replacing – as well as the four Dutch doors – meant repairing and/or building brick arches. I didn't have a clue about how to build an arch, but fortunately Tage did, and he was pleased to show me.

When I took out one of the old windows (I started with one of the three in the future living room, facing Korngatan), I discovered (no longer to my surprise – I was becoming rather cynical about what to expect from that house) that the old walls had been built on homeopathic principles: the mortar between the bricks was about 99.9% sand, with just a trace of cement, like the merest hint of a whiff of a dead fish. The outer walls had the thickness of the length of a brick, which meant the thickness of the width of two bricks. And indeed, the outer walls were double: fired bricks outside and mud bricks inside, with an occasional fired brick turned perpendicular to the others to bind the two wall "layers" together. I'd never seen or even heard of mud bricks before. They were apparently used because they were cheaper, but they could only be used indoors; exposure to rain might turn them back into mud. Sometimes I didn't know whether to laugh or cry.

The more I'd worked on this house, the clearer its history became to me; not that it told me a lot about any of the individuals, but that the constant reminders of its poor quality in every respect spoke volumes about the lack of respect the *haves* had for the *have-nots*. The poor quality wasn't due to mistakes; it was clearly calculated corner-cutting. Every expense was spared in the making of "homes" for the poor working-class people who would be living in them. Sweden in 1864 was incredibly far removed from Sweden in 1976, but it wasn't because the *haves* had had a change of heart. It was because the *have-nots* got organized and stopped taking it on the chin, as their forebears had done for generations, for centuries, throughout history.

After removing an old window, I had to extensively tuck-point the surrounding bricks. Sometimes I even had to remove loose bricks altogether and start over. I put in pressure-treated wood blocks at three points along each side in order to have something into which I could screw the new window frame.

When I'd repaired both sides of a window opening, I left a sort of indent at the top to prepare for the arch. Then I took a piece of thin plywood the width of the wall and a bit longer than the width of the opening, so I could bend it into a curve that would press against the two sides and form an arch above them. This was the frame for the brick arch, supported from below with a vertical board in the middle and two diagonal boards supporting each end of the arched plywood.

Next I'd get a pile of bricks ready, as well as one brick that I beveled slightly along both edges of one of the long sides. Then I prepared my non-homeopathic mortar (with real lime cement in it this time!). I worked quickly from both sides, laying bricks against each other on the plywood support, alternating from each side for balance, until I reached the middle, then placed the beveled brick there, tapped it gently into place to put some pressure along the arch in both directions, and immediately removed the arch support before the mortar dried, in case there was further settling to be done. I then went back and tuck-pointed with mortar where needed and proceeded to add wedges of brick on both sides to come up to a straight wall line, level with the top of the arch.

One by bloody one I built these arches and put in these windows. By the time I finished, I knew how to do it. It was pretty much the same for the Dutch doors. The two big windows earmarked for my studio upstairs were trickier, since they were so big and heavy that I could barely lift them on my own, and was terribly afraid one might tip over and crash down to the concrete slab that our yard still consisted of. I was glad to have practiced on all the other "normal" windows (all of which were triple-glazed). Minimizing our fixed costs seemed to make long-term sense if I were to go on painting for a non-living.

Hamadi finally decided that having his home at his school, and vice-versa, was no longer feasible now that he and Saloua had a baby. The need to find another venue for the school may have been accelerated by the fact that in searching for Hamadi one morning, I mistakenly opened the door to one of the classrooms – a *former* classroom, as it turned out – to the great alarm of a stark naked Saloua. So Hamadi found a new location for the school in the old part of central Malmö, on Gråbrödersgatan. We continued to use Per's Krog as our lunch place, which meant a somewhat longer walk. But a brisk walk was almost always welcomed and beneficial, and walking through Kungsparken was usually very pleasant.

Among my first pupils at that new location, for two weeks in mid-March (if I remember correctly), was a friendly young man named Carl Bennett, about five years younger than me. He was a good student, and we had many a lively discussion on many an interesting topic. One that stands out in my memory was our discussion of drugs – narcotics. Although neither of us had any first-hand experience of anything closer to a narcotic than alcohol or tobacco, I held that cannabis-based products should be de-classified as narcotics, while he vehemently opposed lifting the ban.

He cited the prevailing argument, that pot was a gateway or portal to heavier drugs. I admitted that he might be right – but only because pot was illegal, meaning that someone wanting to try pot would have to buy it from someone who was already breaking the law, and would prefer to have a customer for life by selling him heroin or other hard drugs. Carl claimed that heroin wasn't a problem in Sweden. I countered that it would soon *become* a problem if Sweden didn't legalize pot to break the connection to those dealers. That was about where we left it. [*He went on to become the chairman of Getinge AB, a world-leading medical supply company that for some years in the 1990s became one of my biggest clients. But I never met him again. Sweden didn't legalize cannabis; and heroin became a problem.*]

Jeanette was nearly finished with her amazing self-appointed task of knocking down all the old plaster from the façade. (I only did the parts high above her reach; stepladders were fine for her, but we were in complete agreement that I should deal with the five-and-a-half-meter-high peak along Källargatan that required an extension ladder.) One day while we were both away at work, we came home to find that the municipal power company had been working in the sidewalk outside our end wall along Källargatan, near the corner, and had installed a neighborhood connection box along our wall, directly in front of the very part of the wall Jeanette was working on and hadn't had time to finish. They'd installed the box so close to the wall that it was impossible to reach in behind it and knock down the flaking plaster.

I phoned the power company and described the problem. They said they'd send somebody over to have a look. A little while later, an old Saab V4 pulled up, and out of it stepped a lean, middle-aged man who was almost a caricature of the stereotype Civil Servant: beige trenchcoat, hat, horn-rim glasses, brown leather satchel, stiff and bureaucratic manner. I saw him arrive, so I went out to greet him.

He asked what the problem was. I gestured towards the new connection box. He looked puzzled and asked again what the problem was. I told him that, as he could surely see, we were in the midst of restoring the house, and suddenly this box appeared and made it impossible to repair the wall behind it. He whipped out a measuring stick and measured the distance from one back corner of the box to our wall: 10 centimeters. "*It's 10 centimeters,*" he said. I said I had no reason to doubt him, but the fact remained that it was too close to the wall to permit access to repair the wall. "*That's not our problem,*" he considerately observed. "*We have an agreement with the Swedish Homeowners' Association that these boxes may be placed 10 centimeters from the wall of the adjacent property.*" I asked whether we could put some flashing to cover the gap between the wall and the box to prevent water from getting in behind the box and causing further damage to the wall. He was most emphatic that that was not allowed. I asked if we could fill in the space between the box and the wall to prevent damage. That would under no circumstances be allowed. "*You can have the box moved temporarily – at your own expense – but it will cost you thousands,*" he suggested, almost gleefully. I was struggling to keep from exploding.

In all my work on our crazy house, one thing was quite clear to me: there were no 90-degree angles. I saw my chance. "You measured 10 centimeters from *that* corner of the box to the wall?" I asked innocently, pointing to the corner in question. He nodded. "Please measure the other corner!" He looked puzzled, but again whipped out his measuring stick. It was 9.5 centimeters. "Please move it!" I said. "*But half a centimeter isn't going to help you with your problem!!!*" he spluttered. "Ah, but there's an agreement with the Swedish Homeowners' Association that these boxes should be *ten* centimeters from the wall, *not nine and a half*!" I pointed out with ill-disguised jubilant satisfaction.

Mr Bureaucrat didn't say another word, apart from a vehement "*Hhrrumph*!!" as he made an about-face, marched straight to his Saab, flung himself in, and roared off. I had no idea what that meant, nor what would happen next. Had we won? Would our request be granted? Or was our plea going to be ignored?

Early the next morning, we awoke to the sounds of a truck pulling into Källargatan and braking. By the time I'd thrown some clothes on and raced out to the sidewalk, several workers were already breaking up the newly laid asphalt around the new connection box and were beginning to dig out the sand around it. I chatted with them and told them about the problem, which was pretty obvious to *them*. They asked me how far out from the wall I wanted the box to be, and they began wriggling it to a place that was still fairly close to the wall, but just far enough away to give us the necessary access to the wall behind it.

Then they asked me if I was going to fix the wall while they waited, or if the new position should be the permanent one. I suggested the latter, which they could easily understand, so they obligingly filled in around the box, packed it down with a compactor and departed. About half an hour later another truck pulled up and a guy with a vessel of steaming asphalt shoveled the contents all around the box, started up his compactor, and soon all was in order. No sooner had the asphalt guy driven away than I saw a familiar Saab pull up. Mr Bureaucrat got out. With eyes bulging and color draining from his face, he spluttered, "*What?! They've filled it in again?!*" I told him that they'd asked me if that was where I wanted it to be, and considering that I not only needed access to the wall behind the box to repair the wall *now*, but that there would also always be maintenance, I answered in the affirmative. He spluttered again, loudly, the drained color returning to his face like a tsunami, threw himself into his car without a word, and roared off, never to be seen (by me) again.

An anecdote like that can be funny – but only later, with the *benefit* of hindsight – when the outcome is good and the nervous emotion of the moment has passed. Other incidents may go by unnoticed, barely making a visible mark while they are happening, but turn out later – with the *bane* of hindsight – to have had incalculable significance, life-changing, possibly life-threatening significance. How is one to know which is which, not later, but *at the time*? How many such anecdotes and incidents are there in people's lives, sometimes on a daily basis?!

Much of April was devoted to leveling out the sandy ground of the entire downstairs, then carefully covering every square centimeter with the insulation mats. When that was done, the plumber and electrician put down all water pipes and plastic conduits for the wiring, crisscrossing the floor in ways we deeply hoped they understood. Finally, we put down reinforcement mesh in preparation for pouring a 10-centimeter-thick concrete slab. Like most of the other tasks that we'd never understood we'd be facing when we bought the house, casting a slab was another entirely new venture for me.

Tage again helped a great deal with advice, and showed me how to prepare "tracks" using parallel vertical boards, so that when the concrete slurry was delivered on Monday morning, May 3rd, it could be poured between the tracks. Then, by vigorously pulling and jiggling a wide plank back and forth along the top edges of the two boards, the concrete could be leveled to achieve a flat surface. It almost worked. It was desperately heavy work, especially since the concrete couldn't be pumped directly into the house, but had to be hauled indoors, one wheelbarrow at a time, within an "open" time of just a few hours before it all began to harden. Allan and Per came in to help me; we worked like animals and collapsed when it was done.

It wasn't a professional job, but it wasn't too bad for a first-time-ever experience of concrete work. Considering how crucial the downstairs floor was to the rest of the building – how much would literally be based on it – the reasonably good outcome felt a bit lucky too. I knew that concrete had to "cure", or harden, but the Swedish word for it was *bränna* ("burn"), which sounded crazy to me. As the concrete was continuing to harden that evening, I felt it with my hand and immediately understood: it was almost as hot as an iron. I now also understood why it was necessary to keep it wet for the first week or so, to avoid crack formation.

In April, Bob moved from his two-room apartment on the 13th floor to a three-room apartment on the 12th floor, on the opposite side of the building (there were four apartments on each floor). It gave him a deeply longed-for extra room for books, records, TV and video viewing, and our visits. Mrs Theinert, the lady whose apartment on the 12th floor (directly below Bob's old apartment) and who had always bitched at him for making the slightest noise, was now living on the same floor and was suddenly as gentle and friendly as a lamb.

On May 10th, Grandma Erisman died, three days before her 90th birthday – a release from long and silent suffering and disability, and a release for Mom from a burden she'd willingly been bearing for the past decade, the last few years of which she bore on her own. Suddenly, at the age of 63, Mom was alone, in a way she'd never been before in her life, in an empty house that hadn't ever had time to feel like home to her, unable to drive a car or ride a bike, with nothing but things that go bump in the night. Ralph and Maxine lived a few hundred meters down the road, and ever since my fiercely independent mother had made her move to the countryside outside Knoxville, she'd been extraordinarily dependent on her brother-in-law to take her anywhere beyond her walking distance, which meant just about everywhere. In her memoirs she wrote, "*I tried not to mention my empty house.*"

Jeanette seemed to me to become extra gloomy after my grandma's death, which I found strange. They hardly knew each other at all, and had only met twice – once in 1969 on our way to Sweden, and again in 1974, on our first trip back. They'd never even had a real conversation. Neither had I ever had one with Grandma, despite having met her hundreds of times. What could explain Jeanette's sudden wave of gloom, the kind that arose after my dad's death, then intensified after her father's death? Was it just another glimpse or mortality? Was it *just* "just"?

Once the concrete was good and hard, we could start in earnest to build up everything new, starting with the fireplace. The kit we bought called for a fresh air intake, which I'd already prepared though the outer wall and under the floor insulation, coming up through the concrete in one corner of the kitchen near the middle of the house, facing the dining corner of the kitchen. I built a brick base that interlocked with the brick wall to the entry, thus elevating the hearth about 80 centimeters above the floor level, so that anyone sitting on the far side of the kitchen table could get a full view of a fire in the fireplace. For a mantelpiece, I enlisted Saabyes' help in cutting out a piece about 30 by 100 centimeters from the thick iron plate that once covered the entrance to the cellar from the yard. The idea was that when a fire was going, the plate would heat up and could be used to keep pots and dishes warm while we were enjoying a leisurely meal.

After I finished the fireplace and the wall to the entry, I installed the vertical 20-by-20 cm wooden beam to support the iron girder (the I-beam that was positioned incorrectly but couldn't be moved). It was a great relief not to have to worry about the sagging girder anymore. I could then remove the rotting part of the upstairs floor, then the rotten part of the beams, which I cut off where they rested on the girder, and put in new ones (actually old but healthy ones from the demolition company) above the kitchen dining corner. Then I started laying the new floor upstairs. I built up the remaining section of the upstairs load-bearing wall in connection with building the new chimney from the fireplace and on up through the roof.

There was a small problem. Fire safety regulations required a gap of at least 10 cm between a chimney and a load-bearing wooden construction (a beam, rafter, stud, joist, truss, etc), but when I was getting ready to start building the chimney, I saw that the joists between the upstairs and downstairs were not aligned with the rafters. In order to maintain the required gap, I thus had to build the chimney on a slight angle from the upstairs floor in line with the rafters in the roof. I first cut an opening in the floorboards upstairs, corresponding to the format of the chimney. Then I measured the permissible distance from the rafters, marked those four corners in the roof boards, and pounded in 30 mm roofing-felt nails (they have large flat heads), so I could tie a strong string to each nail and pull it taut, fastening the other end of each string to a nail in each corner in the opening through the joists. I then built the chimney by following the four lines to achieve a slight lean that would not impair the joy in the hearts of the inspectors.

The chimney construction itself was a bit complex, as it required three flues. Regulations called for the flue from the fireplace to have an area equivalent to the size of a whole brick. The flue for the fans that would be placed above the kitchen stove only needed to be the size of half a brick, as did the third flue, for ventilation of the airspace in the peak of the roof. "Airspace" always suggested to me something that the planes of hostile countries invaded and had to be chased out of. Now I had to learn that an airspace was needed in a roof between the insulation and the roof boards, to prevent condensation from rotting the roof boards.

By addressing endless questions to people who seemed to know about such things, I found out that I needed to nail one-by-one-inch strips of wood along each side of the rafters, up against the roof boards, to which I could then attach sheets of hardboard that would thus leave the prescribed one-inch airspace. These sheets had to run the entire length of the rafters. Along the eaves the opening had to be protected from wasps and other pests by a polymer mesh.

The sheer complexity of this problem kept me awake at night trying to figure out how to resolve it. The fact is that ever since we'd started working on the house, I was beset by problems of similar magnitude (but entirely different nature) almost every night. My sleep patterns changed. I no longer had deep sleep and REM sleep; I had problem-solving "sleep". Many a night I would wake up at 2 or 3AM with a sort of *Eureka!* solution to whatever had been plaguing me when I went to bed.

The roof peak was one of those problems. Some roofs were built with ventilation of the airspace along the whole length of the peak, but that wasn't feasible for ours since the neighbor's roof peak abutted ours. Instead of building the upstairs ceiling all the way up to the peak, I therefore left a space about a foot high at the peak of our roof, and put in a vent in the peak of the end wall facing Källargatan, to vent out the two-thirds of the airspace between the chimney and the street. The problem was that the chimney itself blocked any possibility of a connection to vent the remaining one-third on the other side, towards the Saabyes. That's where the third chimney flue came in.

The chimney construction went well using the old bricks, with actual mortar this time. After about every three rows, I would "wash" the insides of the channels with mortar to fill any cracks and get a smoother surface. When I came right up to the roof, I removed the temporary covering and sawed out the opening to fit the new larger size. Indoors, I plastered the entire chimney. It looked good, slight slant and everything.

It was time to remove the strings from each corner. Standing on the floor upstairs, it was easy to remove the floor-level nails. Instead of fetching a ladder to reach the nails in the roof peak, however, I didn't think it could be that hard just to jerk on each string and pull loose those four nails. That's what happened for the first three corners. In the fourth and final corner, the nail wouldn't budge. I gave it a hard jerk. At the same moment it loosened I felt a sharp blow in the bend of my right arm. I looked down and saw the nail, with the string still attached, buried up to the head, straight into the bend of my arm.

I experienced much more surprise – bordering on shock – than pain. The first thought that popped into my mind was *Have I had my tetanus shot?!* I had, but I knew the nail had to come out immediately, so I just gritted my teeth and pulled it straight out again, with the help of the string. I was expecting a gush of blood to follow, but there was not one measly drop of blood, just a small droplet or two of some clear, slightly yellowish fluid. I rushed to clean the wound and bandage it up. But my arm hurt a lot. I couldn't make a fist or grip anything hard without terrible pain. Although that lasted about a month, it was my only direct, *physical* (modifiers can be important!) injury during the whole building project.

The next step felt to me like a milestone, turning the corner: framing up the walls with two-by-fours for base plates, top plates, studs and noggins. [*Although Sweden, like most of Europe and the non-Anglophone world, was almost completely metric, there were a few exceptions. In the case of two-by-fours (2 x 4"), inches were still used for certain dimensions of lumber, as well as most diameters of pipes in plumbing. That has since changed. As I write this, the last vestiges of inches in Swedish are in the diagonals of TV screens and the diameters of tires. Don't ask me why.*] I learned these and most of the other technical terms in Swedish first, then had to look them up in English. "Noggin" sounded weird to me; my dad used to say that someone was "off his noggin" when he considered that person at least temporarily crazy. The base plates rested on the new concrete floor; I nailed the top plates to the undersides of the beams, sometimes having to insert an extra piece of wood to compensate for differences in beam sizes. Behind and between the studs would go the mineral-wool insulation, about 15 cm of it, to keep our energy costs down.

I calculated that we would need a whole truckload of bales of insulation, but I had no idea where to put it all. Another neighbor was just starting a major renovation project as well, and also needed a truckload. His property included an entire warehouse-like annex, with plenty of room to store both his insulation and mine. So I negotiated a good price with the supplier, my neighbor and I shared the cost of transport, and they delivered a whole truck-and-trailer of the stuff, with a huge amount of it coming directly to Korngatan one day.

Our neighbor, the illustrious Elvis, a.k.a. Klas Rundström, sauntered over to find out what was going on and how I could *possibly* have use for so *unbelievably* much insulation?! I told him that I considered it the minimum for keeping heating bills down, and that it would pay off quickly. In his extremely cross-eyed way he stared at me (I think), then burst forth in his broad dialect with "<u>*My* roof is <u>*very*</u> well insulated, just great! Why, when it snows in the winter, it melts immediately</u>! Just runs <u>right</u> off! Now <u>that's</u> insulation!"

Once the framing was in place, it was time to get Bengt Lenander (our electrician) back to install all the plastic conduits and boxes for outlets, light switches, junctions, ceiling fixtures and wall-mounted electrical heaters. Getting him to come when he said he would was another matter. He could be an hour late, or a week, or more. I had to learn always to have another task to turn to when he didn't show up. He had a smoldering temper, and always seemed to be raging against one thing or another. His favorite assessment of nearly all others was "*klabbarpare!*" (probably what Basil Faulty meant when he called Manuel "a waste of space!"). Woe unto me if I failed to put in a noggin where he expected there to be one, of if I wanted more outlets than he thought a person of my foreign birth ought to be entitled to!

One of the jobs Jeanette and I could begin while waiting for Lenander was the whitewashing of the façade. Tage again had to show me how, so I could then show Jeanette, because she wanted to do everything that could be done while standing on the ground. I accompanied Tage to Denmark to buy the raw material (a thick chalk paste that reminded me of what came out of the tube of titanium white I painted with) because Tage said they didn't sell it in Sweden. A large dollop of the paste had to be mixed in a large bucket of water, to make something that looked kind of like skimmed milk. If you dipped your thumbnail into it, you knew you had the right concentration if you only had grainy traces of white left on your nail when you withdrew it from the liquid.

When I began splashing the stuff onto the wall that Jeanette had cleaned, using a special wide brush that looked like it should be on the end of a broom-handle, it just seemed to make the wall wet, not coat it at all. But Tage explained that when it dried some 15-30 minutes later, it would be white. He also said it had to be done many times, to build up many thin layers, because too thick a layer would only flake and fall off.

Fortunately, Lenander showed up before his summer vacation, in time to complete enough of his installation work so that I could get on with the insulation, then a plastic film moisture barrier, and finally the plasterboard. To help us keep costs down, our grumpy electrician revealed another side of himself and gave me a long spring (with 50 cm of wire attached to one end) that fit snugly inside the plastic conduits. He then showed me how to bend the conduits to the desired angles and how to secure the junction boxes to the studs at the right depth. Then he returned to inspect them and to have me assist him in pulling a guide wire through each conduit, which he would later use to pull all the electrical wiring through when the time came for the fixtures to be mounted.

Each sheet of plasterboard was a puzzle to cut, since the top edge was so irregular, and there were all the holes to be made for the junction boxes. Accuracy was important to minimize the amount of puttying required later, and to minimize Lenander's grumbling at me. But each new sheet of plasterboard that was nailed in place gave an enormously gratifying feeling of hope – that this project was on its way to completion after all. Each time I finished all four walls with plasterboard, we suddenly saw a *room* – not just an area of the construction site. Just over half of our two-year time limit to complete the house had already elapsed.

One day when I was out working on the front of the house, an elderly lady was strolling by and stopped. I looked up and greeted her. She told me that she once lived in our house, when she was a little girl, in the early 1900s. She was one of nine children – a family of 11 – living in an apartment that comprised one half of our downstairs. There'd been another family of similar size living in the other half of the downstairs. Then there were two more families upstairs. They pretty much covered the floors with mattresses each night, and every morning the mother shooed the kids out to fend for themselves, perhaps to go to work, even though they were children. Only a few went to school. It was a hard life. She emigrated from Sweden to America as a young woman and lived there most of her life, but she found that life as a pensioner in America was far too tough and brutal, so she came home at last to live out her days in Sweden. Her English accent when speaking Swedish was greater than mine.

I suddenly realized something on a human level that I'd only before read or heard about as cold hard facts. I'd already observed how little had been done to give the families who originally lived in our house anything but the bare minimum shelter. After all, it was built for "mere" workers, the working-class poor who didn't count for much back in the days when Sweden was ruled by the well-heeled right-wing Conservatives. There was no public welfare or universal healthcare, no free education for all. Child labor was common, as were horrendous working conditions and long hours with dismal wages, with no such thing as vacations or pensions. Sweden wasn't a democracy before 1900. Only wealthy men were entitled to vote, and the ruling class, the Conservatives, were quite content to keep it that way. They had only their power and wealth to lose. This was the environment into which that elderly lady was born, in the crowded, dirty, chilly house that barely gave shelter.

Sweden's Social Democratic Party was founded in 1889, some 25 years after our house on Korngatan was built. The early leaders of the movement were fined and jailed, but the movement continued to grow. They refused to be repressed any longer. But it wasn't until the 1920s – when that nuisance called democracy was pushing its way into the parlors of high society – that the Social Democrats became a force to be reckoned with. Their leader at the time, Per Albin Hansson, painted the picture of a just society, of Sweden as a home for everyone:

> *"The good home knows no privileged or slighted, no favorites or outcasts. People don't look down on each other, nobody seeks to gain privileges at the expense of others, and the strong don't trample on and plunder the weak. In the just society, there is equality, consideration, cooperation and helpfulness."* [my own free translation]

It took enormous dedication and commitment for Swedes to wrest power from the Conservatives who for centuries had been content to let the vast majority wallow in poverty, servitude and injustice. But unfortunately it would take a mere half a century for the Conservatives to begin to wrest it back again, thanks to growing apathy on the part of those whose ancestors had been victimized. Once again, Santayana's words rang a clear alarm: *"Those who cannot remember the past are condemned to repeat it."*

On July 3rd, 1976, the day before America's ballyhooed Bicentennial, the US Supreme Court ruled that the death penalty was not inherently cruel or unusual, but was a constitutionally acceptable form of punishment – another milestone in America's regressive shift. I couldn't help thinking how wonderful it was to now be living in a civilized country that hadn't executed anybody since 1910 – and how important it is never to take past gains towards a more just society for granted!!

Ten days after I finished the chimney and fireplace, the chimney sweep arrived to inspect and approve them, the first in a series of approvals we needed for the project. We'd now been living in our cramped and primitive quarters for more than 15 months and if we'd had time to stop and reflect on it, we might have despaired. Or we might have celebrated all the progress we'd made. What was our perspective? How much about ourselves or each other did we truly know?

The bed in our tiny bedroom in the little house was flush against three walls, with only the one long-side open to the room, and with only enough floor space for passage between the door from the hall and the door to the tiny bathroom, as well as the cabinet for the water meter and water heater. One day that summer, after a long day's work on the house, Jeanette seemed to be having greater-than-usual problems with her mood swings. She was sitting on the toilet making a list or something, while I was standing at the sink combing my hair back after a shower, so I wasn't more than 20-30 cm from her. Everything I said seemed to infuriate her, even though I was doing everything I could to calm her and speak gently to her.

Suddenly, without warning, she swung her arm forcefully at my naked thigh, stabbing me with her pencil. The lead (graphite) tip broke off in my leg and a little blood came trickling out (it was by no means a serious wound), but she was much more horrified than I was. It was as though the sight of a trickle of my blood woke her from an awful nightmare. She started crying uncontrollably and telling me how horrible she was, and how sorry. I grabbed some toilet paper and easily stopped the bleeding with one hand, while trying to caress and console her with the other.

She was beside herself, and I didn't know what to do. She was begging me to forgive her, which I did, immediately, unconditionally and emphatically, again and again. She said she couldn't understand what kept coming over her. She said she thought she had a brain tumor. I looked at her with alarm and said that if she thought there was the slightest possibility of such a condition, then we should immediately make an appointment for a check-up. She balked at once, changed gears completely, and begged me just to forget about the whole thing, she was just being "a silly goose" – whatever stupid, silly thing came over her was gone now, completely, so couldn't we please just go back to the way things were?

Oh, how I wanted to believe it could be that easy!! Every fiber in my being desperately wanted to believe that this was an anomaly, a one-time-only aberration that would never happen again, that my darling wife was fine and healthy in every way, that peace and love and harmony would engulf us and put everything right. Perhaps, when you want to believe something that badly, it turns out that way. Or perhaps, you become blind to any signs that maybe it *isn't* going to turn out that way. It's so much easier to tackle a problem when you think you can see a solution, *or* when you can banish from your mind the possibility of any problem at all, and thus don't find anything to tackle.

Hindsight, that terrible word that only presents the possible or perfect solutions once it's too late to solve the problems, was in the months to come the only venue in which I would see how Jeanette's rampant jealousy was beginning to morph in her mind into nightmarish fantasies about her health – incurable diseases that everyone knew she had, but nobody would tell her about, horrifying treatments she would soon have to undergo, how she would be kept alive in a conscious but otherwise vegetative state against her will.

Each time these moods, these horrors, came upon her, they started out as explosive anger. I learned to recognize them. I talked with her to calm her down. I encouraged her to have tests to dispel her fears, to find out whether they were imaginary diseases or real ones. I begged her to let us get professional help, to get counselling for her, or for *us*. And then her destructive mood would evaporate into thin air, sometimes for weeks. And she would *plead* with me not to pursue the matter any further. And I thought I was doing what could be done.

CHAPTER 13

"You can picture Jeanette"

On Saturday, August 14th, 1976, Rob and Chris threw a party at their apartment. They'd moved from Lundavägen quite a few months before, and now had a modern apartment in the Caroli City apartment-and-shopping-mall complex, another of the building complexes built and administered by Henry's company. Their apartment, which we hadn't seen before, felt luxurious to us – almost surreal – even though it typified mothing more than the latest Swedish standard. But Rob and Chris had already decided they'd had enough of Sweden, and would soon be moving back to England, to London. We would thus be losing friends as well as tennis partners (although our contacts had already become far less frequent).

In the autumn of 1976, Jeanette was working at a feverish pace: night school four evenings a week (learning German), her part-time job, work on the house, reading everything she could get her hands on – yet her jealousy had time to return in full force. I thought I might try to deal with it by ignoring it, leaving the room when it got to be too much for me. I suggested that she work out her jealous fantasies by writing about them, so she started writing playlets and poetry. In one short play about marital strife, the wife slips and falls to her death. I, the self-anointed expert psychologist, thought it was healthy for Jeanette to be able to get this sort of morbid fantasizing "out of her system".

In late September, we went to Skånemässan, a big annual home furnishings trade fair held in Malmö's sports complex, where we had high hopes (that were fulfilled) of getting great deals on all our appliances: stove, fridge, freezer, washer, dryer, kitchen fan, even a mixer and a sauna unit. (Our deal included the condition that we could postpone delivery until December.) Our plumber also gave us an excellent price on a 200-liter water heater for the big house. We made use of our government loan money sparingly, keeping it within our self-imposed 70,000 limit, only as a supplement to what we could afford with our paychecks. And we were managing quite well to keep on even financial keel.

By the end of September, the insulation and plasterboard were in place on all walls downstairs (and most of the upstairs), except the living room, which we decided to use as a work room until the other rooms were finished. We were at last ready to start laying the Höganäs tile floor everywhere – a prerequisite for ordering and installing the kitchen cabinets and the new stairway. (We'd been using a ladder since ripping out the old steep stairway from the courtyard, and had already walled up that door opening.) It was starting to look and feel like an exciting home, more exciting and spacious than we'd ever dreamed of. The goal, the Promised Land, was in sight! Success was close enough to taste!

We'd already worked out exactly – to the millimeter – what kitchen cabinets we needed, a step that was necessary for making the drawings to be laminated for the worktops, splashbacks, and cupboard doors. There was no hurry, but Stig Svensson told me they were making progress on them. He also said that we'd not only be getting the laminates, but that they'd be sending them to Perstorp's facility in Trelleborg to have them bonded onto high-grade chipboard, with a backing veneer as well (to prevent warping), so that they would arrive as complete worktop units and cupboard doors, with only the edges for me to finish as I liked.

On October 8th, we celebrated our 10th wedding anniversary, and on the 10th we celebrated again, this time for the 12 years since we first met each other on Ellis Street. For many years it had felt to me almost like we *were* each other, like each other's reflection in a mirror, which made Jeanette's increasing mood swings all the more confusing to me. But what was my "confusion" compared to what *she* was experiencing? For her it must have been *terrifying*, far beyond my comprehension or my work-obsessed horizon. Things were going on inside her head that I knew nothing about, much less understood. [*It now seems likely that she didn't either*]. She was drawing and writing a lot of stuff in notebooks that she kept to herself. Only occasionally would she share any of those secret thoughts with me, like this one:

> *You can picture Jeanette*
> *picturing her view,*
> *but you cannot picture her view.*

It reminded me a little of a haiku. The face-value, intellectual meaning was clear enough, but what did it mean to *her* – emotionally? Why did she show it to me and then not want to talk about it? Why didn't I understand it? Why do I understand it *now*?

She told me that she was becoming increasingly, thoroughly dissatisfied with her job, largely because her boss was such a wheeler-dealer and a crook. I urged her to change jobs, telling her that her sense of loyalty in staying there was misplaced. Then at the end of October, seemingly (to me) abruptly, she handed in her resignation at work, giving one month's notice, without having another job to go to. She hadn't mentioned any intention to study full-time, nor did she sign up for anything new. Although we were pretty dependent on having both our incomes, I was prepared to work extra. But was something else involved?

Tiling the floor was hard work. The finish on the underlying concrete wasn't nearly as smooth as it would have been if we'd had it done professionally – or if I'd realized how much more difficult it would be to tile a rough surface. [*I estimate that 10% more work on getting the concrete slab smoother would have saved me 90% or the work on laying the tiles.*] The adhesives normally used for tiles are based on a smooth substrate that only requires a thin layer, but I had to use a lot of rather expensive adhesive to make up for the irregularities. Tage advised me instead to lay the tiles in pure cement – Portland cement – which was cheap, but extremely stiff to work with, so it went slowly. At first, it took me a couple of hours to lay a single square meter (and there were some 70 square meters to lay). I started with the entry to get the feel of it in a limited space, then moved on to the short hall to where the new stairway would be, so we could be ready to install that as soon as it was ready for delivery.

Next came the floor in the kitchen, so that all the cabinets could also be installed more or less on arrival; delivery was scheduled for November 2nd – the same day Jimmy Carter was elected President. I didn't put the tiles all the way to the walls where the cabinets would be standing, but only far enough in from where the cabinet baseboards would be (we barely had enough tiles). Then I evened out the remaining distance to the wall with cement. In one area of wet cement, I drew a heart with our initials in it.

Also in early November, after further discussions with Jeanette, I finally got around to inquiring about a vasectomy. The procedure was permitted in Sweden, but only once we'd both met with a counsellor to discuss our reasons, and to assure them that we both understood what was involved. Jeanette's mind was firmly made up not to have children. As far as I was concerned, if she didn't want children, then neither did I. But the waiting list for vasectomies would mean six to eight more months of condoms, a bit of a disappointment once we'd made the decision to go ahead with it. We had a good, active, and mutually satisfying sex life, so I presumed we were both looking forward to the opportunity for greater spontaneity. (Just as Jeanette was marking her pocket memo calendar with a frowning or crying doodle of a girl for the days when she got her period, she sometimes marked our desk calendar with a tiny little heart for each time we'd made love – around 10 hearts per month.)

In mid-November, the staircase arrived and, after a lot of squeezing, it turned out to be a perfect fit. It felt like such a luxury to *ascend* a staircase instead of climbing a ladder. It also made it easier to run up and down to get more bales of insulation from the living room, which was serving as our temporary depot. We felt we wouldn't be needing to use the living room for anything but storage until everything else was ready, so the tiling of that floor would have to wait till last.

Above the mantelpiece of our new fireplace, I made an inscription (in Swedish) in the plaster: "*Jeanette and Stan Erisman have rebuilt this house. 1976*." We made our first fire there in November, and it seemed to warm the whole house. Jeanette made tea and sandwiches and we set up a table in front of the fire. I had to fight back the tears. Jeanette seemed joyful.

December 1st came, and Jeanette no longer had a job. When she gave notice, she seemed excited and relieved to be quitting, but none of that was visible now, although she did write on our desk calendar, "*A happy end to work*". She said she wanted, by herself, to find ways of "dealing with the void", and she became even more introspective and moody. In between her deep mood troughs, the peaks were no longer high.

Our appliances were delivered on Tuesday, December 7th, and since I'd already installed the cabinets, we just rolled the appliances into place. Even though we had to wait for the electrician (and the plumber for the washing machine), the kitchen was beginning to take on the appearance of living up to its name. We were almost home.

We were scheduled to spend two weeks with Bob, from December 18th to January 2nd, something Jeanette had always looked forward to with considerable enthusiasm in the past. Yet this trip to Basel was strange; her mood was heavy and gloomy when it might have been jubilant. Why was it different this time? After all, we were now within spitting distance of the achievement of a lifetime: creating a lovely, livable house out of a ruin.

The extra room in Bob's new apartment served him well, but he was in dire need of advice (and muscles) to get his furniture where it could be useful for him to have it. At first it felt like he'd merely acquired an extra room to fill with cellulose chaos – books and papers everywhere – but since I'd come to understand

Bob's wishes pretty well, I no longer had inhibitions or hesitation about helping and putting things right.

Jeanette left most of it to me this time. She barely smiled, and seemed sullen and withdrawn. I felt nervous about it and probably tried to compensate for the heavy atmosphere by forcing unfelt lightness upon it. I'm not sure how Bob reacted, or how much he noticed, what he thought, or what he understood. He maintained a sort of diplomatic silence. I just flitted and fluttered nervously, deluding myself that my forced cheer might be contagious.

I woke up on New Year's Day 1977 with a violent, debilitating headache which lasted three days. I went to the hospital about it when we returned to Malmö, and while I was there, on January 4th, Jeanette wrote an urgent poem about not allowing "them" to take me away from her.

> *You aren't going to let them convince you you're sick.*
> *You aren't going to let them take you away from me.*
> *You aren't going to let them label you as one of theirs.*
> *You aren't going to let them give you a chance to give up.*

But they found nothing wrong with me; I came home and forgot all about it. *For me* it was a question of having a problem, going to see those who were trained to figure out such problems, and confirming my hope that it was nothing serious. Although I didn't understand it at the time, *for Jeanette* it was an existential crisis; in her world, the doctors were out to get me, and her fear that it was serious was not at all allayed when they sent me home. *What <u>didn't</u> they find?*

A stack of Christmas cards was waiting for us when we got home from Basel, and we went through them, sometimes making comments, especially on those that included more than the printed messages. One card in particular that seemed to capture Jeanette's attention was from Dave Henderson, Norm's cousin from Oak Park who visited us at Christmas in 1970, but from whom we'd heard almost nothing since. There was no personal message that Jeanette reacted to; it was the motif on the front of the card: a drawing of six little children of different ethnic backgrounds, almost excessively, syrupy sweet, but somewhat melancholic. "Peace on Earth", roughly sketched, was inscribed in the background.

[*Some 40 years later, looking through Jeanette's pocket memo calendar for 1977, I discovered that she didn't make a single entry for any date that entire year. There are only a few addresses at the back (most of the usual ones had been omitted): for her family members, my mom, and Hamadi (my work contact). Various writings are also scrawled at the back. Everything is in pencil, very faintly written, almost illegible.]*

Jeanette dropped her evening classes and most of her work on the house to concentrate on reading physiology and writing poetry, most of which now concerned death. She stopped being jealous, but developed her new, vivid and obsessive fantasy: she had a terminal illness that everybody knew about and wouldn't tell her. I would sit down and discuss this fantasy with her, and after a while she said she realized that it was "only" in her mind. I told her I wished she would go on being jealous; she reacted with surprise and wondered why. I said that her jealousy was directed against me and I'd learned to handle it, but the new fantasies were directed against herself and I had no antidote – I didn't know what to do.

On January 21st, the day after his Inauguration, President Jimmy Carter issued a pardon to all Vietnam War draft evaders, which meant that even if I hadn't gotten off on a legal technicality back in 1973, I probably would have been off the hook now. I tried to discuss it with Jeanette – a topic that would normally have ignited her – but she just shrugged apathetically. Every attempt I made to probe into what was going on inside her was fruitless; she only retreated further into herself. I felt a sense of alarm welling up inside me, thoughts I didn't dare to think, unspeakable fears lurking at an unknown distance, that the person who was my life was becoming – *had become?* – unreachable. I began to feel something like panic.

I could find nothing better to do than to redouble my efforts to finish the house so we could move in. After all, hadn't Bob felt so incredibly much better when we got his home in order? Hadn't his deep depression dissolved and faded away when his external chaos was outflanked by structure? Wouldn't that work for Jeanette too, please, please, *please?!*

By the start of February, she was writing more and more, and drawing more as well. Sometimes she threw out her work. Sometimes she showed me a bit of it. Most of her drawings were grotesque self-portraits, some of her crying, some with tortured and horrified expressions, some vacant and apathetic. Her writings reflected her obsession with death and illness, as though she were mesmerized by it. I thought they were well-written and *hoped* that it was good that she could express herself in that way. I earnestly and anxiously hoped that it could be a way for her to deal with it, a safety valve. I again suggested that if she *really* thought she was sick, she should see a doctor, but again she declined, saying that most of the time she realized that her inner horrors were "just" ideas that came over her. But she made me solemnly promise her that if any major illness did befall her, I would not let *them* keep her alive like a vegetable.

Jeanette reminded me again that she was absolutely certain she didn't want children, and wondered whether I was going to do something about getting that operation, so we went to the hospital together for the compulsory interview, and a procedure was scheduled for June 10th. While we were in the hospital area, Jeanette noticed a job ad posted on a bulletin board, for a very short-term secretarial position at the cytology lab within the pathology department. Not having a job to go to was making her restless, so she applied for it and got the three-week job.

[*In what I would later come to recognize as my usual head-in-the-clouds manner, I gave no thought at the time to the possibility that a person obsessed with illness and death might not benefit from working daily and hourly with documents and possibly photos dealing with diseases and death on the cellular level, too small to be seen with the naked eye, but lurking there all the same.*]

The kitchen cabinets, minus the doors and worktops, were all in place. The plumber installed the stainless steel sink, the water heater and the fixtures in the upstairs lavatory (the sink, bidet, and toilet). In mid-February we installed the appliances. Since the electrician had also done his stuff, we suddenly had a full-size fridge-freezer combination, a stove with a double oven, a kitchen fan, a washer and a dryer, all installed and ready for use.

But Jeanette was reluctant to begin using anything, as if it was somehow jumping the gun before everything else was ready. We were used to the cramped quarters upstairs in the little house. One afternoon when I was just leaving our makeshift living room up there, Jeanette was entering, and I stopped to give her a hug. She hugged me back in such a strange way, squeezing me hard, but at the same time she felt like she'd gone all limp, melting. I pulled back my head to look at her and saw that she was crying. I caught my breath and asked her what the matter was. She just shook her head and said she was being "a silly goose". I was more than dumbfounded; I was *terrified – and therefore banished it from my mind.*

In the early days of March, we ordered a mattress for a new and bigger bed in our new and bigger bedroom, upstairs in the big house. It would take three weeks for the mattress, and we wanted to have it ready. We learned always to have several projects running concurrently, so that if there were a delay – waiting for materials or craftsmen – in one of them, we could keep going on one or more of the others.

One of the only things that remained to be done upstairs was to put up the wood paneling (which we'd already purchased – new) in the southern, steeply sloped half of the roof on the side along Korngatan, where our bedroom would occupy the western two-thirds, and Jeanette would have a room of her own at the top of the stairs, in the third nearest to Källargatan, with a dormer window overlooking Korngatan and the street corner and on up Källargatan towards the square. It would be a bright and cheerful room, with three old exposed tie beams running through it. I would eventually build in some cabinets for her along the outer wall, as per her request, as well as a couple of cubbyholes at the foot of the sloping ceiling, to give her maximum storage space.

Apart from the stairway and the small lavatory, the north half of the upstairs was earmarked to become my studio, with big north-facing windows towards the yard and the little house. The only other tasks left upstairs were the sanding of the floors and the puttying and painting of the walls.

No sooner did we order the mattress than the bonded laminates for the kitchen arrived. Since all the cabinets were ready and waiting, the countertops could be glued and screwed into place directly. The main countertop was over four meters long, with a short perpendicular extension for the cabinets that came out from the wall to where the big vertical beam stood, the one I'd put in to shore up the sagging iron girder.

Then I put up the splashbacks along the entire length of the countertop, from the surface up to where the wall cabinets were mounted. These were held in place by moldings screwed into the wall. The effect of having these in place decisively turned the building site into a striking kitchen. I was incredibly thrilled, but my excitement was instantly quenched when I saw Jeanette's utterly dampened, apathetic reaction. She looked like she was struggling to look pleased, but that the work to do so was just too much for her.

Was she unable to visualize what I was seeing – the finished kitchen, us living in it, laughing, joking, cooking joyfully, everything rosy? Was she visualizing something else, something I couldn't begin to imagine? (*"You can picture...."*) Didn't I dare to imagine her imagination? Maybe unbridled optimism is not always the appropriate response?

About a week later, in mid-March, I was upstairs in the little house, sitting at the table we sometimes still used for coffee breaks, and Jeanette came in, came directly over to me, sat on my lap, and put her arms around me. A few seconds later I again felt that same heavy, limp, melting feeling from her, and again saw that her eyes were all teary. I tried to talk with her about it, but she made it quite clear that she wouldn't discuss it. I felt such overwhelming helplessness emanating from her. *What was happening to her, to us?!?*

The laminated, bonded doors required a bit of work. Each door consisted of a sheet of chipboard faced on one side with my laminated drawing, and on the back with laminated backing veneer of the same color as the background color in my drawings, making a sandwich construction about 20 mm thick. But the four edges of the board were unfinished, and to these I glued strips of dark-brown stained wood about 10 x 25 mm. Into one long edge I screwed lift-off pin hinges, added a simple, dark-brown-stained wooden door knob, and attached magnets for closing. One by one, I got them done, working feverishly against a clock I couldn't see. The cupboard doors doubled the brightness and cheeriness of the new kitchen, but Jeanette didn't seem able to take it in.

On Saturday, March 19th, Hamadi, Saloua and the baby dropped by to see us. They said they were about to leave on an extended trip of 4-6 weeks to Paris to see Hamadi's brother and some other relatives there, and they wanted to say goodbye, and to have a look at the progress on our house. Hamadi also said he was interested in buying a couple of my paintings, right then and there, and was willing to pay a good price for them. I had listed prices in my catalogue, mostly to scare off would-be buyers, but Hamadi thought my prices were quite all right. But he didn't have that kind of cash on him, so he asked if he could he pay me later? I suggested that we talk about the whole thing later, when they got back from their trip, because parting with paintings was no easy matter for either of us. He looked disappointed, almost irritated, but shrugged and changed the subject. They soon departed – in a brand-new Alpha-Romeo (he'd just traded in his old VW Beetle on it) – with Hamadi basically leaving me in charge of running the operations of the school in his absence, although fortunately somebody else was in charge of the administration.

The next day we got a surprise visit from Stig Svensson and his wife Signe, from Perstorp. Stig wanted to see how our kitchen was turning out, and to show his wife. He was proud of the results, which made the kitchen truly unique. They were around 15 years older than us, warm and friendly people, and although we'd never met Signe before, she was one of those people whom one immediately feels like one has known and liked forever. Stig talked about having our kitchen photographed for use in some of Perstorp's promotional material to illustrate the versatility and potential of decorative laminate.

The following day, March 21st, we received a letter from Mom, in which she wrote that she was hoping to visit us for a couple of weeks in September. She enclosed a good portrait photo of Dad for us, and reiterated that she would like the three of us to take a trip together to Jerusalem and other places in Israel in connection with her trip to see us. Jeanette wrote a reply the following day, a friendly letter welcoming Mom to stay with us, and expressing how much she (Jeanette) was looking forward to the trip together. Her letter ended with: "*Spring has finally come, and with it lightness of heart and weather. Hopefully, we'll be able to experience many warm, comfortable days together while you're here.*" [Jeanette sent this letter before I saw it; because Mom was traveling at the time, it didn't reached her until at least 10 days later. Mom kept it and gave it to me at a later date.]

One day during the following week, Jeanette said wistfully that she thought it would be nice to die on the same day that Beethoven died, March 26th, the coming Saturday. I found her remark silly but also disturbing, like she was engaging in some sort of Byronic posturing. But on that date, that Saturday, some friends dropped by in the afternoon, and in the evening some neighbors asked us over for coffee. The neighbor lady was going to teach Jeanette how to knit. And in about one more month, our house would be ready for moving in.

When we woke up on Sunday morning, March 27th, I went across to the big house and got the paper that had been pushed through the letterbox in the door, then came back to bed with it, our usual Sunday morning routine. I saw an ad for the Tuesday evening concert at the theater in Malmö, featuring Emil Gilels, the famous Russian pianist we'd seen several years before in a Beethoven concert that was still the best we'd ever been to! We were *both* thrilled at the prospect of going, and agreed that we'd stop by the theater to get tickets on our way home from our usual hour of Sunday tennis, now just the two of us. After reading the paper, I got up to go and work on the house, and Jeanette was going to read some more and then do a few things in the kitchen until we went to play tennis in the early afternoon.

When it was almost time to go, just after noon, I found Jeanette still in bed with the light off. She was awake, deep in thought. I told her we'd have to hurry.

She played hard and well, but she didn't laugh as she usually did whenever she hit a ball out of my reach. When we started cycling home, her mood was not one I recognized – a numb, vacant kind of look, as if she were somewhere else. We forgot all about getting the concert tickets. When we were cycling along the last stretch along Lundavägen, just before turning onto Vattenverksvägen, I noticed that she was lagging behind a bit. I turned to find her crying. I stopped and asked what the matter was. She said she was just tired, and that when we got home, she'd have a nap while I worked on the house.

I, who almost always question and probe, let her go lie down on the couch upstairs, while I hurried off to continue one of my countless urgent final projects. About three hours later, at 6 PM, I came in to see how she was. She said she had a headache, and would I please go out and get her some aspirin, because our supply had run out. Or instead, could I get her some sleeping pills? Her request surprised me. She'd always refused sleeping pills. I told her I didn't think it would be a good idea, but I would get the aspirin. She just shrugged. In the main square (Stortorget) there was a pharmacy that was open on Sundays as well, and I hurried there for a jar of aspirin, came back and gave Jeanette two with a glass of water. She said we'd eat at eight, and that I should go back and work on the house.

When I entered the little house at eight, it was strangely dark. I went upstairs to see about supper, saw Jeanette still lying on the sofa. I thought she was sleeping. I switched on the light and saw a bowl with *vomit* in it, and vomit on the carpet around it, then something that froze my blood: beside the bowl was the jar I'd just bought, which had contained 100 aspirins. *It was empty!!* I *flew* to her side, shook her, and she moaned and mumbled something. For a few minutes, I stood there in absolute panic, making groaning sounds, mostly to myself, for Jeanette was dazed and numb and only half listening.

I finally fought the mounting tide of panic and hysteria enough to call a taxi. While we were waiting for it, the phone began to ring. It would be Bob, it was right on schedule for his usual Sunday evening call. Jeanette managed to muster enough coherence to plead with me not to tell anybody about this, so I let it ring.

She felt cold and far away as we rode to the emergency section of the hospital, where they pumped her stomach. The staff told me that she might feel a little numb for a few days, but there was no grave danger, that everything would be all right. *And because those were the exact words I wanted to hear, I allowed a barrier of calmness to settle over me, to insulate me and isolate me from what I couldn't bear to see.* They then told me that Jeanette was to spend the night there; I was welcome back in the morning. I walked halfway home, and when my normally indefatigable legs would no longer support me, I took a bus the rest of the way, my head spinning, trying to think of nothing.

When I got home, my head felt like a bottle of soda water that had been shaken for a long time. I went upstairs in the little house to where Jeanette had thrown up. I cleaned up the carpet and the bowl. They told me at the hospital that I could come and pick Jeanette up at nine-thirty the next morning, Monday morning. I went to bed totally drained, set the clock-radio for seven, and slept a stunned, dreamless, comatose sleep.

I woke up with a start at 6 AM, March 28th, 1977. (It was also Mom's birthday.) I would be at the hospital an hour early, I would show her how glad I was to see her. I was determined to hide all my anxiety, and not to rebuke her in any way, temporarily forgetting that I wasn't a person who could hide anxiety if I was feeling it. I tried instead to blank out my mind of everything I could. I glanced at the morning paper before leaving. Two jumbo jets had crashed on a runway on Tenerife, huge casualties. Setting out on my bicycle without even thinking about it, I stopped at a florist on the way to the hospital, and bought a single red rose, like the one I gave Jeanette, my own Rose, the first time I met her after work in San Francisco. I called Isobel at work, asking her to fill in for me at work in the morning because I would be late. I didn't say why.

Jeanette looked weak and pale, but managed a smile when I entered the room, and seemed glad for the rose and the change of clothes I brought for her in a small bag. As a matter of routine under such circumstances, we were told, she'd been referred to the psychiatric section of the hospital before release. I didn't know what to think of that because I'd completely forgotten how to think. I was numb, totally paralyzed with fear, trying to put on a façade of normalcy.

With a nurse accompanying us, I wheeled Jeanette in a wheelchair through the long underground passages that connected many of the separate buildings of the Malmö hospital complex. Jeanette claimed that she felt all right, apart from a numb tingling all over, which they'd told us would wear off in a few days.

We were first taken to a counselor, who wanted Jeanette to remain at the hospital for a few days, but the counselor didn't have the authority to make such a decision. That would have to be made by a psychiatrist. The psychiatrist, a middle-age woman, said she wanted me to be present for the interview, which I was. I held Jeanette's hand. Jeanette said that she didn't know what came over her, that in a way she just wanted to see what it was like, but that it was done with now, over.

The psychiatrist apparently thought that Jeanette – or even I – was capable of making crucial, rational decisions at a time like that, in states of horror, panic, numbness and denial like that. She than *asked* Jeanette whether she *wanted* to remain there!! Preferably not, Jeanette replied softly. The psychiatrist said she didn't want to go into anything that day. She said that it was clearly a question of some sort of schizophrenia, but told Jeanette that she could go home and come back for a chat two days later, on the Wednesday morning. Jeanette seemed relieved, but said nothing. She and I left the hospital.

I asked her if she'd like to stop at the theater and get those tickets for the concert the following evening. She said that that would be a good idea, so we started walking slowly, Jeanette setting the pace, me leading my bike, to the theater, just a few blocks from the hospital. We got good seats, and Jeanette seemed happy about it, but sounded weary, weak, fragile and distant. She hadn't eaten anything, so I ran over to a bakery near the theater and bought her some fresh rolls. Jeanette took only a couple of bites and said she didn't feel like eating now.

Then I asked her the worst and most ignorant question of my life: *Would she like me to come home with her?* She said there was no reason for that, I didn't need to worry, she'd behaved like a "silly goose", but it would never happen again. And I had to promise not to tell anyone. I felt relieved *because I so urgently, desperately wanted that to be true!!* She said she wanted to go home and rest now, and that I should go to work, so I hailed a taxi for her.

We kissed goodbye in the street in front of the theater, I told Jeanette I loved her, and I watched as she was driven away.

I felt anxious and confused and dazed as I went to work, but I fought and repressed it, since I knew she absolutely didn't want me to let anyone know. As soon as I arrived at the school, I called home. The phone rang for a long time before Jeanette finally answered. She said she'd just gotten in the door. She sounded quite a bit better, I thought, her energy seemed to be returning, and she said she was going to make herself a couple of sandwiches with the rolls I bought and then sleep the rest of the afternoon. I felt an enormous wave of relief sweep over me. Just before we hung up, I said once again, "*I love you, Jenny,*" and she said "*I love you, Stan.*"

"You can picture Jeanette"

During my attempt to give English lessons that afternoon, my mind was unable to focus on anything. I was trying to think of what to say to her that evening, what might help to make her cheerful. I achingly hoped that the concert the following evening would do her a lot of good. I finished work at five-thirty, and while cycling furiously home, I decided I would shower Jeanette with all the affection and attention that she may have been lacking due to all my labors on the house. I'd already worked myself into an eager and joyous mood when I arrived home at ten minutes to six.

As soon as I opened the garage door and entered the garage with my bicycle, a blow of sheer terror struck me, freezing my blood, prickling my skin, raising my hair. Around one of the iron girders that supported the garage roof was a broken piece of rope. Directly beneath it, Jeanette's bicycle lay on the garage floor. The door to the little house stood wide open. I ran through the garage, got a glimpse of a cord that didn't belong there hanging on the bare high wall towards Saabyes. I charged into the little house hoarsely shouting for Jeanette. No answer. I bounded upstairs to the sofa. She wasn't there, but what I saw seared my mind. The same bowl was on the floor next to the sofa again, with fresh vomit in and around it. There was a half-empty bottle of acetic acid. A vase with the red rose I'd given her that morning. Dave's Christmas card with the children. *But Jeanette was not there.*

I flew back down the stairs, out the door, across the yard. The back door to the big house was also wide open. I threw myself into the kitchen. Shouting her name in a voice rising rapidly in pitch and volume and terror, around the downstairs, my feet scarcely touching the floor, up the stairs, three at a time.

There! In *her* room! My hands outstretched, my skin peeling off, my heart exploding out my throat. *Jeanette's hand was cold, her semi-closed eyes were vacant, her face was grayish blue, her tongue was protruding slightly from a cruel grimace, her feet were dangling high above the floor, she was suspended from a tie beam by a cord around her neck. A fallen stepladder lay on the floor.*

I just stood there, my love and life and world and hopes swirling into chaos and destruction, my arms around my darling.

And I screamed. And screamed! *And screamed!* *And screamed!!!*

CHAPTER 14

No place to go

I have no idea how long I stood there screaming. Or even if my screams were audible outside my anguished brain. My world no longer existed, my north, my south, my muse, my life, my love, my soul, my reason for living – everything was gone, crushed, exploded, imploded, rotting, decaying, destroyed, disintegrated, pulverized, eviscerated, incinerated. I had no place to go, no place to run, no retreat. *No wish to go <u>on</u>.*

In the same millisecond that one thought began forming in my festering brain, it was electrocuted and pulverized by another thought, then another, then another, in a whorl of chaos, with flashes of reality that ratcheted up the pain in rapid cycles and waves that knocked me down and drove nails into my eyes, where the grotesque image of my darling hanging there was searing my retina.

I stumbled backwards out of the room as if being violently shoved by what I saw, fumbling, to the stairs in a state of howling, shivering shock. Something told me I had to *do* something. I found myself upstairs in the little house at the telephone, dialing the emergency number. It took what seemed like several minutes for the operator to make any sense of whatever was coming out from deep inside me, from my very sobbing core and marrow, only occasionally in the form of recognizable words. After she finally succeeded in getting the address, she told me an ambulance was on its way. I let the receiver fall back in place as I sank to the floor.

An awful nameless fear was creeping over me like a brushfire, burrowing under the thickening layer of shock, and *that horrifying image* kept coming back and back. My feet dragged my body outside, out the front door, to meet the ambulance. I found myself in the middle of Korngatan, writhing in pain. My eyes were so wild I could see I was scaring the few passers-by, but I didn't know who they were or if they were real. I recognized nothing and nobody; my whole world was gone. An ambulance came. There was a lot of running about and low murmurs of instruction. I felt like I was falling into a coma, an abyss. One of the men was holding onto me, holding me up. *Couldn't they just slip me something that would make me die, end this searing agony, this unspeakable heartache, my fucking life?*

Soon another ambulance arrived, or it might have been a police car, or both. I was eventually loaded into one of the ambulances. I don't remember if I was sitting or lying down or who was around me or who was saying what. I was taken *back* to the emergency psychiatric clinic at the hospital, the very place Jeanette and I had been that very morning before they sent her home. I was given a sedative that seemed to have no effect. At least not on my pain, just on my already slurred speech.

Minutes and hours behaved like years. I was sitting there, my body and brain on fire, moaning, in a softly lit, sterile-looking corridor with various medical people walking about, speaking in hushed whispers. Or was it that my hearing was impaired? I didn't dare to shut my eyes, or take my focus from the light yellowish linoleum floor, because if I did I would only see the horror on my retina. Her face, her contorted, vacant face. That empty grotesque look, that look of death, of the void, of *gone forever*. Various uniformed staff members came up to me and said things, but I had too much churning inside to respond to anything outside. Some of them may have put an arm around me or a hand on my shoulder or checked things that medical people check, except that this was psychiatric. I was unable to suppress the cynical thought that *maybe they don't check anything*.

Somebody told me that a couple of police officers wanted to have a word. There were two of them, in dark blue uniforms. They looked worried, concerned, and I knew that they were just trying to do their job, trying to get a statement from me about what happened and when. I tried to tell them, but I kept breaking up, breaking down, breaking apart, falling to pieces. I have a vague memory that they expressed how sorry they were for me and for making me go over it all again. They seemed to be very kind and considerate and all, but there was no good way to do that job or to do anything, no good way to tell whom I'd found or how. Only searing pain.

Somebody asked me if I wanted to call anybody, maybe someone in my family or a close friend, and my practical brain briefly sputtered to life. *Not Mom – she couldn't handle it. Not Bob either – same reason. Not Al – I couldn't handle him. John* – yes, phone John, he's my brother, in California. Yes, USA. My pocket memo calendar was always on me, and I began fumbling with it. They took it and said they'd find the number. When I was taking it out of my pocket, I discovered the concert tickets for the following evening and gave them to one of the staff to give to whomever might be interested. *It would be so great; such wonderful music; Jeanette loved it so much.*

Some undetermined, unbearable amount of time later, someone handed me a phone. I heard my sister-in-law Marj's agitated voice on the line. *Maybe they've already told her.* I sobbed out briefly what happened, and asked her to notify the others – Jeanette's mom, my mom, Al. I don't remember a word of what she said. Then I hung up. Before my practical brain retreated back into its vat of molten lead, I had the presence of mind to ask someone from the staff to call Isobel so I could tell her I couldn't work the next day or that week, or that month, or maybe nevermore. *Quoth the raven.* They dialed, they talked, they handed me the phone. Isobel got out of me what had happened and told me to just sit there; she and Björn were coming at once to fetch me. I had no clue what she was talking about.

I'd hardly known Isobel as more than a colleague at that point. Jeanette and I had socialized with her and Björn a few times, but they were no more than casual acquaintances. In my condition I was incapable of surprise about the fact that even though they were expecting their first child that summer and barely knew me, they were suddenly there in the hospital corridor, sitting on either side of me, each with an arm around me. They were trying to talk to me but I could hardly respond to anything. My nose and eyes were swollen with tears. They were speaking to some of the staff, writing some notes, and then they were helping me on with my coat, and I was being led down the corridor to the stairway, and out of the building into the night air. I had no strength left to scream.

They drove me to their small apartment on Munkhättegatan, and poured numbing Irish whiskey down my throat, and I kept wanting more to dull everything, not to have to feel. *O, that this too too solid flesh would melt!!!* They wiped my face with cool wet cloths. I have a vague memory that Al phoned – he must have gotten Isobel's number from the hospital, or did Isobel phone him? – but I can't remember speaking to him. I must have asked Isobel to phone Bob, but I don't remember speaking to him either or what might have been said. I couldn't stop my terrified sobbing.

Isobel lit a candle "for Jeanette", which was beyond my comprehension. I probably thought it was related to some sort of Irish Catholic superstition. I might have been irritated, it might have flashed through my mind that if lighting something would help, I'd light *everything* on fire. But I had no strength to say so. I kept drinking as much whiskey as they placed within my reach, smoking as many cigarettes as I could, and crying as long as I remained conscious and perhaps beyond. This was long before anybody knew anything about the dangers of secondary (a.k.a. secondhand smoke or passive smoking), or even smoking and pregnancy. I believe that Isobel also smoked, but my memory of that it unclear.

No place to go

At one point I think I asked for a sleeping pill – preferably a jar of them. *Now I knew what she meant. Too late. Too late for everything.* Björn and Isobel just held me all night until I passed out in a stupor of grief and booze. I don't remember Tuesday.

On Wednesday morning, I asked Björn to drive me to the hospital to see the psychiatrist. An appointment had already been made – for Jeanette – but now I decided it must be for me. How did I remember that? My memories of that brief meeting are vague and sketchy, but there are patches of clarity. I remember entering the psychiatrist's pale yellow-and-white, high-ceilinged office, with a few shelves full of books and binders. I seem to recall that I remembered that office and that psychiatrist from two days earlier. She was sitting there at her desk, I sat opposite her – alone this time. I don't remember a word she said, except that it was all a garble of platitudes, empty phrases and defensive excuses. I'm fairly certain that she was already aware that Jeanette was dead, because I presume she would have reacted more if I'd been the one to tell her.

She didn't react outwardly to my being the patient instead of Jeanette. I remember formulating my questions in the past tense accusative, wondering why the hell they'd let Jeanette go home, why couldn't they see what she and I were incapable of seeing, that she was in no state to deal with reality? Hadn't this shrink said that Jeanette showed clear indications of schizophrenia? *Yes.* What the hell kind of rational choices could then be expected? *No answer.* Couldn't they have seen how desperate she was? How desperate I was? How much I was in denial? How unfit I was to know what path to pursue? How utterly lost? *No answers.* Even psychiatrists sometimes get ambushed by hindsight.

If my memory of that meeting has anything to do with what happened, I'm afraid I gave that poor psychiatrist the worst day of her life. She looked deeply shaken. Maybe I was vengefully trying to make her day as bad as mine, to drag her down with me. But I thought my questions were justified, even if I might have formulated them differently. At least I had a right to ask them. I don't remember whether she had any advice to give me. (Or maybe she only asked me what *I* thought I should do.) She placed me on sick leave for two months on grounds of "mental insufficiency". I asked if she expected me to be capable of work after two months. She said the medical leave of absence could be extended if needed. We would see.

At some point somebody from the hospital asked me about "the arrangements".

Once I understood the question, I told them cremation, in accordance with Jeanette's frequently stated wishes. There would be no funeral; I would be taking the urn to America. (I told them this because I feared they would try to prevent me from scattering the ashes at sea, as Jeanette wished.) They said they would see to it.

I seem to recall that Al arrived first. Was it on the Thursday? I think Björn either picked him up at the ferry terminal after his flight landed in Copenhagen, and took us to Korngatan – I was *not* prepared to be there alone! – or Al took a taxi to Björn and Isobel's place and *then* Björn drove us to Korngatan.

I do remember that after arriving at Korngatan with Al, he and I – just the two of us – went upstairs in the little house. I tried to explain what I'd found, how I'd found her. But the picture burnt onto my retina that was so clear *there* was incapable of reaching my lips. Al talked about something or other, and I cried. After a time, I excused myself and went down the stairs, across the yard and into the big house, upstairs to Jeanette's room, the room where she ended her life, the room where she was hanging the last time I was in that room, the last time I ever saw her. That vacant look in her eyes, a look I couldn't put into words, her skin that was cold and lifeless to my touch the last time I'd entered that room. The pain was excruciating and terrifying, the sadness was crushing. After a few minutes, I heard Al hurrying up the stairs to find me with a rope around my neck, standing on the floor, staring up. And I remember that Al picked that choice moment to begin talking to me about the Lord. I don't remember his or my exact words, but I remember the nature and tone of my response clearly, and will try here to put together what words I feel I was likely to have used to convey such a bitter, horrifying response:

> "Al, please understand that the <u>only</u> reason that I haven't <u>already</u> taken my own life now is that I find it <u>impossible</u> to believe in an afterlife! If I did, if I believed for a <u>second</u> I could somehow rejoin her, I wouldn't hesitate to take my life as well, right now. It's only my <u>unbelief</u> that's keeping me alive!"

That shut him right up, or at least shut the sphincter of his evangelizing. I couldn't begin to imagine how he could juggle the books of right and wrong to construe how there could be a good god who had any interest in humanity or sparrows, and who had any control of anything, and yet would stand by watching (or causing) my darling to suffer unspeakably. It was perverse, malicious, obscene, sick, psychopathic, heinous – and fiction.

No place to go

Jeanette's twin brother Michael showed up a day later. I have a vague memory that he was very sad and displayed more emotion than I'd ever seen. I think he asked me a number of hesitating questions, perhaps to get a clue about the circumstances, but I have no memory of any real conversation with him.

Bob arrived shortly after. He didn't say much, but conveyed his strong support without words. I was hardly capable of speaking. I only sat at the window upstairs in the little house, in our temporary kitchen, staring out into the street, waiting (and hopelessly watching) for Jeanette to come home. Bob encouraged me to keep drinking plenty of whiskey, telling me that a man who'd broken every bone in his body shouldn't try to walk and needed any form of analgesic he could get. I longed to hide from all this in Jeanette's arms, but neither these three men, nor anybody, could help.

When it was getting to be late in the evening, I poured myself an extra-large whiskey, probably around 20 cl, into a tumbler. Bob didn't react, but Al's and Michael's eyes went wide. I'm pretty sure I was already drunk enough to loosen my tongue a little, but not drunk enough to stop thinking. I told them, *"I don't need a nightcap – I need a night <u>helmet</u>!"* I needed to get comatose so my brain could get some rest. As soon as enough of the alcohol wore off, I would begin to dream – *what dreams may come* – the worst imaginable nightmares of her tortured face, and I would be startled back into drunken, unendurable, excruciating semi-consciousness.

I have no memory of what sleeping arrangements we had, except that I stayed in our (my and Jeanette's) tiny bedroom downstairs. Bob might have stayed at a hotel. I remember that Ellen Saabye stopped by with a hot meal for all of us, but I was drinking mine, and smoking constantly, only cigarettes, probably Prince (a Swedish brand similar to Marlboro). After a day or two, Al and Michael had to get back. Michael asked me if I wanted to accompany him to San Francisco. Al suggested Seattle. But I chose to leave with Bob to Binningen instead. Obviously. Plane tickets were arranged for me (probably by Bob, possibly with Al's help), the others left for the States, and Bob took care of me. This would probably have been on April 2nd or 3rd.

I don't remember anything about our flight to Basel, except that Bob was talking to me, calmly, slowly, yet nervously, soothingly taut, the whole way. My normal spontaneous Pavlovian impulse to start tidying up his place the instant I arrived was simply absent. In daylight, I spent a lot of time on Bob's balcony looking down, but I couldn't bring myself to splatter myself all over the concrete on the ground 12 stories directly below. I told myself it would be too messy in every way for Bob to have to deal with. When it was dark, I just drank and smoked and sobbed myself to sleep.

Except that I couldn't *stay* asleep. I was reenacting, *reliving*, that horrifying day, that agonizing moment, that blood-curdling sight, every minute, several times a minute. I was reliving what I tried to imagine had been going on in her, what secret horrors were consuming her, but I couldn't know, couldn't *ever* know. It was tearing me apart, smashing my thoughts, destroying my ability to think the simplest thoughts through.

Everything in Bob's apartment – and in all my other thoughts – reminded me of when Jeanette and I did this or that together: fixing up Bob's apartment, enjoying the music and the wine and the conversation. Everything had been so bloody meaningful. Now none of it meant anything. I was staring at my paintings on Bob's walls, thinking about how much she loved them, thinking about all her love and affection and encouragement to keep painting. Now my muse was gone. *How could I ever paint again?*

After staring for a while at *The Underwater Man* and *Old Man with a Pipe* on the wall in front of me, a brief burst of creative energy welled up in me. I grabbed a piece of paper and a pencil and scribbled down a poem – in spurted sections, but with few revisions – expressing how I was expecting to feel for most of the rest of my life, which I hoped would be short. I called it *There Is No Help*.[68]

> I.
>
> There is no help.
> The underwater man,
> Buried to his neck in the spongy bottom
> Of life's riverbed,
> All but his raging thoughts immob'ly held,
> Finds his eyes are blinded
>
> By what he's forced to see.
> And what he's forced to see is that
> There is no help.

---

[68] Please refer to *The Underwater Man* (#35) and *Old Man with a Pipe*.(#33) in Appendix 2.

They are perilous ways we build
Around the horrors that we must not see.
Can hours of constant panic ever quite be filled
With good enough illusions of why we ought to be
Here, when life and love are gone?
The building goes awry,
The hours remain unfilled,
And hope
With vacant eyes and swollen tongue
Is dangling from a rope:
And there is no help!

II.
The old man with a pipe
Sees Nothing before him,
Half-hidden to his near-vacant eyes
By the twisting smoke.
Behind him is what's lost,
Before him nothing that he will not lose.
Faith isn't much
But it's all he hasn't got, and yet
There is no help.

The torture that drove life's love
To anguished acts those years and days ago,
Now drives him to remain –
To see, to hear, to feel what we must never know:
There is no help!

Binningen, 4-8 April 1977

I think it was at around this time that I made a couple of sketches as a way to visualize my horror, capture it on paper so I could at least have a shot at dealing with it. One rough sketch shows Jeanette's grotesquely contorted face, vacant eyes, tongue pressing against slightly bared teeth, cord around her neck. In the background, Jeanette's limp figure hanging from a beam, a fallen stepladder in the background, my tortured **NO!!** screaming off the page. The other shows an open grave, open to the abyss, the void. No details, no life.

I was so restless that I didn't, couldn't, stay with Bob for more than a week. Before flying back to the Copenhagen airport, I phoned Björn and Isobel and arranged to spend a night at their place – I couldn't face being at home at Korngatan alone either. I left the next day for San Francisco. I must have called ahead, but don't remember with whom I spoke, nor do I remember how I booked the flight. The film of my memory got damaged in the explosion.

But some things remain crystal clear. In the arrival hall at the San Francisco airport, I was accosted at least three times by purveyors of different brands of religion. One was the Hare Krishnas, as if fuzz and fluff were what I needed. Another was a young man with a turned-around collar, a player for the Roman Catholic team. He stepped forward to intercept me, put a hand on my shoulder, and made the brilliant observation that I appeared to be unhappy. I could only agree. He asked why. I told him I'd just lost my beloved wife. He said I should pray for her soul, and one thing and another, and I told him that all I wanted to do was die to join her. He stopped abruptly, tried to disguise a note of triumph, and announced: "*Ah, but if you took your <u>own</u> life, you <u>couldn't</u> join her, because it's a sin and you wouldn't go to the same place!*" I told him that *she'd* taken *her* own life. I thought he would sink through the floor down to the baggage claim area.

I think it was Michael (it might have been Vic) who picked me up at the airport. We didn't have much to say in the car on the way home to Seville Street. I'm sure I looked a mess. Rose, Jeanette's mom, looked almost as much of a wreck as I felt. I don't remember meeting Rosanne, but I'm sure I at least met Marilyn. Being back at Jeanette's childhood home only made me think of all the roads not taken. Then I started the blame game. How much better off she would have been if I'd never come into her life, how all her family members were thinking exactly that, how incredibly much I longed to feel her arms around me. They put me in Rose and Mike's old bedroom, where Jeanette and I had stayed when we came back to the States for Mike's funeral, in November '74. I immediately recalled how we'd found the gun Mike kept in the top dresser drawer. I opened that drawer hoping I'd found the solution – *in my mouth or through my temple?* – but the gun was gone.

With the exception of Mike, Marilyn and Rose, Jeanette's family seemed to be avoiding me; at least they *all* avoided speaking with me about Jeanette. It wasn't – she wasn't – a subject anyone wanted to talk about, there was nothing that anyone could do or say anything about. Rose asked me a couple of cautious questions about whether I intended to move. I was totally shocked. *Just leave the house we'd worked so hard to fix up, the dream we'd almost made come true? It was completely unthinkable. Besides, I had no place to go.* I couldn't imagine that any other place would ever feel like home.

Rose was silent. She uttered a few platitudes, but was otherwise lost for words. And yet she was right. What words could possible convey anything meaningful, helpful? It was all just one big fucking, unspeakably tragic mess. I drank like a fish and smoked like a chimney and made everybody within 10 meters of me nervous, the way a driver would become on approaching a major highway accident with bodies lying in the road showing large open wounds. I didn't know what I was doing there, what I was doing anywhere, why I was still living. I was *on my own, no direction home.*

From San Francisco I went to Novato. I think John may have picked me up at Rose's place. The venue of John's new home was totally different and new for me, but I again felt like an awkward, disruptive mess that gate-crashed an orderly home, like someone who should be kept in quarantine, placed in solitary, confined for the duration of a fatally infectious disease of the soul. Jeanette never saw their place in Novato, so at least I wasn't plagued by those kinds of memories.

John and Marj told me they were coming to Sweden in the end of June to be with me for a week or two. It would be their first-ever trip to Sweden, and their first-ever trip to Europe. They would pick up a rental car at the airport. John suggested that maybe we could drive down to Switzerland together to see Bob and maybe see a bit of Europe too. I said OK. I didn't know what else to say.

I knew from past experience that my big brother had a very hard time talking about certain stuff – feelings, emotions, empathy – all that well. Such aspects of human encounter made him extremely uncomfortable and made him look like he was searching for the door, preferably an emergency exit. It was by no means that he didn't care! It was just that talking about caring made him nervous, like he would rather be talking about diodes or engineering stuff. Or religion, but only to those who agreed with him. I think Al must have tipped him off on how inappropriate a subject religion would be at a time like this, or perhaps how dangerous it could be to John's own faith.

The final leg on my American trip was to Bellevue, to be with Al and Nancy. They tried to get me into some "normal" situations – helping them out, playing with the kids, barbequing salmon. Both of my brothers did their best to cheer me up every day, but my nights were sleepless sobbing, especially since I kept running out of booze (even though I'd stocked up somewhere), and their straight-laced morality got in the way of their humanitarian need to keep me supplied. Unlike John's home, Al's was full of Bible verses on the walls, constant reminders to me of what a monster they worshipped. *If people are going to worship an imaginary man in the sky, couldn't they at least have made up a nice one?*

There was a moment of comic relief. I didn't have to search for it, it hit me on the head. Al's darling little girl Amy, who'd just turned 3, wanted me to read her a story. I read it to her, trying hard to disguise as much gloom as I could. When I finished, she looked me in the eye and said, "*Read it again*!" I did so. After the second reading, she repeated her demand: "*Read it again*!" I read it a third time. She demanded a fourth reading. When I failed to comply, she hit me over the head with the book.

Al helped me to track down Norm's phone number. I felt I had to tell him about Jeanette. When I finally got through and heard his voice, I just started letting all my tragic story flow out of me. I didn't give a moment's thought or consideration to what Norm might be going through at that moment, during that period of his life, whether I'd pulled him out of an important business meeting or off the toilet or from some possible domestic chaos of his own. I just dumped it all on him, out of the blue (Jeanette and I had had no contact with him since our strange evening with him and Barbara three years earlier, in July 74). His response was distracted. He was taken aback, but seemed to be too dumbfounded and numb to find anything to say beyond a few well-worn clichés. The conversation ended quickly.

I phoned my mom several times while in the US. At the exact time Jeanette died, Mom told me with great awe and conviction, she was on the train looking out the window – and behold! – there was a rainbow, a clear *sign* from *the Lord* that Jeanette must have been saved in the last split-seconds of her life, and since we had no way knowing with 100% certainty that that could *not* be true, it therefore *was* true! (For all she or anyone else could *know*, with an equal amount of certainty, the rainbow could have been a sign from God that there was a sale on socks at Sears.)

It almost made me throw up. I may have mumbled something about the nine-hour time difference. I might have said something (I certainly *wished* to!) about the Lord's unutterable cruelty if he'd known precisely what was going on, could have prevented it and didn't. I doubt that I said that, however, or that the rainbow had been given by mom's god as the sign of a promise that, after once having murdered all of mankind except eight people, he wouldn't do it again, at least not by water (big of him!). I probably refrained from saying something about how totally repugnant Jeanette found Mom's Lord to be, as well as Mom's mumbo-jumbo. I certainly thought so too. Maybe I was considerate enough to say nothing. Maybe it's a screwed-up world when the purveyors of nonsense get to speak freely, while the debunkers have to shut up so as not to offend them.

I understood for the third time in as many years that America was not the place I wanted to be if I were looking for sanity. But now I was aiming for oblivion. I returned to Malmö in May. I continued to consume copious quantities of medicinal alcohol, and my smoking surged from the equivalent of two or three cigarettes a day (or one pouch of pipe tobacco in about six weeks) to about 50 cigarettes a day. My behavior was admittedly, consciously, urgently, self-destructive; *I did not want to live.*

When I got back to Malmö, I went directly to Korngatan, on my own. It took every ounce of self-discipline I could find, but I didn't want to keep leaning on Björn and Isobel. I phoned Isobel, however, to let her know I was back, and that I intended to stay on my own at the house. She said she understood, and that she hoped I was feeling a little stronger. She also told me that in my absence it had been discovered that Hamadi and his family had *not* gone to visit his brother in Paris, but had absconded, just disappeared, and that the school consequently no longer existed. *That too.* Normally I would have been clamoring for more information, but this wasn't "normally". I just couldn't take it on board. It didn't matter to me. Nothing mattered.

Isobel also told me that all direct contact with the undertakers was being conducted through Björn. The cremation took place on April 6th, and the invoice was sent to Björn a week later, something like 1200 kronor. I reimbursed them immediately. Isobel said that Björn would eventually be picking up the urn and bringing it to me. I just felt numb. *It's come to this. Ashes to ashes, literally. Nothing matters. Meaningless. What's the fucking point?*

I opened the cabinet where Jeanette kept her sweaters. Traces of her fragrance came wafting out to meet me. I froze, couldn't move for a couple of minutes. I buried my face in her sweaters and cried until I had to come up for air. I pulled on one of her stretchiest sweaters, then put a shirt on over it so that I had her smell with me, close to me, at least for a while, and it gave me a strange kind of comfort, a memory, an illusion.

I phoned Bob in the evening, when I knew he'd be home from work. We talked for a long time. He was already encouraging me to try to find moments of happiness, or at least not of pain, or at least of less pain, and to try to build on them. I knew it made sense, but it just sounded like he was reading from the script of a movie about somebody else's life. Then he gave me a piece of advice – expressed more like a direct order than anything he'd ever said to me: "*Self-pity is your worst enemy, Stan! No matter <u>how</u> good your reasons for it – and you've got more reasons for it than most – you've <u>got</u> to fight it! Grief – true, overwhelming grief – can quickly, subtly, secretly, turn into self-pity. It will wrap itself around you like a blanket. It may even start to feel comfortable. But it will <u>destroy</u> you, slowly but surely. You simply <u>have</u> to fight it!* **Please***, Stan,* <u>**fight it**</u>*! With <u>all</u> you've got!*"

His plea had become emotional, tearful, desperate. I said I would try. I probably sounded gloomily indifferent, but somewhere inside me, a real thought was trying to form. And strangely enough, the very relentlessness of the pain I was feeling so intensely awoke in me a sense of empathy towards Bob – *I can't do that to him!*

I told him of the plans to come down to Binningen with John and Marj in late June or early July, and he sounded relieved. It pleased him to know that I had plans. He didn't like the prospect of me being on my own at the house either. I told him I was about to spend my first night alone there, and it made him uneasy. I told him not to worry, I'd be staying in the little house.

After my phone call with Bob, I poured myself another large whiskey and began going through the mail that had arrived in my absence. There was a letter from Mom, dated April 6th, in which she wrote: "*Sometimes waves of sorrow overflow – then waves of comfort, but I know comforts will abound. I have <u>confidence</u> and <u>peace</u> as I think of <u>dear Jeanette</u>!*" I thought bitterly, "How bloody nice for <u>you</u>! Your Great Comforter wasn't dishing out a lot of that stuff to Jeanette! How can you *possibly* believe that shit with a straight face and a clear conscience?!"

There was also a letter from Charles, Bob's brother: "*The sorrow which you know at this time can only be fully known and comforted by a loving God. [...] This is solid; this is real! [...] May the Lord bless you and guide you as He unfolds to you each future step.*" I could hardly believe my eyes. A "loving" God?! Which fucking god did Charles have in mind? What diabolical nonsense!!

Even though I knew that both of them "meant well", their letters made me angry. *"Don't worry, Stan, the pink jackrabbit knows all and will put things right in the end!"* What a pathetic attempt to offer comfort! I thought again of Bob's words less than an hour before: *real* advice, sound advice, *almost* helpful, and how Bob cared for me solely as a *person*, not as the fictitious *soul* I represented to Mom and Charles.

I decided to continue going to the psychiatrist for regular visits after I came home from the US. I had two reasons: firstly, she was the one from whom I had to get extensions of my sick leave from a job I no longer had or felt able to look for; and secondly, I wasn't ready to let her off the hook, to forget too easily having sent Jeanette home. But the sessions themselves gave me nothing. She said little, and if I sought advice, I only got back inane questions (like *What do you think?* or *How do you see it?*), which were no help to me at all.

It wasn't as if I were bottling things up, or was unable to talk about what happened. I was doing little else! I was practically going door to door, seeking out all my neighbors and friends (acquaintances) to tell my story, like the Ancient Mariner. They listened, *like one that hath been stunned*. They listened, which in itself did me more good than talking to someone I didn't know, someone who didn't know or had never even met Jeanette. But only a few of them returned my visits. The one person who really helped me in terms of advice was Bob.

To my bewilderment, people I thought of as friends tended to retreat more than people I knew less well. But the Saabyes were there for me. They listened patiently, even though they were busy. I hung out a lot in their workshop, and occasionally exchanged a few words with them as they scurried about and did what auto mechanics do. Gustaf and Magna Jeppsson welcomed me into their little kitchen table and let me talk, let me cry. No platitudes, just ears – big, warm, comforting ears. Gert Isgren listened, and just shook his head, which meant so much more to me than "It's always darkest before the dawn" and all the other well-intentioned platitudinous tripe I heard. Nobody had a solution. How could they? There *was* none! Anybody who claimed to have one was either lying or deceiving themselves, and trying to get me to do likewise. I wasn't looking for a solution, just contact, human contact.

I was unable even to think about getting back to work on the house. I could hardly face entering the big house at all. Going up the stairs was so painful it made me dizzy, and for some time I had to retreat before I got halfway up. I couldn't look at that room, Jeanette's room, at the top of the stairs. Some people asked me cautiously if I was going to sell the house, as if they meant *when* was I going to sell it. My response was the same as when Rose asked me: Sell the house that Jeanette and I had worked so hard on, *our* dream almost come true?! That was far more than unthinkable!

But I had to make the house *different* before I could be there. Somebody who understood what I meant put me in touch with Ulf, Ola and Bengt, three young men in the neighborhood who were architects and builders. They had their own company from which they designed *and* built stuff, and I was able to hire them to put up the paneling we'd already bought for the sloping south-side ceiling upstairs, in the rooms that were to have been Jeanette's room and our bedroom. I'd already done the structural work on reinforcing the roof beams, constructed the airspace, put in 30 cm of mineral-wool insulation, and covered it all with the plastic-film moisture barrier – *before*. The slope of the roof didn't go all the way to the floor; there was a vertical part around 80 cm high in which I intended to make cubbyholes for storage, so I told them not to panel that part, I'd eventually do it myself. I kept out of their way, and they did an excellent job, but it cost more than I expected.

While on sick leave, I was still getting something like 90% of my average salary, or at least what my salary would have been if there'd still been a school. My expenditures were largely limited to whisky and cigarettes, my beloved coffin nails. I was starting to get flashes of memory of Jeanette in happier times, which gave me the tiniest windows of joy before the fact that I no longer had the joy of my life brought reality crashing down around me again. The roller coaster was operating.

Björn and Isobel continued to visit me, or I them, nearly every day. Bob also called me nearly every day for a brief chat, and at least once a week for a long talk in which he would keep badgering me not to succumb to self-pity, and to value the life I still had even though I could see no value to it. He sent me helpful books and letters. One book, *The Aristos*, by John Fowles, argued for life: *having only this*, one must live life to the fullest; this life is not only the best thing we have, it's the *only* thing we have.

In one of the drawers in the makeshift kitchen, upstairs in the little house, under a stack of old receipts, I found a collection of Jeanette's writings. Uppermost was a small notebook, lined A5 format, of the kind often used by secretaries for taking shorthand at meetings. Staring me in the face was a note, in

Swedish, faintly written in pencil and dated 10 days before she died. It would be the closest thing I would ever find to anything resembling a suicide note. I had to sit down to read it. Jeanette's original (mostly Swedish) text is shown here, with my translation:

18 mars 77	*18 March 77*
Kära Stanley!	Dear Stanley,
Ta min hand, lev vidare	Take my hand, live on
med mig i Ditt hjärta.	with me in your heart.
Glöm aldrig, att jag nu och	Never forget, that I now and
i evighet bara älskar dig.	eternally only love you.
Lär ut konst till världen	Teach art to the world
för att hjälpa oss alla.	to help us all.
Var i fred och ta hand	Be at peace and take care
om Dig själv.	of yourself.
Yours forever	Yours forever,
Din älskling	*Your darling*
Jeanette	*Jeanette*

I began weeping as I started to read it. By the time I finished I was sobbing uncontrollably. I ached for her, for her touch, her arms, her smile, her voice, her eyes, her hair, her love. What did she mean by that injunction, "*teach art to the world*"?! How the hell was I – *who* the hell was I – to teach art to anybody, to teach anybody anything? *My muse was gone*!! What was she thinking? What did she mean? Why couldn't she have told me what was going on in her poor, troubled mind?! How could I – and everyone else she knew – have been so fooled, so in the dark, so unsuspecting?!

I discovered other poems.[69] One written during the last weeks of her life made me shudder to my marrow. Then I found another that chilled me even more, because it was from 1967 – the year after we got married, and the year before we moved to Canada – two years before we came to Sweden.

I understood less and less, my emotional roller coaster was careening out of control. How was this possible? How had I not seen how big the problem was? It was no comfort to me to realize that nobody else who knew her well – *Did anybody know her well*?? – seemed to have had a clue either. "*I shall leave no children*

---

69 See Appendix 3.

behind to wonder." I thought of how she'd been gazing at Dave's Christmas card. Did she want children after all? Not likely, not after all the emphasis she'd put on not having any. Or was it because she felt *she* was unfit, more than the *world* being too bad a place for children?

I couldn't make myself stop looking for answers where none could be found: pure speculation was posturing as analysis. But one thing I knew: if I couldn't have children with her, I would never have children. I remembered that my vasectomy was scheduled for June 10th – Jeanette and I had gone to the hospital to book it together – and I was damn well going to go through with it. We'd already had the screening interview, months ago, and I hoped the hospital records weren't cross-referenced so they might find grounds to deny me the procedure in my current state. I didn't tell anybody about my forthcoming operation, not Bob, nobody.

A few days before the operation, I quit drinking (or took a hiatus) so nothing would show up if they ran a blood test prior to surgery, and cause them to start asking probing questions. I was numb, even before they gave me the local anesthetic (or was it a spinal?). I put on my bravest face, although they probably hadn't memorized my original face and wouldn't know what I used to look like.

While I was off to the hospital having my operation, it turned out that Björn was picking up the urn. The operation didn't take long. I'd heard (from John?) that when the anesthetic wore off, it might feel for a few days like I'd been kicked in the nuts by a mule. It was of no concern to me, but I certainly felt it, and I felt I deserved all the pain I could get. I happened to make that particular observation to Bob, and he immediately flew into a rage at my self-pity. Correction: not a rage (not his style), but an extremely firm and agitated admonition; he wasn't going to let me get away with it. Sometimes I understood what he was going on about, sometimes not. I was making forward progress, then receding, then back, then forth, to and fro, hither and yon, inside-out, upside down, raw nerve endings everywhere.

Björn and Isobel seemed to feel awkward when they had to ask me what to do with the urn. I knew that Björn would be picking it up and thought I'd asked him to bring it to me, at Korngatan. I didn't really know what to do with it myself. My only thoughts were that I wanted to die, and then have my ashes and Jeanette's scattered at sea together, so I couldn't very well scatter hers now. I asked Björn to bring it to Korngatan and told him no more. But I couldn't have the urn standing around either. I decided to put it in a plastic bag, tape it shut, and then place it under the slope of the roof in the corner of her room nearest the street corner, then wall it up with paneling, and leave a message about it for Al to deal with when the time came.

Midsommar was approaching. Björn and Isobel told me they were taking me up to Björn's family's place in the country, which was where his grandmother lived, in a place called Skepparkroken, just north of Ängelholm, in northwestern Skåne, along the coast. His whole family was going to be there – parents, a brother, two sisters, possibly an uncle or aunt or two. They always had fun at *Midsommar*, Björn assured me. I tried to protest that I would be a one-man recipe for ruining the festive spirit for everybody, but Björn wasn't having it.

Midsommar always falls on a Saturday between June 20th and 26th, near the summer solstice, and *Midsommarafton* (Midsommar Eve) is the big day of celebration, the day before. In 1977 it fell on June 24th. Björn and Isobel picked me up in the morning in their bright yellow, special-edition VW Beetle, with jeans upholstery. Skepparkroken was a bit more than an hour's drive north of Malmö. The family "cottage" was an elegant old frame house on a sloping lawn with a view of the sea I would normally have relished. Björn introduced me to various family members. I had no idea who they were, nor was I terribly approachable. I just wanted a drink. Was my presence a surprise? Must have been a pretty unpleasant one in that case! But I presumed they'd all been briefed about me and my "situation".

The actual festivities wouldn't begin until the late afternoon, and they would last halfway through the night, so time was weighing heavily on my hands – and Björn's. He tried taking me for a walk along the sea. It was low tide, and the shore didn't look all that attractive. He tried taking me on a car tour around the Bjäre Peninsula, stretching from Båstad in the northeast to Ängelholm in the southwest. Skepparkroken is near the southwest corner.

We drove up over a ridge to Båstad for me to see the sights along the way and in the town. Not much registered. We drove along the north coast of the peninsula to a village called Torekov, which I would have found beautiful if "beauty" were still in my operative vocabulary. I was slightly and tragically aware of my inability to react, in the way that people with early Alzheimer's become momentarily aware that they are slipping away, and their partial awareness of it makes their sorrow all the more profound.

We drove past a country church in Barkåkra on the way back to Skepparkroken. Björn stopped at a house almost next door to the church, to see if Lena, one of Björn and Isobel's neighbors from Malmö, was there. Barkåkra was the home of her parents, but nobody was in. Björn had no paper or pen, so he wrote a short message by dragging his foot in the gravel driveway to spell it out. The message invited her to come down to Skepparkroken in the afternoon.

When we drove on, Björn explained that Lena would be leaving for America in the fall. She and her American fiancé Larry had been Björn and Isobel's neighbors for some time. Larry had already moved back to Sacramento, California, and Lena was going to join him in mid-September to get married and settle there.

An hour or so later, Lena turned up at the gate to the yard in Skepparkroken. Björn and I were in the yard, and of course Björn recognized her. She was blonde, very pretty, but only my eyes reacted. Björn explained that I'd emigrated from the States and now she was immigrating there. She giggled. I just stared in the general direction of my feet and the grass. And then she left.

The festivities began. That meant a lot of herring and meatballs and boiled potatoes and beer and schnapps. I had no appetite, but the schnapps part worked fine for me. The more the others ate, the more they drank, and the more they drank, the more they sang funny and sometimes brazen songs from their little song booklets that were compiled and printed (sometimes even given new lyrics) for the occasion. In other words, what was happening was completely in accordance with Swedish Midsommar traditions – traditions that Jeanette and I might have enjoyed immensely once upon a time. Or like our first Midsommar in Sweden, in Elsa's cottage, just seven year ago. My grief was overwhelming me, right when all the others were at their merriest.

I had to leave my place at the table, I had to get out of their sight, I couldn't drag people down with me, it wouldn't be right. It was nearly midnight now, still some twilight in the northern sky, a balmy evening, Midsommar Eve at its best. Except it was at its utterly worst for me. I went out on the lawn, away from the others, and fell down, sobbing into the grass and soil. I think one of Björn's sisters and came out tried to comfort me. I was crying out my heart and soul in some place I'd never been and didn't want to be. I had no place to go. I didn't want to be *any*where; I didn't want to *be*. I was in the deepest rotten rut – where all ladders end – down in the foul rag-and-bone shop of the heart.

END OF BOOK FOUR

APPENDICES

Slings and Arrows

APPENDIX 1 – Our home at Korngatan, before and after

Downstairs: how it looked when we started in April 1975

Kållargränd

Workshop | Junk | WC

Garage | Yard

Neighbor's house

Workshop | Storage? | (WC)

Kållargatan

Storage

Workshop | Entrance hall | Workshop

Korngatan

Plate over hidden | Chimney | Girder | Window | Doors

Appendix 1

Upstairs: how it looked when we started in **April 1975**

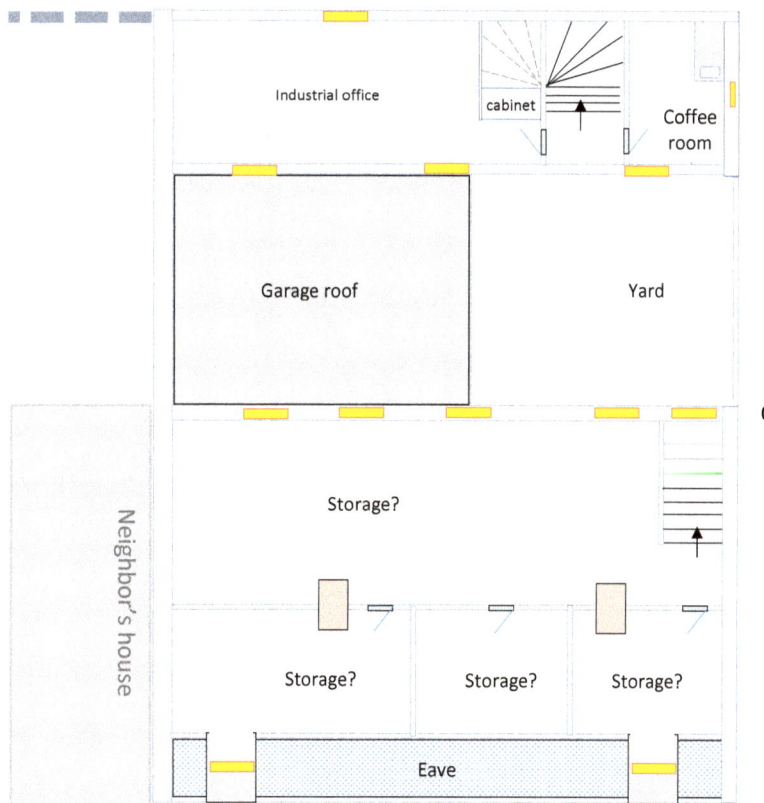

Slings and Arrows

Downstairs: how it looked in **April 1977**

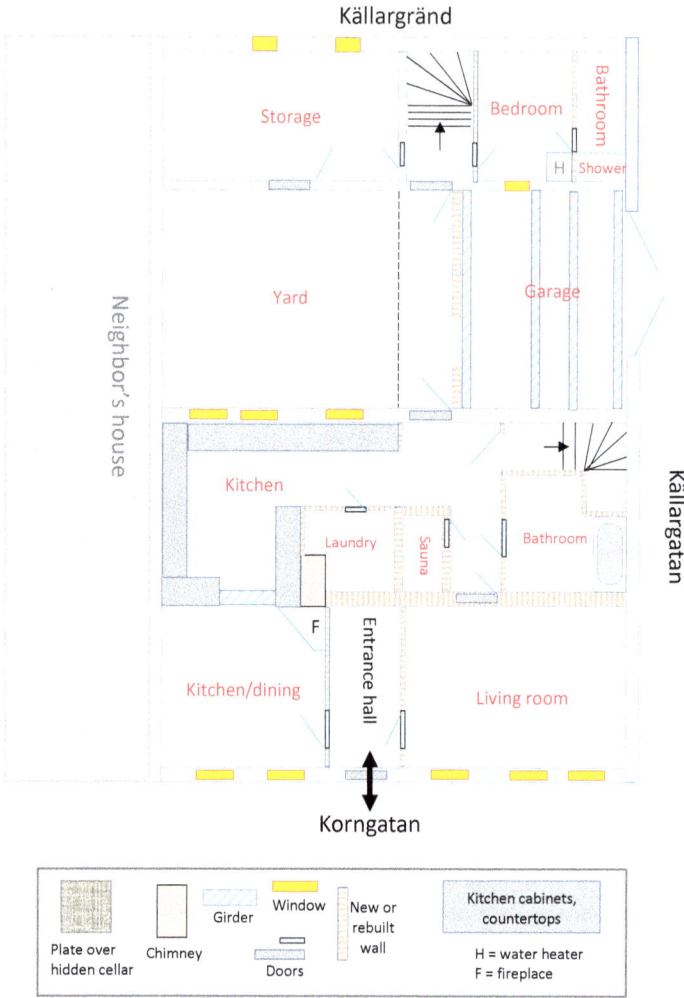

Appendix 1

Upstairs: how it looked in **April 1977**

Kållargränd

Living room | closet | Kitchen /dining
cabinet

Yard | Garage roof / terrace

Källargatan

Neighbor's house | Studio | WC

Master bedroom | Study

Eave

Korngatan

APPENDIX 2 – Paintings 19-78

Paintings #19-77 were painted at our apartment on Vårgatan, #78 was painted at our house on Korngatan.

#19 The Giver of Music

#20 A Face

#21 A Cry

Appendix 2

#22 Memory of a Friend

#23 Smile

#24 Love   #27 Hate

Note that Hate (#27) is not shown in numerical order in order to juxtapose it with Love (#24).

Slings and Arrows

#25 A Choice of Illusions

#26 Green-Eyed People

#28 Competition

#29 Pipe and Bottle

Appendix 2

#30 Man Reading a Book

#31 Sun, plant and lamp

#32 Loneliness

Slings and Arrows

#33 Old Man with a Pipe

#34 Eden

#35 Underwater Man

#36 A Red Horse

Appendix 2

#37 Esau Eating

#38 Public Image

#39 The Victims

Slings and Arrows

#40 The Midian Children

#41 Garden Visions

#42 Boxes

Appendix 2

#43 Outrage

#44 Sitting at the Windows

#45 Regret

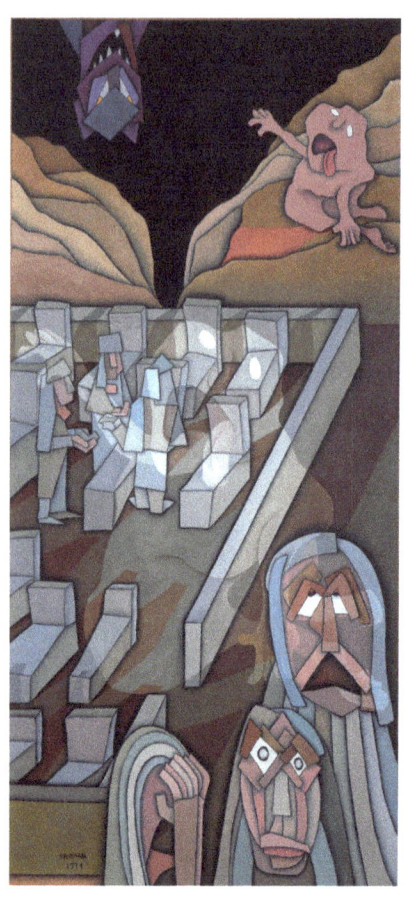

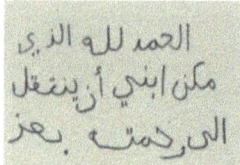

Epitaph on Tombstone

#46 The Funeral

#47 Train Compartment

#48 Empty City

Appendix 2

#49 Still Life with Fruit

#50 The Club

#51 Exhaustion

#52 Having Waited…

#53 The Late Guest

Slings and Arrows

#54   The Irrepressible Memory

#55   Autumn in the Park

#56   Man in a Waterfall

#57   Writing a Letter

Appendix 2

#58   Imagine our Surprise

#59   Shifting Void

#60   The Garden of Euphoria

#61   At the Pub

Slings and Arrows

#62 The Unexpected Meeting of Long-Lost Friends

#65 The Blue Room

#64 And We See *you*

#63 Residential Area

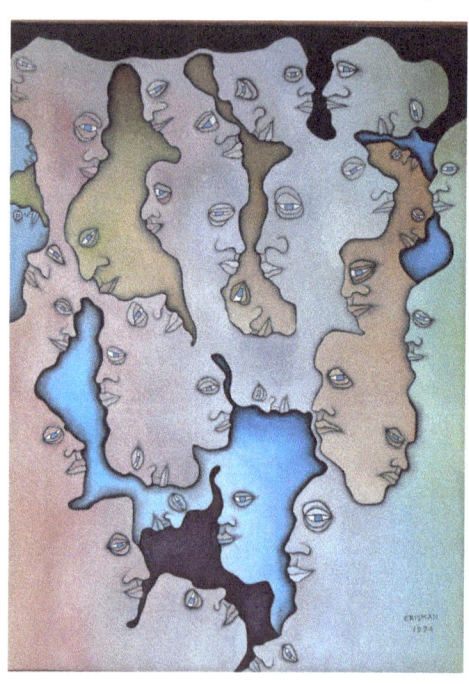

Appendix 2

#66 The Game

#67 Wanderers

#68 Inconclusive Anticipation

#69 Table for One

Slings and Arrows

#70 Departure

#71 Dialogue

Appendix 2

#72 But Maybe I Don't Want To See

#73 Stranded

#74 It Depends on Your Point of View

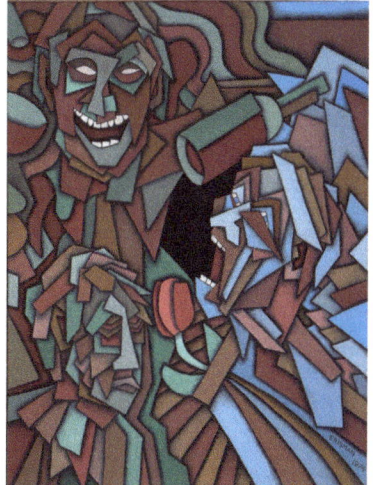

Slings and Arrows

#75 Nobody Home

#76 Neighbors

Appendix 2

#77 Despair

#78 Tell Us Another One

APPENDIX 3

Jeanette's poetry

I found these 12 poems among Jeanette's papers weeks and months after her death. I'd never seen most of them before. Many of her references remain unclear to me.

1. [no title]

> *I shall remain an egotist*
> *And die a rodent.*
> *I shall leave no children behind to wonder.*
> *I shall want nothing*
> *But to be left alone;*
> *And yet only wanting to be*
> *With someone.*
> *I don't know where*
> *To seek what is good,*
> *Perhaps not really wanting to.*
> *Too many questions, no answers.*
>
> c. 1967 (San Francisco)

2. [no title]

> *A silent form*
> *Engulfed in the flame of the fire,*
> *Hypnotized by the footless sparks leaping to and fro.*
> *Burning through the heart*
> *Fleeing from within, evergoing –*
> *Never will it end.*
>
> 28 October 1968 (Vancouver)

3. [no title]

> *Let me think in my mind*
> *No words uttered from without.*
> *To hear such praise*
> *Would cause only pain;*
> *To hear rebuke*
> *Would only kill what's within.*

Appendix 3

Express the tearful experience,
Escape from expression;
Limit your feelings,
Speak only what's expected;
Forsake your creative subjects,
Erase the beauty in your mind.

                        2 November 1968 (Vancouver)

4. To Marilyn

We are many miles apart when young,
Reasons where distance only knows.
To become sisters, friends, mothers,
Is to receive the gentleness of all.
To be driven farther than youth
Is to long for voices to be heard.

                        November 1968 (Vancouver)

5. Christmas

The cold white snow is dropping in heaps from a pale
Sky on the ground and the trees and the houses of men.
Inside the houses, humanity sleeps. Every nail
Is in place, every board and shutter checked again and again.

Christmas is always pure and white like the emission
From a wound that never may heal. The church-bells peal
And the town salivates. From the windows they find that their vision
Is blinded by the crystalline whiteness which need not be real.

The churches are filled with blurry-eyed dabblers, taking
The time to go through the motions they've learned from their youth:
Flaunting the soul like dirty pajamas while making
The sound of brass in their pockets – their viable truth.

"Manger" is mentioned by a gold-robed high priest to appease
The child-god. To the others, prayers and candles are offered;
But the tinkling sounds in praise of the god they most want to please
Muffle all others that the drowsy-eyed crowd may have proffered.

> The priest chants of glory which echoes off marble and gold,
> While the gallery watches enthralled as the censer shakes.
> Outside, the beggar, stumbling by starlight through the cold
> And the snow, knows marble's inedible and his body still aches.
>
> 23 December 1968 (Vancouver)

6. "On reflection of myself during study of [Kafka's] The Trial"

> *I lie on breasts of*
> *Falsehood*
> *I rest on thoughts of*
> *Love*
> *I dream on visions of*
> *Brotherhood*
> *I awake on feelings of*
> *Hate*
> *I arise on emotions of*
> *Emptiness*
> *I go on gestures of*
> *Hope*
>
> 4 January 1977 (Malmö)

7. "After seeing S's dr's appointment in the calendar – <u>Headaches</u>!"

> *10:15 appointment at the*
> *Hospital*
> *You aren't going to let*
> *Them convince you you're*
> *Sick*
> *You aren't going to let*
> *Them take you away from*
> *Me*
> *You aren't going to let*
> *Then label you as one of*
> *Theirs*
> *You aren't going to let*
> *Them give you a chance to*
> *Give up*

Appendix 3

> *12:15 you are home*
> *Then you are well*
> *Then you are here*
> *Then you are thine*
> *Then you are free*

4 January 1977 (Malmö)

8. Reflecting on the Purpose of Education

> *I was led to see in*
> *Sightlessness said the*
> *Visionary to the*
> *Blind man –*
>
> *I was led to see in*
> *Sight said the*
> *Blind man to the*
> *Visionary –*

22 January 1977 (Malmö)

The following poems were probably written during the last two weeks of Jeanette's life, March 13-27, 1977. Discovering them after her death was an excruciating experience for me, but far less so than the experience for her of her inner world when she wrote them.

9. [no title]

> *My mind is so fertile*
> *That planted seeds are*
> *Cultivated indiscriminately*
>
> *Once the difficult problems*
> *Have been resolved*
> *There remains a chance*
> *To manage the simple ones*
>
> *I live in a shadow of myself*
>
> *He who loves most needs most*
> *He who needs most loves most*

My life will end at
Either 38 or 48
To which is then....

1977 (Malmö)

10. Arteriosclerosis

How can I sense death?
I'm so cold, it's so very cold
I'm going to die.

How can I feel fear?
I'm so cold, it's so very cold
I'm about to die.

How can I be alone?
I'm so cold, it's so very cold
I'm afraid to die.

How can I cope now?
I'm so cold, it's so very cold
I'm waiting to die.

1977 (Malmö)

11. [no title]

I await the rain
the flow of life
the stream of hope
the drop of blood
the fall of death
- - - - - -
Death beckons me
and looks away
Death shadows me
and fades away
Death cries out
and stands away
Death hands out
and takes me.

1977 (Malmö)

Appendix 3

12. [no title][70]

> *We were going to grow so old*
> *together.*
> *We were going to work so hard*
> *tillsammans.*
> *We were going to play so much*
> *zusammen.*
> *We were going to laugh*
> *with each other.*
> *We were going to cry*
> *med varandra.*
> *We were going to live*
> *mit einander.*

1977 (Malmö)

---

[70] together = tillsammans (Swedish) = zusammen (German); with each other =med varandra (Swedish) = mit einander (German)

Slings and Arrows

Hindsights
the six-part autobiography of an unknown artist

Book 1
Natural Shocks
by Stan Erisman

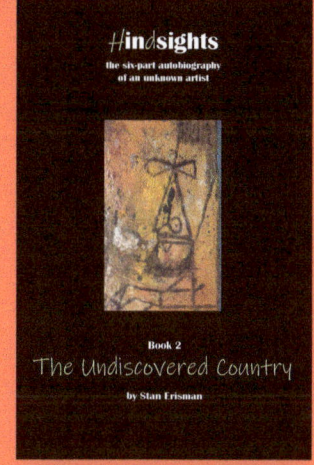

Book 2
The Undiscovered Country
by Stan Erisman

Book 3
No Traveller Returns
by Stan Erisman

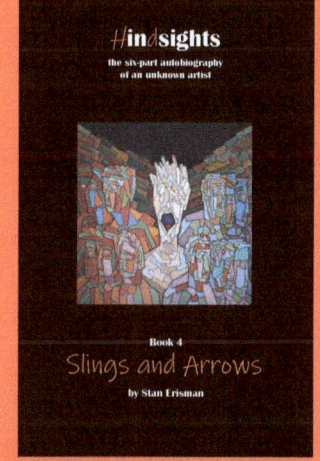

Book 4
Slings and Arrows
by Stan Erisman

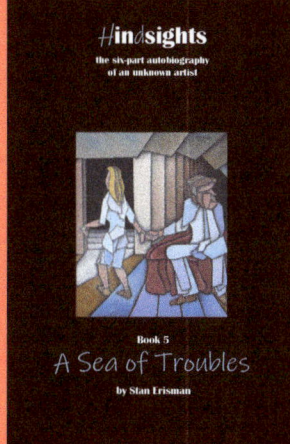

Book 5
A Sea of Troubles
by Stan Erisman

Book 6
Perchance to Dream
by Stan Erisman

www.ingramcontent.com/pod-product-compliance
Lightning Source LLC
Chambersburg PA
CBHW040252170426
43191CB00019B/2386